For Laurence
from
"Unc" Norman
with affection

Understanding Rosenstock-Huessy

Understanding Rosenstock-Huessy

A Haphazard Collection of Ventures

NORMAN FIERING

WIPF & STOCK · Eugene, Oregon

UNDERSTANDING ROSENSTOCK-HUESSY
A Haphazard Collection of Ventures

Wipf & Stock
An Imprint of Wipf and Stock Publishers
199 W. 8th Ave., Suite 3
Eugene, OR 97401

www.wipfandstock.com

PAPERBACK ISBN: 978-1-6667-1390-9
HARDCOVER ISBN: 978-1-6667-1391-6
EBOOK ISBN: 978-1-6667-1392-3

03/11/22

In loving memory of Renée who for
sixty years uncomplainingly abided
my ardent engagement with the work of
Rosenstock-Huessy

Our times are plural. Every timely human type is owed its own ways, its own space, and its own ages. The more we recognize their full number, the more we may spread peace. We can only become peaceful, quiet on our own little acre, and full of the resonance of our hour, when we preserve the inheritance we have received: the full complement of times. . . . We should begin to think of each generation as a body of time and of *the* Spirit as the one that connects all these bodies to each other. . . . We are continually in the desperate position of having to move from genius to genius and at the same time remain united in One Spirit. It becomes harder with each century, and we must allow our young people a deliberate degree of ignorance lest their own genius be stifled. But we must all proceed out of one spirit, regardless of the multiplicity of times and places.

—Eugen Rosenstock-Huessy, *The Fruit of Our Lips*

Any philosophy is deteriorated by the fact that it is memorized by the disciples. They store it in a part of their body which is unable to produce similar effects in their own life as the philosophy produced in the thinker himself. Only when the philosopher can get his hearers to do something about it, to feel it, to remember it, and to register, only then has he found heirs to his bequest to posterity.

—Eugen Rosenstock-Huessy, "The Listener's Tract"

Contents

Preface

THE INSPIRATION FOR THIS book dates back more than sixty years to when I was an undergraduate at Dartmouth College in the 1950s and fell under the spell of Professor Rosenstock-Huessy's lectures. His influence has stayed with me all of my life, but I did not attempt to write about his thought until I retired in 2006 from a long academic career as a historian. Although my decision ultimately to get a Ph.D. in history—after a few sallies in other directions—followed from his inspiration, my academic research and writing, including two books and a number of journal articles, did not focus on the thought of Rosenstock-Huessy. His ideas infused everything I wrote, but I rarely made overt reference to that fact or gave him credit. In my published work, until very recently, I cited him only two or three times.

Why this abstemiousness? First of all, because in American academe Eugen Rosenstock-Huessy (1888–1973) had no place, no category, no disciplinary niche. He held two degrees from Heidelberg and had taught at Leipzig and Breslau as a legal historian and medievalist, but as early as the 1920s he was already on his way to a radical rethinking of many of the presumptions of Western culture. The catastrophe of the Great War, in which he served as an officer in the German army and witnessed the tragic horror of Verdun, changed him permanently and profoundly. This was followed barely fifteen years later by another trauma, the rise of Adolf Hitler, in response to which in 1933 he immediately emigrated to the

United States, thoroughly convinced that business as usual was impossible. The ivory tower with its distancing from the world became for him anathema. Teaching at Harvard for three semesters he made some lifelong friends, but he also clashed with colleagues he found unresponsive to the urgency of the world crisis, lost in their pedantry or besotted by the promised Communist utopia. It was also evident to him that they were in denial about the force and persistence of religion in human affairs. He was fortunate that the offer of a permanent position at Dartmouth College beginning in 1935 rescued him from what might have been a personal disaster in the United States, which not a few émigrés suffered no matter their distinction in Europe. At Dartmouth he was given the made-up title of professor of social philosophy and free rein to teach however he was inclined until his retirement in 1957. We have to thank Dartmouth for this enlightened arrangement. Under the sponsorship primarily of Prof. Page Smith, a former student, Rosenstock-Huessy lectured for a few more years, on and off, at UCLA and at UC-Santa Cruz. He also had various short appointments in post-war Germany at Göttingen, Münster, and Cologne, and he continued to publish, rounding off his *oeuvre*.[1]

The point of this brief biographical recitation is that Rosenstock-Huessy, despite his deep learning and his productivity, did not have a secure reputation in this country. His overt dismissal of many academic shibboleths led to a kind of ostracism. He became a school of his own, tracked by a small band of admirers in this country and abroad, only a few of whom were academics. My own career as a historian might have been tainted had I openly identified myself with the thought of Rosenstock-Huessy, who was assumed by many of those in power to be a bad-tempered crank with wildly idiosyncratic notions. He challenged the fundamentals in the fields of linguistics, sociology, religion, history, and more. It also did not help that Rosenstock-Huessy uninhibitedly espoused Christianity and its unique message in an academic world that was committed to secularism or to atheism of the Communist variety. But even his devotion to Christianity was unorthodox and suspect. In his authoritative essay on Rosenstock-Huessy in the *Stanford Encyclopedia of Philosophy*, Wayne Cristaudo cited Karl Lowith's charge, in a review of Rosenstock-Huessy's *The Christian Future* (1946), that the author's thinking was essentially pagan and that "he secularizes and vaporizes Christianity."[2]

1. Epstein, *A Past Renewed*, has useful basic information about Rosenstock-Huessy's academic career.

2. Lowith, review of *The Christian Future*.

One of the worldly principles I learned from Rosenstock-Huessy's lectures is that if you wish to criticize a person or a set of ideas, you must first prove yourself to be the equal or the master of that which you are opposing, lest you appear to be envious or merely carping from below. If you want to criticize the current practice of historiography, for example, first demonstrate that you, too, can be one of the professional practitioners before you reject the norm. My achievements as a scholar are modest, but they have nevertheless given me enough respectability in the profession such that if I praise the work of Rosenstock-Huessy and defend his thought I cannot be *automatically* discounted as a mere uncredentialed amateur. I have earned the right to a respectful hearing, although that may not get one very far.

A second reason why I did not devote my years as an intellectual historian to interpreting the thought of Rosenstock-Huessy is less edified. My knowledge of German has always been rudimentary, and to write about his life and work thoroughly and fundamentally I would have had to work hard to achieve a much higher degree of competence. As a historian I confined myself almost entirely to relying on English and some French sources. One book I wrote on the teaching of moral philosophy at Harvard in the seventeenth century required a great deal of neo-Latin translation, for which I got help from a specialist.

I had long before vowed to myself that upon my retirement I would devote my new free time to promoting the work of Rosenstock-Huessy and interpreting him for the benefit of others. And since 2006, in a position to be listened to, I have been doing that on and off. This book is a compilation of various pieces written in the past fifteen years, some as a participant in international conferences devoted to the life and work of Rosenstock-Huessy, some for private circulation to the Rosenstock-Huessy Society of North America, which I founded, and a couple for publication in the journal *The European Legacy*. The order in which I have placed these essays is neither topical nor chronological; they are arranged in such a way that I intuit may hold a reader's interest. Two of the chapters are pieces written entirely by Rosenstock-Huessy himself, not by me, which are included because they concisely distill fundamental elements in his thinking. Of course, throughout the book he is extensively quoted.

No one could be more conscious than I am of the inadequacy, incompleteness, and superficiality of this book in relation to the massive, brilliant, complex thought and writings of the man who is its subject. His mind was surely among the most fertile of any author in the Western canon. I touch here on only a small proportion of his fundamental ideas. I have often skimmed and skipped, failing to interpret in sufficient depth or breadth. I have done little or no research on the topics here. It is not a learned work but essentially personal testimony and an effort to uphold or justify Rosenstock-Huessy's insights. There are single paragraphs in Rosenstock-Huessy's work that alone deserve twenty-page essays. It has not helped that I began this work in my seventies and at this moment I am eighty-seven. One's intellectual fortitude diminishes with age no less than the physical body's. I can only hope that these pages arouse the interest of better and younger minds.

One failing in the work for which I seek the reader's forgiveness is tiresome repetition. I know that I have repeated myself from chapter to chapter. Since each of the chapters was originally written to stand alone. I fall back again and again in separate pieces on the same metaphors, same bits of information, same explications. The work is in no sense then a continuous monograph.

The underlying premise of this effort is my belief that Rosenstock-Huessy is one among a small handful of twentieth-century original thinkers who has a message, or a set of messages, so essential that if heeded can profoundly change the human condition for the better. More than messages, he conveys a singular attitude, hard to describe, which takes a while to be absorbed, but once it has been learned changes the way a person looks at the world. It is a unique combination of both skepticism and affirmation, skepticism toward all the bunk and hokum we are afflicted with daily and toward the mindless acceptance of hypocrisy and group mentality that clutters our view, and affirmation of the potential of the human spirit to make real progress toward peace and community globally. This collection is an argument, an effort to persuade the reader that we should heed Rosenstock-Huessy who speaks as a prophet from a vantage point far ahead of the present moment. To quote a favorite motto of his: Listen mortals, lest ye die (*Audi ne moriamur*).

1

Rosenstock-Huessy in the Classroom

[Some of this material was previously published in the Introduction to a special issue of the journal *Culture, Theory and Critique*, vol. 56 (April 2015) devoted to the work of Rosenstock-Huessy.]

DARTMOUTH COLLEGE

Rosenstock-Huessy lectured to Dartmouth "boys" for twenty-two years (1935–1957) in courses with broad titles like "The Circulation of Thought," "Universal History," "American Social History," and "Comparative Religion." In 1949, for the first time, some of these courses were tape recorded, initially by C. Russell Keep, one of his students, and then by a succession of later students, including Bernhard Bergesen, Leon Martel, and Paul Margulies. Over three hundred hours of such recordings have survived. In the 1980s, Mark and Frances Huessy undertook the gargantuan task of transcribing all of the recordings, and now both the audio and the transcriptions are preserved together online at the Rosenstock-Huessy Fund website, www.erhfund.org/lecturelibrary.

Rosenstock-Huessy's lectures, as one might expect, are revealing of the man and teacher as none of his books can quite be. To begin with, he took for granted the confidentiality of the classroom. He is unguardedly forthright, one might even say outrageously opinionated, as few people would be in a book, and he did not fear that he would be quoted out of context. Because he spoke so pointedly and personally to the young men before him—persuading, provoking, teasing, admonishing, advising, as well as precisely instructing—these sessions of about seventy minutes had a degree of intimacy not usually found in a college course.

This intimacy and the inherent seriousness of the process were heightened by two unusual facts. First, Professor Rosenstock-Huessy spoke extemporaneously, with no text before him other than a few notes on a single index card, if that. There are professors who virtually memorize their written lectures and speak in class in a measured way without a text before them. Rosenstock-Huessy's lecturing was not the recitation of a pre-existing script but a continuing string of rhetorical inventions and ruminations on a theme. He had several topics in mind for the day and then elaborated on those topics with fecundity, insight, and originality, pulling into the discourse whatever struck him at the moment as relevant. He digressed but never lost his way. He told illustrative stories from his own experience or from centuries past; he drew on his extraordinary knowledge of etymology; he recalled arcane facts from history and cited passages from the world's classic literature; he commented on the morning news; and he provided a vast framework for understanding God, man, and the world (or nature), the three irreducible pillars of his thought.

The second fact that added to the excitement and intimacy of the moment, in addition to the spontaneity of his lecturing, was the awareness on the part of the student audience that their teacher was imparting to them privileged wisdom, deep and wide-ranging learning that could not be found anywhere else other than in that classroom at that moment. Here was an original "philosopher," or "sociologist," or "historian," or "prophet" speaking from his heart as well as his mind with an intense desire to be understood and heeded. One felt privileged to be so included. He did not hesitate to say often, "No one else will tell you this, gentlemen," and it was true.

Rosenstock-Huessy's tone sometimes had an urgency akin to the message: "Listen mortals, lest thou die." He constantly disabused his audience of the errors or absurdity of their inherited, conventional views. He saw into events with a penetration that made layers of opacity fall away. He seemed to have a preternatural understanding of human affairs, and he quickly got to the heart of the matter, whatever it was. There is hardly one of the hundreds of his lectures that does not contain surprising, profoundly instructive observations. His goal was to make a lasting impression on his young listeners, teaching them, he said, what he believed they needed to know not so much at twenty, but later, at age fifty or sixty when they would have commanding roles in society. College education, he always stressed, must not be just for the benefit of the student but for the long-range benefit of society.

The recordings have technical deficiencies—scratchiness, interruptions, and faded sound when the professor turned his back to write on the blackboard—that make them sometimes difficult to listen to. The set-up was primitive—a garden-variety microphone sitting on a wooden table in front of the room, and nine-inch reel-to-reel tapes to capture the sound. Often, too, Rosenstock-Huessy spoke with an intensity that students are not used to and from which one needed frequent respites, that is, time to pause and absorb. The accompanying transcriptions are invaluable for helping the listener to follow and ponder his words.

Reading a lecture is much faster, of course, than listening to it for seventy minutes. But reading is a whisper, and Rosenstock-Huessy believed that good teaching must be emphatic lest the power of strong speech be left only to the demagogues. The transcriptions are needed for close study, but they bury the rhythm and stresses in his speaking, his voice rising sometimes almost to a shout. His voice tone, too, makes clear the difference between merely amusing, sometimes daring, asides, intended in part to entertain his student audience, and serious, considered pronouncements. But one point about Rosenstock-Huessy is vital for understanding him: even when he is at his seemingly most extreme, he should never be summarily dismissed. He used exaggeration and dogmatism as a device, countering the usual academic cautiousness with its "perhaps-es" and mandatory even-handedness. Underneath every seemingly wild assertion or generalization there is a kernel of truth that deserves to be brought out.

One other apologia: Repeatedly in his lectures Rosenstock-Huessy took to task the failings of American society. For the young men in the audience in love with their country, this was sometimes hard to accept. To some small degree these attacks may be attributed to the European intellectual's reflexive snobbery toward the perceived superficiality and vulgarity of U. S. culture, and it must not be forgotten, too, that in ca. 1950 Prof. Rosenstock-Huessy was in his sixties and sometimes impatient with the follies of the young generation in front of him. Moreover, rhetorically he seemed to need a foil against which to draw contrasts.

Yet however much the denigration, it was offset by his evident appreciation of the United States and its political and literary heroes, such as Jonathan Edwards, George Washington, Emerson, Lincoln, William James, Homer Lea, and dozens of others who were featured in his teaching. It was impossible to sit in his classes and not come away with some appropriate deflation of ignorant chauvinism and at the same time, much new understanding of what has been achieved on these shores. Part of the message to college youths was: Your country has faults; don't sit on your hands, make it better.

BARNARD COLLEGE

For twenty-two years teaching at Dartmouth College, Rosenstock-Huessy addressed young men only. The college did not become co-educational until 1972, long after he had retired from regular teaching. Occasionally in his classes there were women auditors—a girl friend, a wife, etc.—but that was not common, and the circumstance of his speaking regularly to an all-male audience naturally affected his approach. He has been accused of insensitivity to women, but there are many passages in his published work that put the lie to that charge. At worst, he was something of what the feminists call an "essentialist," that is, he believed that men and women were fundamentally or essentially different and by nature complementary to each other. To resort to present-day parlance, his position would be that conventional gender roles are not entirely social constructions.

However that may be, we have at least one good example of Rosenstock-Huessy lecturing at a women's college. In the spring of 1962, he was invited by a former student, Harold Stahmer, at the time a professor in the Religion Department at Barnard College in New York, to give three lectures to Stahmer's classes. These three lectures are a good condensation of aspects of Rosenstock-Huessy's thought on the nature and significance of speech, a short course, as it were, on the grammatical method. The style, the digressions, the stories and provocations are much like his lecturing at Dartmouth. At moments, however, here and there he introduced remarks addressed specifically to the young women before him. I extract below a few illustrative passages. Whether he judged his audience well is hard to determine. He could as easily have offended these young people as elated them. But as usual, he was not reticent.

"Everyone of us begins where the world leaves off," Rosenstock-Huessy said in the first of the lectures, meaning by "world" mere nature, which is quantitatively measurable and always ends in death. "Everyone of us contradicts the world as it exists around you. If you are ugly, if you are pretty, resist it, because that's no mark for your real life to say, 'I am pretty,' 'I am ugly.' Fifty years later, my dear people, you will all . . . look alike, neither ugly nor beautiful, but old. And that's a different quality, to look old. It's something of great beauty, and of something more. You are then a child of God, and no longer a child of this earth." And then he warns the women: You run the risk of trying "to be so terribly beautiful at fourteen that you don't look beautiful at sixty." Needless to say, Professor Rosenstock-Huessy would not warn Dartmouth men in ca. 1950 about giving primacy to the quest for personal beauty.

At one point he comments on intonation as an important and revealing element in speech. "Intonation is a secret by which you can express all feelings, nearly, without words. . . . You can express by mere intonation love and contempt, loyalty . . . and revolution." "Tone is something between you and me. It presupposes that we all have the same soul, the same resonance. We all are organs on which many, many keyboards may be found." Then, again, targeting this particular audience, he says: "When you hear yourself sneering or gossip[ing], you better stop. These are the dissonances on the keyboard which you can overdevelop," as is true of so many ladies who by sixty have unlearned all the other keyboards except gossip. Tone, Rosenstock-Huessy continued, is a betrayer, because the tone you use towards the world will reflect on your face. "You will see . . . at sixty in every human face whether he has co-suffered or whether he has co-sneered about the world at large; or whether he has remained indifferent and has no face at all. There are many people at sixty who have lipstick, but no face."

At the heart of this lecture was the distinction between words, names, and figures, meaning by "figures" enumeration or quantification. The introduction of quantification in areas where it does not belong was an error against which Rosenstock-Huessy frequently railed. In that spirit he avoided the academic style of beginning a discourse with a definition, like axioms in geometry, because, he said, "a definition is an attempt to degrade a word to the rank of a figure. A defined word is a desperate attempt of modern philosophy to reduce the beauty of Shakespearean language to definable words." "A definition, then, is an attempt to assimilate . . . speech by words to the speech of the mathematician. . . . It has gone on since Plato's days, who also believed in the five platonic bodies in mathematics and tried to reduce the beauty of the Athenian women to something that could be sold on the meat market. The most awful enemy of modern feminine youth is Plato. I warn you against him."

Rosenstock-Huessy did not eschew Plato in his teaching, of course. He assigned topics on Plato to his students. But he argued uncompromisingly that the West, even to this day, was far too much under the sway of the values of ancient Greek culture and of Plato in particular. Plato, he said, is the enemy of the grammatical method (that is, Rosenstock-Huessy's speech-thinking) and the arch proponent of the mathematical method, that is, the method of trying to live by definitions, of trying to "to reduce living speech to definable entities, which would make them into figures." Definitions obviously have a place, in the courtroom and in the natural sciences, for example, but it is a limited place in relation to the full needs of human society.

For Rosenstock-Huessy, speaking and listening were inseparable experiences. Neither is understandable without the other. The sense of hearing was thus sharply distinguished from the other senses. In fact, each of the senses connects to us in a different way, to different parts of the body. The conventional belief that all of the senses report to the head is a "big lie." "They do not report to the head, first of all, and second, they immerse us in five different networks of reality, and not into the same." The point here is not where the pathways of physical nerves may go, but to what degree thought or mind has a role in sensory experience.

> Smell is connected with the genitals, that is, with the great honor we have to perpetuate the race. The eye is the only organ which leads from its sense organ to the brain. And that's why anything we *see* is subordinate, is second-rate. Prettiness is not all, we have said. . . . Hearing goes through the heart, just as contact goes through the skin . . . and taste goes through the tongue. . . . To know the world by smell contradicts all the truths about the world by sight. . . . Anybody who hears what a person says must forget how he looks.

The power of music exemplifies the nature of hearing. Between the listener and the music there are no barriers. "And you, young lady, despite all your harness of beauty and fashionable dress, allow it to enter you and to lay down the barriers of resistance. And you say, 'I am now not a separate entity, but as of this moment, the music is allowed to float through me . . . without any limitation.' . . . In music, the individual person is of no importance. And that's a condition of her listening to the music. It's the exclusion of the personal which makes music possible. . . . God created one universe permeated by sound and swallowing up your little resistance."

Music has nothing to do with the brain. "It has to fight the preconceptions of your brain." In general, "to listen means to break down the barriers of the visible world. And you cannot listen to God, or to religion, or to poetry, or to wisdom or to a command given by a commander in the field if you cannot for one moment deny that there is a wall between the speaker and the listener. For this one moment, the man who makes the sound, . . . and the man who intercepts it must be united." Thus, "in any speech recurs the musical experience that the listener and the speaker form one body politic."

"God has given us this faculty of melting down—in humility, in obedience, in enthusiasm, in conviction—the walls of our being. And you should not marry if your husband has not been able to break down the walls of your virginal resistance. There are too many marriages that are based on your will. Don't marry when you feel at the altar that it is just by your free will that you marry. If it is by will, it will end by will. To will is not enough. You have to submit to some higher will, or you can't get married." Tragedies ensue from the wrong theories of speech. We are led to believe that a man speaks, the woman thinks it over, and then she decides. But such decisions when made by "thinking" are always the wrong decisions. "The only decision you must make is when you say, 'I can't help it! I can't pass him up. He is the man.' And it's perfectly, usually indefensible. He is usually a rascal. But you have to marry him. And the man who is not a rascal, but a very virtuous boy, don't marry him. He is too tiresome."

The remarks above are from the first of the three Spring 1962 lectures at Barnard College, and in order to keep this survey brief I have necessarily excluded much of interest. The topic for the second lecture, Professor Rosenstock-Huessy announced, is "the difference between lust and love and the difference between peace and war." These were topics he often addressed at Dartmouth as well, and here, too, I am radically cutting, excerpting only a few passages from the whole that are framed a bit differently, I think, because the audience was female.

To speak in the classroom on love and war, Rosenstock-Huessy said, we have to be "full of reverence for the dangers of life—death, cruelty, prisons, murder, war, lust—everything that endangers your own existence." The confusion between sex and love matters for every woman. The grammatical method helps us to make the necessary distinctions. To speak of "sex" rather than use the proper word "lust" is a mistake to begin with. Sex is only a means to an end. "Sex is simply an individual's aptitude to realize love," that is, to ascend. "Lust is the situation in which love is abused, remains on the lower range. Sex is only the instrument of this lust. It would be clearer if you would never use the word 'sex' in your own life. It is not dignified enough. Because the problem of loving each other . . . is a problem of social living, of co-existence, of unity, of society. Sex is the aptitude of an individual body to take part in this great process of love."

In both love and war, speech or its absence is the decisive factor.

> Words have to be spoken in order to allow us to love; words have to be spoken to allow us to live in peace. . . . You have this terrible habit not only to mention 'sex' in relation to love, you also say that you "make love" and that you "make war.". . . Man does not make love; and man does not make war. . . . If you think that you can make love, you abuse language. You declare love, and you accept the declaration of love. . . . If you don't declare your love, you don't know what love is. Because one state of affairs, one moment in the history of every loving experience is that it has to be said. Somebody has to say to you, "I love you," and you have to accept it and believe him in order to know that you are in love.

For Rosenstock-Huessy, it is the expression of love that legitimates sexual relations. He invoked occasionally when discussing these matters a maxim of his invention, I think: "Sex without song is sin." "Everything is forgiven to illegal, illegitimate, unmarried lovers who sing. That's innocence. The legitimacy of love does not depend on the marriage formality. But that a man's soul and a woman's soul meet in song, that makes their physical behavior innocent." Singing is an involuntary action, he noted. It cannot be forced. "That's why I warn you: whenever there is will in your relation to a man, don't marry him. You will go wrong, and he will be unhappy and you will be unhappy. Marriage is the surrender of your own will."

The proper helplessness of will in the face of love, inspiration, passion, and similar imperatives was a recurrent theme in Rosenstock-Huessy's teaching. "Thank God for necessity," he would say, referring to those moments when we know exactly what we must do regardless of our will. Necessity rescues us from aimlessness. The essential meaning of his Latin motto, "*Respondeo etsi mutabor*" (I respond although I shall be changed), lies here. It is linked directly to Jesus's prayer, "Thy will be done." Rosenstock-Huessy warned the women not to imitate the male sex by saying, "My will be done and nobody else's." "It's called self-reliance and some other such nonsense. How can a man in love be self-reliant? He's a victim. He can only pray that the gods may be merciful with him, in his passion, in his servitude, in his humility." Lest his listeners at Barnard College think he was reducing them all to nothing more than prospective brides, an insult even as early as 1962, he said: "A marriage between two—husband and wife—is not the whole story. You can marry a party. You can marry your country."

Love entails not only the forfeiture of will; it also calls for sacrifice. "Love and sacrifice go together because love unites mankind, and the sacrifice only means that the hindrances [to] this love, or [to] this peace, which is the same, have to vanish. To sacrifice for love means to make love possible. And that always costs."

"The declaration of love is that strange moment in which we become aware that our love will cost a price, and we declare that nothing is too dear to be sacrificed. That's the content of a declaration of love. . . . You ladies don't seem to know this anymore, but any man sacrifices his freedom when he gets married. . . . He must be ready to sacrifice his freedom. . . . A man, a boy, of twenty, as I see it, cannot possibly marry, because he doesn't know that he sacrifices something big, his freedom."

Rosenstock-Huessy proffered to the Barnard women what can only be called a romantic view of love and marriage, revealing a side of him not so well known. He sometimes disparaged co-education not because, he said, he has anything against "your meeting boys as often as you like, day and night, but because marriage has to overcome distance. It has to overcome mountains." In a co-educational institution, where you sit next to each other every day, you are not compelled to declare your love under any great difficulties. "To declare love must be not only time-consuming, but it must be dangerous. There must be conflicts; there must be impediments; there must be obstacles. And the higher the obstacle that you jump over . . . in accepting the courtship of a man, the safer you are in testing whether it's real love. . . . The human race demands love, and the declaration of love in a highly, high-strung, poetical, and sacramental manner, and therefore, it has to be difficult that you find each other." The marriage of high school sweethearts was no ideal of Rosenstock-Huessy's. On the contrary, love-matches that crossed ethnic, religious, racial, and national boundaries portended the future of humanity, his Great Society.

The final lecture of the three at Barnard contains no remarks addressed particularly to a female audience. However, it seems fitting to conclude with a few words from it addressed to all humankind:

> There is no reason that the physical event of a man's death should finish his influence. . . . When we speak of people in heaven, of the saints and of the Resurrection at Easter, we mean that there are people who have died long ago and are still ahead of us. If Jesus has any power in your lives, it means that he is still more of the future than you are. We are obsolete as long as we only listen to the demands of our belly. If we, however, can listen to a good name, to a sacred name, then heaven is [that] which is still to come. Heaven is the spoken, promised future. . . . That is the only allowable use of the word 'heaven.' 'Our Father in heaven' means the God who is still to come. It doesn't mean, of course, a god who is a better Sputnik. . . . People really cling again to the idea that heaven is sky. Obviously that isn't true. Now all the saints and all the great souls which you need for your own upbringing and your own achievement are ahead of us.

2

Marriage

Society will have to find a new word now to capture the unique concept of the *union of opposites* that is traditional marriage. The advent of gay "marriage" misses this idea, and by it the word "marriage" is so stretched or diluted that that specific meaning is lost. Same-sex marriage like heterosexual marriage is a declaration of love, and as with heterosexual marriage it obliges the community to recognize and respect that bond, thus helping to create a stable social order, with lines of demarcation and borders, plus legal rights.

But from its beginnings the institution of marriage achieved much more. The invention of marriage was a huge step in the progress of humankind because in addition to creating peace in the community by bringing sexual rivalry and jealously under control, it created the internal peace of the family by harmonizing the essential differences between the sexes. That men and women are intended for sexual liaison is obvious, but it was no easy matter to convert the sexual into the conjugal, to convert the perpetual war between the sexes into some degree of social peace within which a lasting shelter was created to rear children.

Comradeship, friendship, and love between members of the same sex is easy and natural, after all, whereas matrimony between members of what we rightly call the "opposite" sex transcends the natural and is sufficiently miraculous or spiritual to deserve a name all of its own. What that specific name shall be in years to come remains to be seen, now that "marriage" has been generalized.

Like man's capacity to make laws in general, reining in his independence, and to make peace out of his natural inclination to war, marriage was an amazing, once-and-for-all triumph over the terrifying force of unbridled, promiscuous sexuality with its destructive accompaniment of domination, jealousy, bitter rivalries, and the looming threat of incest. The battle of the sexes is eternal, like war itself, but at weddings we celebrate with joy and relief that that battle does not have the last word.

According to the revelatory "Universal History" of Rosenstock-Huessy, it was in the tribal era, over a period of thousands of years, that people learned to marry, that is, "learned the act of marriage, so that one man and one woman can belong so close together that their children can treat them as one." He spoke of the chastity zone of the family, where the names "mother," "father," "daughter," "son," "brother," "sister," are entirely and deliberately de-sexualized. "Incest is the destruction of a sacred space inside of which the passions of sex shall not rage." "Chastity is the creation of a spare room inside of which man is unafraid of the other sex."

The problem facing the tribes, Rosenstock-Huessy wrote, "was to enlighten the act of mating with the word. . . . Marriage means to go from the blind act of the moment, through the whole life cycle to its most opposite point, the childbirth." In heterosexual marriage at least three generations are necessarily invoked—the lineage of the parents of the bride and groom and the anticipated children. Only because of marriage do we even know who our ancestors are.

The marriage of a man and a woman, therefore, not only creates a new inner space, a new private domain, as does gay marriage, it also creates a new time span stretching from a distant past to an open-ended future of progeny. "A bride speaking her decisive 'Yes' or 'No' before the altar uses speech in its old sense of revelation," Rosenstock-Huessy wrote, "because her answer establishes a new identity between two separate offsprings of the race and may found a new race, a new nation." Every marriage," he said (but here we must exclude gay marriage), "is the nucleus of a new race." Gay marriage is sterile by comparison.

Rosenstock-Huessy discussed marriage in a dozen places in his work, but nowhere more interestingly than in his little 1936 book, written in America, *The Multiformity of Man*. Chapter 5 in that work analyzes the "dual" in grammar versus "dialectic polarity" such as feminine and masculine, heaven and earth, light and dark, man and wife. Some of the most primeval words of our modern speech still preserve today a phase in our history when language was deeply interested in the dual. Such words are "mother" and "father," "sister" and "brother." Here a feminine and a masculine both end in "r," the remnant of the comparative form "er," as in "bigg-er." The dual means that diversity is found within unity. The dual is far different from the plural, a distinction that I cannot elaborate on here.

The *Multiformity of Man* formulates three "ecodynamic laws." The one pertaining to the dual reads: "In all relations which are representative of the generation and regeneration of man: Two equals One." Such a law may seem trivial, Rosenstock-Huessy writes, but it is an essential tool for understanding, considering that most sociologists "think of man merely in terms of the equation One equals One," which is hardly adequate for describing the problems that arise in society, notably in the areas of love and sex.

> Marriage organizes the self-conscious half of our existence on earth. In committing herself to a friendship, in falling in love with a great cause, in getting betrothed to a bridegroom, a human being makes the attempt to organize the whole of her conscious life into one unity! The dual does not apply where this decision for better for worse is not made. An acquaintance is not a friend, [a vote] in an election is not a life's service given to your country, and a honeymoon ending in Reno never was a marriage. . . . The dual is a striving for polar unity. It could exist and it practically exists in many lives which know nothing of sex relations.

The dual is needed to overcome the tendency of consciousness to fall into dialectic contradictions. We are constantly thinking in terms of contrasts: "black calls for white, male for female, yes for no." We would be unable to overcome this "hairsplitting method of yes and no" without the dual. "The dual transforms two contradictions into the foci of one ellipse." Man and wife are opposites, which inevitably causes conflicts, but the mutuality is more "prominent" than the suffering. "In any marriage the absent husband is represented by his wife."

Only the dual enables us to transcend the endless paradoxes of our reason. "Antagonisms and puzzling conflicts are re-translated into polarities of a higher unity." The dual allows us "to exchange ourselves with somebody else without losing our personal identity!" Marriage is abused by lawyers or legislators who conceive of it as a contract between two partners. In a sale the two partners to the contract think of their own advantage. "The whole content of a real marriage might be summed up in the statement that the two who are partners are each expected to care more for the other partner's happiness than for their own!"

Moreover, in a contract the expected duties are fixed at the beginning. In a true marriage the duties are in "permanent flux" as the relationship grows and the actions of each partner shape the form of the dual as it evolves. Finally, Rosenstock-Huessy notes, the partners are agents of a corporated body for which each individually stand, such that in the absence of one the other can represent the whole. This is especially evident in a family when one parent dies and the other strives to play the dual role of representing not only himself or herself but also the interest of the parent who has passed away, stressing it even more than might be the case if the dead parent was still alive. In a contract, when one partner dies the other is free. In matrimony a wife surrenders her beauty and her health to her husband for better or for worse. And the man surrenders his adventures, his infinite chances. How can such a perilous exposure of the whole be treated as the result of a willful arrangement between two individuals? In a contract I try to get as much as possible, and to remain as unchanged as possible. In a true marriage, "I throw in my lot today without knowing where I shall be tomorrow."

It is characteristic of the bipolar dual that one makes such an open-ended commitment. The dual is a means of regeneration by personal devotion. Mere sexual relations between two individuals leads to the suppression of progeny because the participants are looking out for their own interests first. "The reproduction of the kind and the reproduction of any social form present a problem of how to produce self-forgetfulness. The bipolar dual is the means of wresting from man this devotion which is against his self-interest and against his instinct for self-support and independence."

Rosenstock-Huessy believed, as he counseled the Barnard girls in the lecture in Chapter 1, above, quite romantically, that the longer the way to overcome the self-interest of the two "who shall be melted together, the more promising is the process." That is why, he said, "in nature and society all duals are based on a long period of courtship!" "The resistance of the two individuals must be genuine and deep to make the result valuable."

Breaking down the "walls of individuality" to create a true marriage is no simple matter. Nature uses so many "extraordinary means of color, smell, and music to overcome the fears of the two who make love to each other that it is obvious that the dual is something adventurous, dangerous, and overwhelming." "Mutual responsibility is the self-forgetting principle of any true marriage. . . . He who learns to renounce his individuality for the sake of somebody else gets it back a thousandfold. This man discovers a new secret every day; he begins to grow."

3

Engagement with the World and Chastity of Mind

A FRIEND WHO IS quite conversant with the thought of Eugen Rosenstock-Huessy sent to a few people the following autobiographical sketch:

> I have been an Episcopal priest for over 53 years. Along the way I took an interlude of 8 years as a stockbroker. That was in part a response to my belief in the worker priest idea, in the conviction that Christianity has for 2,000 years been too otherworldly in our under-standing of the implications of the Incarnation, in the conviction that yes we have to let go, but the letting go is only to lead us by the Spirit into taking hold. I see us as here to take hold in every sphere of society by that holy love at the core of all being. The Buddhist detachment is only half of the story. Medieval otherworldliness is in some ways parallel to that detachment. Every legitimate human enterprise is a place for us to take hold [of] the paradox that we die to self to be born to self. We let go so as truly to take hold, and truly become who we are.
>
> Martin Luther was right. If there is anything priestly about life we are here to be part of the priest-hood of all believers. Simone Weil (Paris, died 1943) regarded it as her Christian vocation to remain unbaptized until the Church (Roman) gained more of a real appreciation and love for the world.
>
> My question: Are these otherworldlinesses merely a response to the very sorry state the world is in, without seeing

> the other side of the paradox of life? In other words, are we so blinded by the realities of evil that we basically opt out when we should be looking for the ways to opt in? The world is holy beyond and in spite of "the fall."
>
> Back to Luther, and to Paul: It is not a real option for us to think that at 10 a.m. tomorrow we can all be as pure as the driven snow. Monasticism is not a real answer, perhaps a pointer. The world operates by justification by faith. If we have to be perfect to be the recipient of God's love, we have no hope. We must simply do what we can and leave it in God's hand. The opposite of sin is not virtue, it is faith.
>
> If we take the world seriously, we need justification by faith, since it is not even a live option for us simply to do the right thing. As a stockbroker I came to see it this way, and I think this is somewhat parallel to the situation in every occupation. A stockbroker has at least a triple loyalty: to himself and his family, to his employer, and to his clients. These loyalties conflict. He has to take home a paycheck no matter what the state of the markets and the economy and of his clients' needs. There is no way he can serve all three loyalties perfectly. He is functioning in a fallen world whose societal structures are part of who he is, reflections of who we are as the human race. You do what you can, and trust that the incredible love is there for you no matter what.

The author of these sentiments (Robert Pollard, I can reveal here) was not asking for a reply; so I am answering gratuitously. But I could not resist applying the pattern of Rosenstock-Huessy's thinking to the situation described. One of Rosenstock-Huessy's recurrent ideas, although not necessarily articulated as such, is that the world always needs countervailing forces, to create a balance. I have been told that he used the word "concordance" to capture this notion, a claim that may not be accurate. This insight enables us to see a historical value or purpose for some beliefs that otherwise would seem to be totally erratic and lacking in synchronicity with the prevailing sentiments in the world. Rosenstock-Huessy is one of the few intellectuals I have ever heard praise Mary Baker Eddy's Christian Science. He spoke not about the particular tenets of the sect, but, he said, if not for the protests of the Christian Scientists *everyone* would be on their knees worshipping modern medicine.

Modern medicine is deified anyway, as we know, because its achievements are wondrous, but we worship this "industry" at our peril. George Bernard Shaw made that clear in his "Doctor's Dilemma" one hundred and fifty years ago. Christian Science, however seemingly irrational, sets a limit to our natural polytheism. It's not a matter of religion vs. science, but the recognition that although we sometimes must have faith in medical science, at other times we must have faith in, let's say, the law or politics or investigative journalism, which regularly expose the fraud, corruption, dishonesty, and greed that infects the medical profession no less than any other, for all its essential, benevolent work. The point here is certainly not to vilify the doctors, but in fact to peer into the underside of all of the professions turned into idols.

This is said as a preliminary to the larger question of engagement vs. disengagement with the world, where counterbalancing is essential. It is a necessity exemplified in the broad and diverse missions of Roman Catholic orders, the Trappists' silence, let's say, as compared to the Jesuits' verbalism. Rosenstock-Huessy, trained originally as a historian of medieval law, lectured explicitly about the particular roles and achievements of the different orders. The eremites in the desert, fleeing the "world," sanctified the wilderness by demonstrating that there is no spot on earth that needs to be feared because of the demons that lurk in it. The desert hermits proved that whatever evil animal spirits may lurk in the wilderness, there is also the over-ruling one God. The whole planet, which to the natural mind is full of terrors, by dint of this Judaeo-Christian message, that is, by faith in the oneness of the divine Creation, was thereby opened for exploration and development. This is another example of the dispelling of polytheism, of the banishing of the lesser gods of nature, which toyed with man.

The monks were not trying to be useful. They were trying to be holy. Nor are the Trappists trying to be useful, but their silence sanctifies speech. We need engagement with the world; we also need disengagement, which is to say the search for purity of being, because only such un-contamination can set a standard of holiness by which all conduct in the world may be measured. Such disengagement is not for everyone and it is certainly not tantamount to indifference.

Rosenstock-Huessy argued (as an anti-idealist, in the philosophical sense) that it is exemplary flesh-and-blood standards, mortal models, that thereafter define what is truly good and hence put in perspective all of the halfway goods. The initial incarnated good, the great, embodied pioneering soul, defines the good, which only much later becomes a meaningful abstraction. St. Francis was not living up to some philosopher's pre-existing concept of humility; only after St. Francis's life do we know what humility is. Socrates taught us what intellectual inquiry is, by which all inquiry thereafter is measured. It helps, as is often the case, that he was willing to die for the right to open inquiry.

In a world overtaken by utilitarian ethics as the supposed ultimate measure, we need to know that retreat from the world, and the rejection of usefulness as a sole criterion, is of parallel value to engagement— not of superior value, but equal value— because from it alone can we gain the measure of the good. Jonathan Edwards, the greatest American Christian thinker, posited "usefulness" and "devotion" in opposition to each other, and argued that of the two, devotion was far more valuable; but he went on, "not that I believe a man would be *less* useful even in this world, if his devotion was to that degree as to keep him all his lifetime in an extasie." Even divine ecstasy—totally non-productive by today's standards—in Edwards's judgment is "useful" by the measure of eternity.[1]

It is the balance of the two kinds of good that saves Christianity from the passivity of some Asian religions (the "ecstasy of indifference," G. K. Chesterton called it) or from philosophies that do not contain, as a counterbalance to monastic retreat, the explicit mandate to re-make the world for the better. Immersion in the world is necessary but it inescapably generates compromise and corruption. Without those living outside this world, striving for purity, how would we know what corruption is?

With Reinhold Niebuhr (and Rosenstock-Huessy), I am not a pacifist. There is not just one absolute response to violence and evil, such as turning the other cheek. But where would we be without the devout Quakers and other pietists who exemplify unconditional pacifism. Without their living example such a stance would be a mere abstraction and not believable. Like the Christian Scientists who refuse to bow down before the god of medical science, true pacifists refuse to worship the god of war or to accept the bloody human sacrifice we perpetually offer to him. These protests against the lesser gods do not diminish their power, unfortunately, but it is important to know when we are compromising, to know that there may be another way and that it has been lived. Rosenstock-Huessy defended priestly celibacy on the grounds that it served to prove that Venus was not universally worshipped. The pacifists, he noted in 1946, "are the indispensable antithesis to the ghastly warhoops of the temporal mind. . . . They are right when they abhor war as the order of the world; it certainly is its disorder. The world was created for peace. But they are wrong when they do not add that the act of creating the world is

1. Fiering, *Jonathan Edwards's Moral Thought*, 348–50.

a perpetual act. What we call the creation of the world is not an event of yesterday, but the event of all times, and goes on right under our noses."[2]

All of the above is also representative of the inescapable tension mankind must live with, the cross of reality in Rosenstock-Huessy's description, wherein our loyalties are tested every day by the vectors of space and time. Space wise, where should I stand and with whom? Time wise, when is the right time to act, if ever? To what or to whom do we pay homage? Who or what are we worshipping?[3] Anyone involved in finance, by enabling the creation of wealth and hence the means of overcoming the misery of material deprivation that has always afflicted the mass of mankind, is in theory engaged in justified service in the world. It is how one performs that service that matters—with integrity, decency, compassion, honor, scrupulosity. Where else are such virtues more needed than where the greatest sins are committed?

I will conclude with a quotation from a Rosenstock-Huessy classroom lecture of October 9, 1953 (from his "Cross of Reality" series, Lecture 2) speaking to Dartmouth undergraduates, at the time all male. As I have earlier noted, Professor Rosenstock-Huessy lectured extemporaneously. The course would move ahead crab-wise, because he often digressed when the spirit moved him. He was wholly captivated by the urgency of his message.

> It's too early for you to understand, but I have to announce it, so to speak. The . . . chastity of a woman's body must be always . . . paralleled by the chastity of a man's mind. Your body, the sins of your body, are not visited on you. . . . I think God is perfectly indifferent whether you go and have intercourse or not with

2. Rosenstock-Huessy, *Christian Future*, 224.

3. Rosenstock-Huessy, *Christian Future*: "Our existence is a perpetual suffering and wrestling with conflicting forces, paradoxes, contradictions, within and without. By them we are stretched and torn in opposite directions, but through them comes renewal. And these opposing directions are summed up by four which define the great space and time axes of all men's life on earth, forming a Cross of Reality. . . . Yet . . . no individual can move adequately in all four directions at once. Therefore life is a perpetual decision: when to continue the past and when to change, and where to draw the line between the inner circle we speak to and the outer objects we merely speak of and try to manipulate. Hence both mental and social health depends on preserving a delicate mobile balance between forward and backward, inward and outward, trends. Integration, living a complete and full life, is accordingly not some smooth 'adjustment' we can hope to achieve once for all and then coast along with, as popular psychology imagines; it is rather a constant achievement in the teeth of forces which tear us apart on the Cross of Reality." (166–69).

> somebody. . . . He is not interested in that, despite all the Puritans. But He is terribly interested that . . . you mean what you say. And you are utterly lost once you have become accustomed to the fact that that you can say that which sells [i.e., that you say what you say because it sells]. As soon as you begin to believe that a man can say that for which he gets a price, you are just a male harlot. [A] man is not a harlot . . . because he gives away his body. He is a harlot because he gives away his mind. And this is the prominent story of this country, and there is not even a warning uttered . . . towards young men that they must not do this.

At that point a student asserted that Dostoevsky wrote for a periodical for money, to put food in his mouth. Rosenstock-Huessy responded: "Well, he vomited. That's why he was so sick. The poor man knew exactly when he did one thing and when he did the other. Don't you think he knew? But of course, the whip of reality is on him. [But] As long as such a man says, 'I am cursed . . . because I have to do this' all his sins can be forgiven him."

Relevant here concerning chastity of mind is Rosenstock-Huessy's essay "Metanoia," an autobiographical piece reprinted in *I Am an Impure Thinker*. The catastrophe of World War I, in which Rosenstock-Huessy served as an officer in the Germany army, shocked him into the realization that European civilization as it had developed into the twentieth century was fundamentally flawed, and that life for him could not continue as it had. Before 1918 "the idol of scholarship held me firmly in its grip," he wrote, "let us call it charitably the god of the research of truth." As a teacher of its law and constitution, he also felt beholden to the German state, and he considered himself an orthodox member of the Christian church. His devotion to the three gods, "the god of scholarship, the god of government and law, and the god in church," had fortunately not killed his "sensitivity to the real sore spot of our society." In 1918, "my whole world organized in church, state, universities, the 'Western World,' that is, collapsed," as was foreseen, he noted, by Marx, by Henry Adams, by Nietzsche, and by Giuseppe Ferrari.[4]

4. Rosenstock-Huessy, "Metanoia." 185. Ferrari (1811–76) was a historian and editor of the works of Vico. Among many other subjects, he wrote on the history of revolutions in Italy.

> The Church, the Government, the institutions of higher learning, all three had piteously failed. They had not been anointed with one drop of the oil of prophecy, which God requires from our governors, from our teachers, and from our churches, if they shall act under the grace of God. Not one of them had any inkling of the doom or any vision for any future beyond mere national sovereignty. . . . The three representatives of [God's] Word on earth, the law of nations, the sacramental church, the universities, all three had been obtuse. They had lost [the] scent. . . . 'For we do not live by sight but by scent, of which faith is the sublimation.' (Luke 12:54ff)."[5]

Yet, predictably, in 1918 Rosenstock-Huessy received splendid offers from each of these three mirages to enter into their service. Nonetheless, he saw that "any role in any of these three doomed institutions would have gagged me and therefore at best be meaningless." Abandoning all three he went into industry editing a factory newspaper, innovative and urgent work in the labor relations sector where strife was endemic. "I did probably not advance much in personal virtue by this about-face towards the future, away from any visible institution. I did not become a saint. All I received was life. From then on, I had not to say anything which did not originate in my heart."

Thus conversion for Rosenstock-Huessy was the integration of speech and action. In the process, he said, he discovered the meaning of original sin. "Under original sin, the offices which we hold in society force us to think one way and act in another." This chain, he said, he had "broken." Repentance clearly does not apply where one confesses "private and usually perfectly unimportant sins." Rosenstock-Huessy emphatically rejected the notion that in 1918 he repented for private sins. He felt he was called into "a new, dangerous form of existence which did not yet exist."

> One cannot stress strongly enough the difference between this situation and the sinning against the Ten Commandments. I was in danger of falling into the sin against the Holy Ghost by doing the dead works of scholarship, state, [and] church. The urgency of the catastrophe challenged me to do repentance not for my sins but for the sin against the Holy Spirit committed and perpetuated by these institutions. The crime or sin against the Holy Spirit always is committed as a social and collective action. And we repent for it by dissociating ourselves from the profession or institution which is God forsaken.

5. Rosenstock-Huessy, "Metanoia." 183. The biblical citation is not exact.

But when institutions, including corporations, encompass most of accepted society, when "no social space or field exists outside the powers that be, and the existing institutions are all there is at the moment of one's metanoia," how is one to express this new faith. It takes "a lifetime and longer," Rosenstock-Huessy admitted, "to extricate oneself from the established institutions and to find new ways of establishing some less corrupt forms of expression for the living faith."

Metanoia, he said, is not a positive act of will. It is rather a refusal, "the unwillingness to continue," and this unwillingness "is not an act, but an experience." One feels that the usual words make no sense, "the atmosphere is stifled. One chokes. One has no choice but to leave." Yet there is no blueprint for the future. It is a "decision" in the exact Latin meaning, a "being cut-off from one's own routines in a paid and honored position." But one has faith that this "subzero situation is bound to create new ways of life."

This kind of "conversion," or turning point, Rosenstock-Huessy writes, can only apply to mature people in the world, who must write God's history of salvation. God cares little for the minor personal sins of youth. It is only the sins against the Holy Spirit committed by grown men and women that cannot be forgiven, for the obvious reason that their ramifications are so great. Thousands, millions of people can be affected by the failure of integrity that allows people in positions of social, economic, or political importance to continue in their "work" when it is perfectly evident to them that what they are doing is empty, at best, and woefully destructive at worst. As almost always in Rosenstock-Huessy's thought, the essence of metanoia comes down to voluntary death so that new life may emerge. One dies to the old ways and is born anew, although not without suffering and risk.

Professor Rosenstock-Huessy returned to the academy later in the 1920s, teaching at Breslau, and then after coming to the United States in 1933, at Harvard and Dartmouth. But anyone who attended his classes knows that he conformed not at all to the protocols of academe. He was a rebel, or better, a prophet, in the midst of what he saw as a higher education that had lost its way. He believed that the mechanistic, positivistic, relativistic standards of the social sciences caused tragedy after tragedy in the world.

4

The Structure of Significant Lives

[Originally prepared for the ERH Society conference on "William James and Eugen Rosenstock-Huessy, The Moral Equivalent of War and the Social Representation of Truth," held at Dartmouth College, November 12 and 13, 2010. Revised July 2016 and published in the journal *The European Legacy*, 22, no. 4 (2017), 406–26. I have made some minor changes in this version.]

THE CITY UNIVERSITY OF New York a few years ago received a gift endowing a new "center" focused on the study of "biography." For anyone interested in the patterns of actual lives, that might appear to be an encouraging development. Its declared aim, however, is simply to build connections between independent and academic biographers and to encourage discussion about the art and craft of biography. This is the usual goal of such programs: improvement and propagation of a literary art, which is to say, the study of texts as opposed to actual lives. "Biography" does have this double meaning, referring both to a book or to the corporeal three-score-and-ten on earth most of us are granted. It's like the word "history," which means both the past and writings about the past.

The question I want to conjure with here is whether the real lives of men or women of great distinction tend to unfold in any particular pattern that is revealing of some of the deeper psychological and spiritual forces that move us. If one undertook to read scores of biographies of major contributors to society, would there be anything fundamentally similar in many of these stories of accomplishment, an impetus beyond the usual recounting? We want, of course, to get beyond mere romanticizing, such as biographical movies typically indulge in, with a familiar triadic formula that appeals to our hearts, a sequence portraying, first, youthful talent and hope, followed by a time of adversity, and then ultimately triumph, with the mandatory help of a good woman.

I am asking this question because Rosenstock-Huessy believed that a pattern may be found in some significant lives, if not all, that reveals to us sources of creativity and effective action beyond the superficial. He was particularly interested in "distemporaries," a word of his coining, referring to geniuses far ahead of their time (or sometimes behind) and therefore embattled in their quest for recognition. It cannot be denied that Rosenstock-Huessy came at the question with an existing theory, his so-called grammatical method; so we have to ask whether the theory really helps, and whether the method is confirmed by specific cases or whether it is no more than an artificial, abstract layer imposed on a less orderly reality.[1]

At Dartmouth College, where Rosenstock-Huessy taught from 1935 to 1957, he approved warmly of an actual course on the subject of biography taught by Prof. Arthur Wilson, the author of a prize-winning life of the *philosophe* Diderot. Such a course was a rarity in higher education anywhere, and Rosenstock-Huessy would have been happy to see the example spread beyond Hanover, New Hampshire. In his preface to *The Christian Future* he called attention to Ambrose Vernon as one who "twice has founded a college department for biography—at Carleton and at Dartmouth." Vernon, according to Rosenstock-Huessy, believed that "the life of Christ . . . would meet the students through the lives of other great souls in history, if the spiritual core of biography could be opened up to them as a lawful order," that is, as an understandable pattern although dependent upon unpredictable movements of the spirit.

1. Aside from specific citations below, for some general reading on Rosenstock-Huessy in English, see M. Darrol Bryant and Hans H. Huessy, eds., *Eugen Rosenstock-Huessy: Studies in His Life and Thought*; Wayne Cristaudo, *Religion, Redemption, and Revolution*; George Morgan, *Speech and Society*; Lise van der Molen, *A Guide to the Works of Eugen Rosenstock-Huessy*; "Recent Publications Relating to the Work of Eugen Rosenstock-Huessy, 1973 to 2013" at www.erhsociety.org/publications. Recordings of hundreds of hours of Rosenstock-Huessy's vibrant lectures, with transcriptions, can be found at www.erhfund.org/lectures.

I don't know what Professor Wilson taught in his class on biography, but I am guessing that despite Rosenstock-Huessy's approval, Wilson was primarily interested in the literary or historical art of writing biography, the methodology and the problems faced by the biographer, as at the new CUNY center, and not so much in the "spiritual core" of the life portrayed. Rosenstock-Huessy was looking for both universal and distinctive configurations in significant lives, particularly the turning points or "conversions," although not in the usual religious sense. He pointed to the meaningful suffering that may beset a person living in advance of his time, and he examined the matter of timing itself, the study of what he called the "too early and the too late." At any given moment, all those alive are not necessarily contemporaries, he stressed. Some will be too far behind or too far ahead to be socially or intellectually accepted and thus can find no solace or sanity in their community. Rosenstock-Huessy, in fact, urged the serious study of the "science of timing," although what that might mean in practice is not clear. Whatever the case, he had no doubt that Shakespeare had it right: "ripeness is all" as is said in *King Lear*. It is the right action or the right word at the right moment that rule the tides of history. If the timing is wrong, even the truest words will fall on deaf ears—until the time is right.[2]

As a historian facing the perennial question of whether it is so-called impersonal economic and social forces that determine the course of events or particular men and women in particular circumstances who principally effect change, Rosenstock-Huessy seemed to favor the latter, if for no other reason than the inspirational: such a faith encourages the individual to make sacrifices and take risks for human betterment. Is God's will evident in historical developments? We can only guess at that, and pray, but if it is the determining factor, it is manifested solely in courageous, groundbreaking, individual *human* action—the "human spirit," as we call it, once more triumphing over the forces of darkness. For Rosenstock-Huessy, "human spirit" is simply the modern euphemism for the old-fashioned "holy spirit" of religious discourse. But despite his occasional recurrence to the traditional vocabulary of Christian doctrine, there is no sign of beyond-this-earth, magical interventions in Rosenstock-Huessy's thought. God exists in time, not in space, and it is

2. Rosenstock-Huessy, "Teaching Too Late, Learning Too Early, " in *I Am an Impure Thinker*: "The time has come to build up a science of timing . . . its Novum Organum will be the timing of teaching and learning, because they are its basic phenomena." 91–92.

He who calls us into a better future. But the voice we hear—beckoning, urging, commanding— is not from the clouds: it could be that of a friend, relative, neighbor, colleague, or indeed a word spoken centuries ago in an ancient text that has somehow, at a particular moment, affected us profoundly and given us new energy and a new direction.

In his essay "Holderlin and Nietzsche," written in 1941 and published in English for the first time in a collection entitled *The Cross and the Star: The Post-Nietzschean Christian and Jewish Thought of Eugen Rosenstock-Huessy and Franz Rosenzweig* edited by Wayne Cristaudo, Rosenstock-Huessy makes a remarkable comment about Nietzsche. He confesses that with few exceptions he was little impressed by the content of any of Nietzsche's books, but what made Nietzsche of imperishable importance in Rosenstock-Huessy's view was not only Nietzsche's brilliant writing but "his life." Reflecting back on his own academic career in Germany in the 1920s and 1930s, with two Heidelberg degrees behind him, Rosenstock-Huessy commented:

> In the heart of the German university tradition, in the [field of] Classics, a man had achieved success and abandoned it. The one universal ambition of any German, to become a professor, he had reached and transcended. . . . An unseen new trail had been beaten by Nietzsche around the times which surrounded me, free from any requirements of institutions, but imperative for our real life in the future. Never have I doubted, never have I shaken off my belief, that in Nietzsche something final had happened, an avatar of the divine ended. He had stepped outside of his time.[3]

Always in Rosenstock-Huessy's thinking the radical changes in the progress of mankind are brought about initially by the actions of a single person, that is, by living, concrete example first, not by detached ideas concocted in the head. The embodiment or incarnation of a wholly new exemplary way of being, evident in the *life* of a person, comes first, from which we may thereafter draw a lesson, or a moral, or derive "values," as we like to say, and thereby be freed from a prior social constraint (or perhaps fall under a new constraint). The point is, nothing is proven or established until it is first lived. Ideas in themselves are plentiful and cheap. "I have been the sworn enemy of philosophical idealism all my life," Rosenstock-Huessy wrote, "because it separates mind and body,

3. Rosenstock-Huessy, "Holderlin and Nietzsche," 18–19.

spirit and incarnation. I prefer a child to an idea, and Lincoln to any abstract principle."[4]

The exceedingly brilliant student of Classics, Nietzsche, permanently undermined a German ideal, or idol, indeed a false god, by his devaluation of an academic career. In this respect, Nietzsche emancipated Rosenstock-Huessy himself. The revelation by deed comes before the later articulated abstract "truth"—there are greater things in life than an academic chair in Classics—although our worship of human "reason" leads us to believe proudly, after the fact, that we knew it all along, adhering to the vanity that values and ideals are generated first by our mind's genius, our brain, and followed later by embodiment. But for Rosenstock-Huessy, the beginning is the *incarnated* word. In his unpublished "Letters to Cynthia" of the 1940s, Rosenstock-Huessy adopted the adage, "Our forebears are our values," which was Cynthia Harris's condensation of his teaching on this point. Since the singular, concrete, pathbreaking accomplishment is usually quickly followed by countless similar feats, the bravery and originality of the pioneer may easily become depreciated. But no subsequent action is as difficult as the first, when it was unheard of. Columbus's 1492 voyage was replicated in the decades after by many subsequent Atlantic crossings, and soon it is claimed, "anyone could have done it," or anyone could have thought of it.

We see a similar perception to that concerning Nietzsche in Rosenstock-Huessy's commentary on two of the greatest philosophical intellects in American history, Jonathan Edwards (d. 1758) and William James (d. 1910). He knew and admired the writings of both men, but he also deliberately called attention to their humanity and to some telling episodes in their lives. The image of the thinker who somehow transcends quotidian life was laughable to Rosenstock-Huessy, and he delighted in referring to himself as an "impure" thinker, one who was subject to myriad unheroic weaknesses, as are all humans. The only serious question is: What enables us, despite our weaknesses, to sometimes lead and to serve bravely, to manifest the best of the human spirit and create new futures for mankind when we are mired in an unacceptable present?

Rosenstock-Huessy saw in the biographies of both Edwards and James (and in many other lives about which he commented: St. Augustine; St. Francis; Jean Calvin; the French social thinker, Henri de Saint-Simon; Cardinal Newman; Homer Lea, for example) defining events that settled

4. Rosenstock-Huessy, "Teaching Too Late," 108.

their course of action or in the end helped to elevate them to greatness. Jonathan Edwards was the most prominent Congregationalist minister in New England in ca. 1745, one of only a handful of Americans at the time with an international reputation, and he was no compromiser. In mid-life, with a large family to support, he was shockingly dismissed by his congregation in Northampton, Massachusetts, over issues of principle about which he would not retreat. Although other choices were open to him, including a pulpit in Scotland, Edwards chose to go into exile in Stockbridge, Massachusetts, a frontier village at the time, in the relatively minor position of missionary to the Indians. The six years in Stockbridge turned out to be the most productive of his life as a writer, and he was vindicated in 1757 by an invitation to become president of the College of New Jersey (later Princeton University). We may see this episode as a kind of profile in courage, a moral example, but Rosenstock-Huessy had more in mind than that in his biographical studies, as will become apparent.

In his 1942 lecture "The Soul of William James," Rosenstock-Huessy describes the debilitating depression James suffered in his late twenties, brought on it seems by a mechanistic cosmological view, much the fashion at the time, and by his struggle with the problem of evil. James was rescued by his encounter with the work of the distinguished French philosopher Charles Renouvier, who became the greatest single influence on James's thought. They corresponded over a period of years, and James finally met Renouvier personally in 1903, shortly before Renouvier's death. Rosenstock-Huessy refers to Renouvier as "the *converter* of William James." And James himself wrote: "Yesterday was a crisis in my life. I finished Renouvier's definition of free will. My first act of free will shall be to believe in free will." And later he wrote, "Since years ago, I read Renouvier, the center of my *Anschauung* [philosophical view] has been that something is doing in the universe and that novelty is real."[5]

The two narratives—concerning Jonathan Edwards and William James—are totally different except that both, in Rosenstock-Huessy's terms, are examples of figurative death and resurrection, or of deep despair and renewal, and are exemplary, as well, of lives (including Nietzsche's) that break the mold, defy the conventional expectations of the time, and open up new paths for others to follow. One of the questions that

5. Rosenstock-Huessy, "The Soul of William James." Much of Rosenstock-Huessy's understanding of James came from Perry, *The Thought and Character of William James.* Perry wrote: "That Renouvier was the greatest single influence upon the development of James's thought cannot be doubted" (633).

Rosenstock-Huessy is implicitly asking here is: What tools do we have for interpreting such personal crises? Empiricist or behaviorist psychologies are not equal to the task.

How could he not believe in the bodily resurrection of Jesus Christ, Rosenstock-Huessy would assert, when he had himself experienced death and renewal in his own life more than once. In his teaching and writing, he drew attention to rebirth in the lives of a number of great, creative men, although there is no implication that being "born again" is confined to the great, and certainly no implication that being born again is somehow strictly or exclusively associated with evangelical Christian churches. Rosenstock-Huessy argued that what the lives of Jesus and his disciples revealed to the world had universal application—that is indeed the very basis of their importance—but the discoveries the gospel contributed to human freedom sometimes needed to be extricated from entanglement in conventional churchliness. Those "born again" in the evangelical Christian tradition are a less exclusive club than they may imagine. To be resurrected in this life is a universal entitlement.[6]

The more famous the name, the more reason to look for the *crucial* moments, "the spiritual core of biography," the crises, the awakenings, the commitments, the sufferings that reveal both the greatness of a man or woman and the actual, concrete means by which humankind slowly, painfully moves towards its destiny. My use of the word "crucial" above is not arbitrary in the case of Rosenstock-Huessy. We are all—the famous and the infamous, the notable and the obscure—inescapably suspended on a figurative cross throughout our short existence on the planet. The most basic opposing or alternative vectors in time and in space—past vs. future, inside vs. outside—threaten to pull us apart with incessant questions of when and where. Choices are regularly put before us that in the end may be reduced simply to those four alternatives. In matters big and small, we must ask: Do I act now or later? When do I take a stand, if ever? Am I for change or continuity? Should I be here or there, inside or outside of this group, this cause, this movement, this marriage? Choices may be postponed, we may achieve a temporary equilibrium, but we are bound to

6. It is possible that I am making Rosenstock-Huessy too much of an Emersonian here. It remains a question, regardless of his avowals, what kind of Christian Rosenstock-Huessy was. See Löwith's review of Rosenstock-Huessy's *The Christian Future*. Rosenstock-Huessy's *Fruit of Our Lips* (available in a new edition in 2021) gives a quite different impression of the depth and orthodoxy of his faith than *The Christian Future* does.

be challenged and tested in the stages of our life if we live intelligently. On the other hand, we see, in some lives, moments that lead to a permanent resolve. Doubt always remains in a sane person, but the sustained singleness of purpose derived from an inspiration, that is, a gift of the spirit, or a moment of grace, may free us from some of the uncertainty.

In an imaginative leap, Rosenstock-Huessy made the crucifixion of Jesus emblematic *in extremis* of the nature of the human condition in a general sense. He believed that, historically, uniquely, it was Christian teachings that set us free from the domination of any single past and from the confines of any one group, which had never before been true of any segment of humankind. With freedom comes choice, but also agony. Christianity, Rosenstock-Huessy writes,

> assumes a turning point in every person's life, or rather it inserts such a turning point into every life. It smashes the generalization "life." The days of a life cease to be merely equal fractions of a "whole," a life that supposedly proceeds uniformly from cradle to grave. A Christian's year is not made up of 365 individual days; a Christian's life is not made up of 70 individual years. The movement of "life" is separated into several creative acts: before rebirth and after rebirth people live in different worlds. The soul ceases to live an incremental life. It progresses in jolting steps, in creative acts.[7]

Always Rosenstock-Huessy disdained the mindless application to human affairs of the physicists' conception of time, made up of equal increments and suitable only for measuring dead things. The "scientism" of the social sciences carried over from the natural sciences is the greatest perpetrator of this destructive practice, which reduces man to an object.[8]

PARACELSUS (1493–1541)

The longest piece of writing on biography in English by Rosenstock-Huessy may be his ardent fifty-page essay on Paracelsus. The work, with the title "The Founder of the Science of Life: The Tripartition in the Life

7. Rosenstock-Huessy, "Ichthys," in Rosenstock-Huessy, *Fruit of Our Lips*, 40–52.

8. Rosenstock-Huessy was hardly alone in his concern about the disastrous overreach of the "scientific method" in the nineteenth and twentieth centuries. Cf. McKnight, "Voegelin's New Science of History" "On a deeper level, arguing against the introduction of the spatial category of measurement to the internal human experience of duration, see Bergson, *Time and Free Will.*

of Theophrastus Paracelsus von Hohenheim, 1493–1541," was composed at Dartmouth College in ca. 1937 and survives in photocopies of an original mimeograph.[9]

Rosenstock-Huessy admired Paracelsus as a pioneering physician and biologist, who is sometimes characterized as the anti-Galen, but the focus of his biographical sketch was the structure of this scientist's life, which he formalized into a paradigm of the life of that rare breed in human history, the founder of something entirely new. My use of the word "paradigm" here will immediately suggest to some readers a connection to Thomas Kuhn's influential work *The Structure of Scientific Revolutions* (1962) with its discussion of "paradigm shifts" in the history of natural science. However, I am talking about a *biographical* paradigm, Kuhn about the prevailing scientific paradigms that govern the approach or assumptions of a large body of scientists, as for example in the history of astronomy, supporters of Ptolemy versus supporters of Copernicus. Nonetheless, Kuhn's well-known work is relevant in that Rosenstock-Huessy's writing on the practice of science as a social phenomenon anticipated Kuhn by decades.[10]

There is much in Rosenstock-Huessy's essay on Paracelsus to distract us from my main point: the question of the frameworks available to us for examining the structure of biography. The Paracelsus essay is, for example, among other things, an instance of Rosenstock-Huessy's determined attack, found in various of his works, on academe's overly vaunted view of Renaissance Humanism. It was the Humanists who, as it happened, hounded and ultimately destroyed Paracelsus because he refused to believe that the study of Classical texts was the key to progress in medicine and biology. Thus Paracelsus's "fatal conflict with the Humanists of his time," Rosenstock-Huessy writes, "is of so gigantic dimensions that modern scientists like [William] Dampier who try to give a history of science, remain helpless before this tragedy." Dampier, subservient to the Humanist mirage, could not believe there could be any falsehood in the official record. But innumerable, deliberate

9. The essay on Paracelsus may be found in the informal publication, "Rosenstock-Huessy Papers," vol. 1, under the title "A Classic and a Founder."

10. Kuhn, *Structure of Scientific Revolutions*. For the scientist as first of all a person, see Rosenstock-Huessy's 1939 essay, "Modern Man's Disintegration and the Egyptian Ka": "The scientist must hold to the faith that every person that decides to become a scientist does so not as a scientist but as a human being who harkens to his deepest calling" (49–50). There is a similar argument in Eric Weil's "Science in Modern Culture," but I doubt that Weil and Rosenstock-Huessy were aware of each other.

falsehoods there were, and Rosenstock-Huessy condemns, as well, the Humanists' successors into the twentieth century, who have ridiculed Paracelsus without reading him, blindly carrying on a tradition of disparagement and perpetuating calumnies.[11]

Paracelsus was so extraordinarily ahead of his time that trouble with his contemporaries was inevitable. He formulated a method based upon observation above all, and not just static observation, but varied observation, that is, looking at varying instances of a phenomenon in as many venues as possible. One must turn the pages of one's art, he said, with one's feet, that is, by travel and by "surveying with [one's] eyes the characteristic element of each place." Today this practice is enshrined in the sciences as fieldwork. Judging most of the existing book learning in medicine as nearly worthless, Paracelsus fraternized with all levels of society, looking for information and clues relating to bodily illnesses. He talked to peasants and to those who, above all, had first-hand experience.[12]

In 1526, this heretic in the eyes of the learned was improbably invited to teach at the University of Basel. Paracelsus had restored to health the famous printer Johann Froben, whose press was located in Basel. Froben was much admired among the Humanists and had even worked closely with the great Erasmus. Paracelsus's clinical success with Froben was enough, apparently, to overcome the opposition and get him a lectureship. Yet, Rosenstock-Huessy observes, "two contradictory forms of thought, of research, of social standards and of faith clashed in the tragedy" that ensued.

To begin with, Paracelsus was required by university rules to lecture in Latin, and secondly, he was not permitted to teach his own findings as a physician. He was expected to descant from the books of the so-called authorities, that is, the ancients, who knew far less than he did about disease and its causes. Paracelsus was a perfectly good Latinist, but he insisted on teaching in German, keeping "his feet on real mother earth, his mind on real data." He was the first man in the Western world who lectured in a university openly in his native tongue, Rosenstock-Huessy believed, and he taught not from the books of others but from his own research. "Smooth talk in different languages does not make a physician

11. Rosenstock-Huessy, "Classic and a Founder," 20. Sir William Dampier (d. 1952) wrote extensively on the history of science. Rosenstock-Huessy is probably referring to *Cambridge Readings in the Literature of Science* (1924).

12. Rosenstock-Huessy, "Classic and a Founder," 27–42.

nor the reading of many books; he is made by the knowledge of the material world and its hidden powers." So Paracelsus told his students.

Unsurprisingly, Paracelsus lasted only one year at the University of Basel, but it was the formative, the generative year for him and it shaped his mission in life or, Rosenstock-Huessy might say, his "commission":

> This one year marks an epoch in the whole rich production of Theophrastus. It seems as if every sentence spoken at Basel, every question put to him in these few months, every idea articulated under the pressure of regular teaching . . . was, by its belonging to this extraordinary year, indelible, forever asking to be further developed. Like the promises which an honest man makes good, these words were followed up by weighty and voluminous works.

Paracelsus's character "crystallized," to use Rosenstock-Huessy's metaphor. He acquired his indelible character and what might be thought of as his "appointment by God," as a result of "his conflicts with the men among whom he had to live by the odd appointment to a professorship." Like the light from distant stars, Rosenstock-Huessy writes, generations may pass before the new illumination from a genius truly reaches us. "Is it not true that the light generated by a human heart undergoes similar laws of irradiation . . . ? When a new light shines up among men, in its first year of appearance it is hardly visible." "It is not to be wondered at that the students . . . [of Theophrastus von Hohenheim] were not prepared to understand the new deity of experience and experimentation and her prophet."[13]

From his dismissal from the University of Basel in 1527 until his death in 1541, Paracelsus wandered in a "sandy desert," according to Rosenstock-Huessy. The Humanist physicians and other enemies labored to destroy him and blocked the publication of his work. The desert presented not so much the danger of starvation as "the permanent danger of complete oblivion." Yet Paracelsus also made friends, a few people "intimately affected by something inexpressibly great in the man. These people became the trustees of his knowledge and the manuscripts which he dictated. . . . During constant medical practice and traveling thousands of miles, he managed to produce about ten thousand pages of manuscript in these fourteen years." The year 1527 thus became "the axis" of Paracelsus's life: "Losing his office as a professor, he made his life the profession of

13. Rosenstock-Huessy, "Classic and a Founder," 47.

the new office that he felt himself to hold." As with Rosenstock-Huessy's comments on Nietzsche, the shape of the life is viewed as a legacy equal to the work, a life such as no one had ever lived before, indeed, a new type of man.[14] Northern Europe at the time had room for but two classes of learned men, Humanists and Protestant clergy, but von Hohenheim could be identified neither with Erasmus nor with Luther. "One might almost assert that [Paracelsus's] light was so far away from his incidental contemporaries that they did not see him at all." Two halves of learned mankind could not place him in their picture of the world.

We can talk about natural science today as though there was always a place for its practitioners in society. What is not understood, Rosenstock-Huessy maintained, is that "a new form of thought must be lived first before it may be externalized into endowed institutions. And that is exactly what Theophrastus did: He lived that same life of immediate, encyclopedic, unprejudiced, experimental research on which modern society bases its existence." One sees in the biography of Paracelsus three "distinct forms of existence," according to Rosenstock-Huessy: the thirty-three years before Basel, when he was still "unchallenged, unattacked, growing"; one year at Basel, when Paracelus was initially honored and expected to carry through with recognized duties; finally, the fourteen years after his time at the university and his encounter with the establishment, "a target of slander, persecution, danger and illness."

"The highest times of men are whenever heaven and earth, world and inspiration, seem to meet," Rosenstock-Huessy writes. When that is the circumstance, "external position and inner life seem firmly balanced on all fours." But such moments rarely last. A person in a position of responsibility, let's say for an institution or an organization, learns that to "succeed," compromise with the "world" is a necessity. The "ordinary, natural" man knows how to distinguish between ideals and realities. He may call himself an idealist, but he acts as a realist under the watchful eye of those to whom he is accountable. Paracelsus at Basel, however, was "beyond the interests of the natural man. The pursuit of happiness [is] now meaningless to him. . . . He will use and exploit and outwit and overreach his own nature to make her the carrier of the message that is entrusted to him."[15] "His own life is a tool now," Rosenstock-Huessy

14. As we will see below, Rosenstock-Huessy said the same of Freud: "That Freuds are able to exist is more important than psychoanalysis" (*Soziologie*, vol. I: 305).

15. It is hard to resist the thought that Rosenstock-Huessy, consciously or unconsciously, is in some general way identifying with Paracelsus. He says of Paracelsus that

writes. Paracelsus experienced "the existence of the divine inspiration beyond any doubt. . . . He is left as a witness of the higher life, as a herald of its promises and potentialities. . . . He is under one single obligation: What the world rebuked and refused to accept has to be proved to be the acceptable gift of future life." The founder may not survive the ordeal. One hopes that there are at least a few loyal followers who will do the work of translating the initial bestowal of grace into a lawful order. No one will again be Paracelsus, nor does the generality of humankind ever experience such extremes. But yet Rosenstock-Huessy believed that a similar tripartition of life, although more pallid, is "a common experience of all true humans."

Paracelsus was "a new type of man, moving in a new world, using new language, and living with his fellow men in a new fellowship." Of course, no institution "will endure the contact with a creature that had never existed before. He is howled down from the chair, and the world does all it can to make sure that he will be down forever. He now faces despair, or compromise, or thirdly, the slow road of waiving comfort, peace, and rest, and re-building, brick after brick, the palace of truth that before had appeared to him gratuitously."[16]

The English poet Robert Browning got it right, Rosenstock-Huessy believed, in his long poem "Paracelsus": "He is sure that God never dooms to waste the strength he deigns impart."[17] Grace, the commission, the calling, the revelation, the infusion of the spirit is thus transformed into a new "descendible law. We repay, by our faithful masonry, ploughing and building up from the ground, our load of gratitude for the inspiration, the abundance of inspiration, that fills us in our best hours."

Always eager to breathe new life into the ancient vocabularies of law, religion, and morality, Rosenstock-Huessy repeatedly in his writing and lecturing attempted to rescue from silly misconceptions certain

---

what he has to offer must be "acceptable to God," whether or not it is accepted by man. This is a heroic challenge because the devil, the "tempter, whispers, of course, smiling: 'Neither man nor god is interested in your craziness.' Under the spur of this inner temptation and the external disaster, the child of genius is turned into the fighting apostle" (46).

16. Rosenstock-Huessy, "Classic and a Founder," 43–51.

17. The quotation is from Browning, "Paracelsus," vol. 1, lines 366–67 ("Be sure that God / Ne'er dooms to waste the strength he deigns impart") in the definitive edition of this long dramatic poem, edited by Woolford and Karlin. Browning did a considerable amount of research on Paracelsus, and the poem was to some degree influenced by Goethe's *Faust*.

irreplaceable descriptive terms—such as "grace," "spirit," "soul," "conversion," "revelation." In what he called our "post-theological" age, none of these enduring words need be associated with the mystical, the paranormal, or the magical, when they can be properly translated into everyday mundane experience. It is a handicap that such terms are not part of the acceptable language of science, which is, alas, almost the only recognized intellectual authority in our time, but since they are not material, measurable, and spatial entities, they are deemed inadmissible. It is stupidly asked: Where is the soul? Or, Why can't I see the spirit? Few people understand the severe limitations of scientific description, how it excludes about three-quarters of human living, which is experienced mostly in categories of time, not space.[18] A moment of grace is not an angelic whisper in our ear accompanied by organ music. It can just as well be an e-mail. Rather, what sets grace apart is that it does not fit into the ordinary, billiard-ball-colliding-with-billiard-ball concept of causation or even into the more sophisticated concept of invariable sequence. It is not reducible to a mental or material cause, nor is it explicable in the terminology of natural science, which, as a matter of quite commendable strict faith in its own methodology, cannot concern itself with any phenomenon not reducible at some point to a universal law. But the permanent uniqueness of an event does not make a moment of "grace" somehow weird, since it is quite commonplace for persons to be reached, touched, moved, and energized into action by speech, whether written or spoken, and it is usually fruitless to look for some concatenation of "causes" behind the event, whether mental or physical. "Speech is the body of the spirit," in Rosenstock-Huessy's words, and mysterious though its effects inherently are and irreducible, speech itself is quite material, made up of nothing more than air and flesh, or breath and the motion of throat, lips, tongue, and so forth. Yet the scientific study of the extraordinary human speech faculty will never tell us anything about grace.[19]

18. In Rosenstock-Huessy, *Practical Knowledge of the Soul*, the author assigns soul, body, and spirit each a place in mundane human experience that is indisputable. See chapter 5, below: "Soul, Body, Spirit."

19. Martin E. Marty, longtime editor of the *Christian Century* and a prolific author, in various contexts has called attention to Rosenstock-Huessy's emphasis on grace as the center of life (see Marty, *By Way of Response* and "A Life of Learning.") Rosenstock-Huessy wrote extensively on speech, and on no other subject, other than perhaps his writing on the subject of time, is his work more illuminating and original. In a world supposedly disenchanted by materialism and positivistic science, the wonder of our capacity for speech (by which he meant more than just talk or "communication")

Rosenstock-Huessy considered it a tragic misconception that Cartesian notions relating to the behavior of matter ended up being adopted by the *human* sciences as universal principles and as a criterion for truth. All that anyone needs to do is to look at their own life experience to see how useless such "laws" are beyond the study of the motion of bodies. When in the course of a moment or a month or many months or even years, we "find" ourselves, as the expression goes, that is, find direction and know what we want to do with our life, or maybe because of some particular encouragement take a chance on the future, such deliverances may be categorized as "gracious" precisely because they are unpredictable and irreducible, not part of a recognizable chain of causation. Human experience, whether in macro-history or intimate biography, is full of events that can never be simply "explained" in scientific terms. To accept that fact does not make one a devotee of the para-normal or the occult.

Already in the eighteenth century, when religion and science came into sharp confrontation, Jonathan Edwards in private notebooks called his "Miscellanies" wrestled brilliantly with the meaning of the term "miracle" and came up with an analysis superior even to David Hume's classic reasoning. Number 1263 of Edwards's "Miscellanies" is ostensibly a defense of miracles, but the total effect of it is to diffuse the idea of a miracle along a graded scale, so that in the end one can speak only of the more or less miraculous in a natural world that is one great miracle in all of its parts, which Darwinian theories do not even begin to account for. The arbitrary law-giving God and the God who is Himself necessarily limited by fixed laws are not altogether separable. The arbitrary act is "the first and foundation of the other and that which all divine operation must finally be resolved into." An arbitrary action, in Edwards's definition, or what I have been calling a unique event, should not be interpreted as an action opposed to God's law-abiding rationality. The original establishment of the laws of nature is itself an instance of arbitrary operation. God's arbitrariness appears in His supreme originality, not in whimsicalness. It becomes clearer, as Edwards progresses, that the meaning of "arbitrary" for him is the "new," the "unique," the "unprecedented," and the "particular," not the unconditioned. Thus, the first act in any series is arbitrary in a sense, or it is more arbitrary than the subsequent acts. As Edwards explains arbitrariness it is perfectly compatible with the strictest exercise of

brings back a great deal of the mystery without a hint of the occult. See, e.g., his *Origin of Speech* and *Speech and Reality*. See also Ong, "The Spiritual Meaning of Technology and Culture," 29–34.

scientific reason. The so-called arbitrary actions of the deity differ from fixed laws only in that they are less common. Spiritual relations are rare and refined occurrences, and in that sense arbitrary, God's will in these matters being largely unknowable on earth. Edwards pointedly rejected the notion that spiritual relations are amorphous and fuzzy. Their precision, he argued, is not below that of mathematical physics, but above it, and because of that fact not measurable with man's rough calibrators.[20] My goal here is not in the least to introduce divinity or magical occurrence but to make room in secular psychology for irreducible, unique, or arbitrary individual events that are determinative of the future.

Thus, although it is necessary and laudable for the historian to uncover, retrospectively, the causes of the French Revolution or the causes of the American Civil War, only a fool believes that the foundations are thereby laid for a science of history that in the future will enable us to predict the moment of revolution or the outbreak of war, let alone the moment of inspiration that shapes the life of an individual. We are now in the strange situation that the investigation of moments of inspiration in the lives of individuals, which beyond all else shape the course of events, is deemed a lower order of research than what occurs in a chemistry or psychology lab and is thereby relegated to departments of religion, where there is supposedly less rigor, and where rigor simply means reducible to quantification or *visual* inspection.

In autobiography, as in history, we may profitably look back and try to understand how our destiny unfolded, often quite unexpectedly in relation to our youthful aims, and why we chose what we chose and did what we did, but such recollections and recapitulations all occur long after the fact. Such a retrospective view, Rosenstock-Huessy said, is the last stage of any event, the analytical or scientific phase, when all the vitality that was present at the beginning is long passed, in fact quite dead: "Genius has its everlasting, spiritual laws. As soon as we place grace where it belongs, in the center of life, as its inspiration, its directing force, life ceases to be arbitrary or accidental or casual or boring." Any important institution in history is founded twice, "once by a stroke of genius, and a second time by the labors of the duty." Over decades or centuries it may have to be founded more than twice, but always at least twice, "one as a free gift from supernal

20. See Fiering, *Jonathan Edwards's Moral Thought*, 97–104.

inspiration, one as honest fruit of great fatigue and error." Rosenstock-Huessy described this as the law of two-fold beginnings.[21]

SIGMUND FREUD (1856–1939)

Let us now look at a case four centuries after Paracelsus, the exemplary life of Sigmund Freud, another noble physician. No one would ever describe Rosenstock-Huessy as an admirer of Freudianism or of psychoanalytical theory. In fact, he tellingly pointed out the inadequacy of the psychological structure of ego, id, superego, and external reality, and the unremitting internal struggle they portended. Yet he gave credit to the man Sigmund Freud, and as with Paracelsus and others, he saw in the elements of Freud's life a paradigm, although he used a different terminology than he did with Paracelsus to describe the pattern.[22]

In volume 1 of his *Soziologie*, long in the making but first published in 1956 (and reissued in a new edition by Thalheimer in 2008–9), Rosenstock-Huessy devoted some ten pages to what he called the "tides of time" and the "transformations of time" that can be extracted from looking at the stages in Freud's life related to the founding of psychoanalysis. The pages on Freud also incorporate commentary on the varieties and meaning of time, a subject about which Rosenstock-Huessy made original and profound contributions, although as yet little recognized.[23]

Our focus here is on the succession of the radically different kinds of time that can be perceived in the stages of Freud's life. Yes, "kinds of time." Rosenstock-Huessy was aghast at the simplemindedness of the common idea that it is adequate to describe time as merely the fourth dimension of space, when time has its own dimensions and is the medium of human culture, the stream in which we live and die, the basis of Judeo-Christian thought and of the Western legal tradition. Even the most distinctive of

21. Rosenstock-Huessy, "Classic and a Founder," 48.

22. It is a wasted effort, I believe, to try to reconcile variant versions of Rosenstock-Huessy's fundamental ideas. Variations are not the same as inconsistencies. He was rarely starkly inconsistent. But it is exactly in accordance with who he was and what he taught that at different times he would see similar phenomena somewhat differently.

23. For these comments on Freud, I have relied on a translation by Susan Solomon of pages 303–12 in Rosenstock-Huessy's *Soziologie*. Much of Rosenstock-Huessy's work on time is not yet available in English. One recent commentary is Leithart, "The Social Articulation of Time in Eugen Rosenstock-Huessy." See also the insightful piece by Stünkel, "Nations as Times."

human traits, our ability to speak, is impossible without the time required by utterance, which is no less true of music. "Man is peculiarly a temporal being," Rosenstock-Huessy wrote, "ever but an exile and pilgrim in the world of space."

To some degree Freud's biography parallels that of Paracelsus, although there is the major difference that Freud witnessed in his lifetime the formation of a clear succession for his ideas, that is, the psychoanalytic movement, whereas Von Hohenheim died far more isolated, lacking the organized community of followers that gathered around Freud. In comparison to Freud, the normal grammatical unfolding in Paracelsus's life was distorted. There are, Rosenstock-Huessy begins, "stations" in Freud's life, as in all exemplary lives. Stations are not in permanent opposition to each other, such as the ego, the id, and the superego, but they are distinct temporal experiences connected by the vitality of a single life. Freud himself, according to Rosenstock-Huessy, fell into his own life-course through an offhand remark by the famous French neurologist Jean-Martin Charcot relating to the origins of what at the time was identified as female "hysteria"—"C'est toujours la chose genitale." From this passing comment at a social gathering came a vocation, Rosenstock-Huessy argues. The process Freud actually went through is compressed in Rosenstock's telling, but there is no doubt that in listening to Charcot's lectures at the Salpêtrière Hospital in Paris, Freud developed the deepest respect for the French doctor, to the point that any words from Charcot's mouth carried exceptional weight.[24]

Freud did not anticipate the influence Charcot would have on him. He applied for a travel grant to Paris to come under Charcot's tutelage for a few months because of the prestige of such an appointment. All that mattered to Freud at the time, according to Freud's biographer Ernest Jones, was "to secure a standing in the medical profession that would hold out some prospect of [his] earning enough money to marry [Martha Bernays]." Little did Freud know, according to Jones, "what a critical moment this [time with Charcot] was to prove in [his] life. It was assuredly the experience with Charcot in Paris that aroused Freud's interest in hysteria . . . and so paved the way for resuscitating Breuer's observation and developing psychoanalysis." Freud was with Charcot for only four months, but he wrote of him in 1885, "No other human being has ever affected me in such a way." Freud was already a brilliant promising

24. Jones, *Life and Work of Sigmund Freud*, 75.

neurologist when he abandoned that direction altogether to concentrate on psychopathology.

Rosenstock-Huessy appears to have missed the irony that what for Charcot was a passing, even slightly cynical, remark, became for Freud the seed of so much of his future reasoning. Charcot never lectured on the subject of the sexual etiology of neurosis. In public he would deny there was any connection between "the disease [hysteria] and the genital organs." Peter Gay describes the occasion in *Freud: A Life for Our Time*:

> Early in 1886, during a reception at Charcot's house,[Freud] had overheard his host arguing in his lively way that a severely disturbed young woman owed her nervous troubles to her husband's impotence or sexual awkwardness. In such cases, Charcot exclaimed, it is always a genital thing, always. "Mais, dans des cas pareils," he insisted, "c'est toujours la chose génitale, toujours . . . toujours . . . toujours."[25]

In this instance, Rosenstock-Huessy writes, time came to Freud as a "decisive moment, as the beginning of a trail, just as a noble Great Dane picks up the scent which the hunter throws before it. With Charcot's expostulation, Freud was thrown onto his life's path." He was, in Rosenstock-Huessy's vocabulary, *prejected*, that is, thrust into a new future. A "preject" is not a "subject," he is not an ego or an "I," exercising will, nor is he an "object," a "him" or an "it." At the beginning of his great accomplishment, the founder of psychoanalysis rather than *willing* something into existence is initially passive, a patient not an agent, a receptor, intrigued by what he has heard and captivated by it. The ego does not come first; the imperative, the call to action, when one is *addressed*, precedes it. In speaking of Paracelsus, Rosenstock-Huessy wrote:

> This absolute certainty that directs our steps is possible only because we are sure that the power behind us is bigger than our weakness. We are precipitated from above. Man being the animal that changes his environment, the phase of inspiration is that phase in which sufficient strength accrues to the individual so that he feels empowered to change the environment for the group. Inspiration does no more than that. It dislocates and places us. We cease to be part of the environment, we are made the center of a new environment which, in our inspiration, is envisaged and anticipated by us.[26]

25. Gay, *Freud*, 91–92.

26. Rosenstock-Huessy, "Classic and a Founder," 50.

"Such a moment is a specific manner of experiencing time," Rosenstock-Huessy writes. Such creative moments "cannot be measured with a stop-watch. [They] can last for years. [They] depend on the concentration of time, the cutting away as mere coincidences of all other temporal events that take place at the same time. He who experiences time as a moment experiences it as a selection," as when one is in love and is blind to all distractions. We are alive, Rosenstock-Huessy believed, only insofar as we are able to experience such moments. The first station in the transformations of time that constituted Freud's life thus consisted in his being gripped by this soon-to-be fundamental concept of psychoanalysis, "c'est toujours génitale," which was to have a lifelong effect on him.

The reception of the inspiration, or the commission, is followed by the tension in what became Freud's life's work. Building on the creative moment, in response to this revelation or command, Freud combed through human history, including Greek myths and the Bible, thirsting for relevant knowledge to establish his claims. The period following the creative moment is suspenseful, when the inspiration transforms into action and Freud strives to make his case, with no certain outcome. Freud's literary achievement pours out from this tension. From a preject, he is now a *subject* with a will, an ego that is driven to communicate. In this subjective time of suspense, the subject asks himself: Will I be able to communicate what I have discovered? Do I have the strength to carry out the commission that has overwhelmed me? Long periods of doubt, worry, and conjecture about the future are integral to this phase. As contrasted with the first station that springs from the imperative mood, when one receives a kind of command—"Sigmund," Freud tells himself, "you must act on what you have heard"—grammatically, the mood in the second phase is the subjunctive, where everything is contingent or conditional. Freud himself pointed out that there is a vast difference between a casual flash of intuition and taking an idea seriously, working through all of the complexities surrounding it, and winning for it general acceptance.

It is indeed true that Freud faced a fiercely negative reaction to his ideas on the sexual etiology of neurosis, especially from the medical establishment in Vienna. Ostracism and snubs were the norm. By 1895, according to Ernest Jones, Freud felt that "he was leading a Crusade . . . against the accepted conventions of medicine," yet, Jones says, "he accepted his mission wholeheartedly." He consoled himself with the conviction, as did Paracelsus, that although respect for the intellectual greatness of those who came before us "belongs to the best qualities of human nature . . . it should take second place to respect for facts. One need not be ashamed to admit it when one sets aside reliance on authority in favor of one's own judgment, gained by the study of the facts."[27]

The third station is still a different kind of time, neither the creative moment, when we feel we have been elected or chosen to bring forth something new, nor the suspenseful time when without knowledge of the outcome we work obsessively to fulfill the commission. This third transformation of time Rosenstock-Huessy calls "immortalization" or "eternalization," when the achievement exceeds any individual will and becomes a movement, in this case with Freud at its center. The movement takes on a life of its own and can become monumental with its own capacity for renewal forever.

As the founder of the cultural institution "Psychoanalysis," Freud was first of all transformed by an inspiration, or commission, and then he was transformed again by battle, so to speak, because in defiance of the world he endured the tension that comes with the effort to communicate something wholly new. But this prodigious suspense did not give way until he entered the third temporal modality when the isolated ego, the "I" in grammar, becomes at last the plural "us" or "we." Freud "eternalized" himself in the emergence of the psychoanalytic movement. "Eternity" for Rosenstock-Huessy is not simply time without end as people imagine, like an unending line in geometry. Such an eternity applies only to dead things or to the infinity of space. In the grammar of the living "only he who can transform himself is eternal." In order to be eternal, one must die and resurrect over and over. The dead stone on the ground is "ever" and "always," but it is not eternal. Eternal life belongs only to one who can survive death. From the time that practicing psychoanalysts, Freud's progeny, have existed, Freud's death has become survivable. Now many more have stepped into the place of the pioneer. In this way, and in this way alone, does that which occurs in human time become immortal.

In this third stage, those who become part of the arc of Freud's creation, the new "we" who share the time from the creative moment to Freud's death, immortalize him. Freud is now the prisoner of his past, the original inspiration has become crystallized. He is caught in the trajectory of his own life's work, part of an intellectual movement, and in Rosenstock-Huessy's terminology he may be described, in the spectrum of time, as a *traject*, driven more by the past than by the future. In the

27. Jones, *Life and Work of Freud*, 231–32, 236, 249.

third stage, the literary form is personal narrative, the autobiographical recounting of what "we" have accomplished.

Finally, in the fourth and last transformation of time, after the creative moment, after the struggle to convince, after the eternalization that assures perpetual revival, psychoanalysis is perceived in detachment, as a development in the past that occupied a particular "space of time" with an objective chronology. Time at this juncture lacks the urgent "now or never" of the moment of inspiration, lacks the anxiety of hope and expectation that may go on for years and years, and it is not the entrance into the eternity of recurrent new life by the formation of an intellectual movement. Really, time has died in this final phase, Rosenstock-Huessy says, or better, has died off. We now have before us the objective history of psychoanalysis, Freud and his creation as existing in space, a space of time, as "object"—in grammar "it" or "they" or "he." Freud and psychoanalysis are now embalmed in encyclopedia entries and thousands of monographs. The grammatical mood of this work is the indicative, as in all scientific writing.

From this final perspective, Rosenstock-Huessy writes, Freud and Freudianism are available objects for historical or sociological analysis. Freud visibly occupies a space of time, comparable to a phenomenon in nature that we *look at* for study.[28] He is a topic for historical examination handed to the scholar or critic. He is available "as evidence and can be retrospectively criticized." But although this "space in time" that is the object of monographic study is no longer vital or living, we will always be impressed by Freud and regard him highly, Rosenstock-Huessy believed, because at the beginning he "happened" in time, and this happening had a particular, grammatical unfolding, a sequence that Rosenstock-Huessy claimed is universal when something new is introduced into the world: from "thou" or "you," to "I," to "we," and finally to "he" or "they," or "it," in other words, from the imperative mood, when Freud is called; to the subjunctive mood of doubt and struggle, when he is transformed from a "thou" who is addressed to an ego or "I"; and, finally, to the personal, plural narrative form, the story of what *we* are doing, when a movement develops in which many personally share, which opens the promise of life over many generations. The very final stage, the grammatical indicative,

28. There is a growing literature on the predominance of the visual in modern culture, to the detriment of the aural. Decades before this phenomenon became a frequent subject of scholarly commentary, Rosenstock-Huessy had written about it as a deleterious imbalance and explained its origins.

is characterized by detached scrutiny and discussion by those who never participated in the movement. This final stage is at best but one-quarter of the whole process of creation, yet oddly it is the mode of discourse given the highest credence in our time, the embers left after a conflagration. The vital origin somehow gets lost.

Rosenstock-Huessy's friend from the 1920s Martin Buber—they had collaborated closely on the journal *Die Kreatur* (1926–29)—argued similarly. Charles David Axelrod in his *Studies in Intellectual Breakthrough: Freud, Simmel, Buber* comments that Buber held "that certain achievements when preserved objectively lose virtually all of their intelligibility." That the "language of objects catches only one corner of actual life." "For Buber, the distinction between objective speech and dialogue is significantly more deep-rooted than the simple relation between fraction and whole. . . . [Buber] refers to their distinction as a formal 'opposition'":

> Dialogue cannot outlive its moment or escape its participants without losing its force and transforming its nature. Thus it is only accessible to its participants and only to the extent that their relationship endures. In contrast, objective speech has no feeling for its moment, or whether during that moment its speakers enter into an authentic relation. . . . Objective speech must be accessible to anyone at any time.[29]

The imperative, by which Freud is first addressed, is inherently dialogical. A command waits for a response. Without the expectation of a response, a command merely delivered into the air is idiocy. One of Rosenstock-Huessy's essential criticisms of Buber's work on dialogue, however, is that Buber formulated the relation as "I-Thou," rather than the more psychologically empirical, "Thou-I."[30]

Rosenstock-Huessy would be the first to accept that his own commentary on Freud, like everyone else's, is, in the end, dependent on Freud's having first accepted a call and creatively entering into a new time. All criticism follows upon what was first personal inspiration and then finally enters the record. The final stage, the indicative mood in grammar, is always retrospective and supplementary. It is the time that engages the students of nature, who investigate only what is found in front of them. The three earlier processes were lived and they are known only from

29. Axelrod, *Studies in Breakthrough*, 51–55.

30. For Rosenstock-Huessy's disagreements with Buber, see his important note in *Judaism Despite Christianity*, 69–70. See also, Rome and Rome, eds., *Philosophical Interrogations*, 31–35.

direct experience. Later, when they are part of the objective record, they are merely cadavers: "Analysis is an appendix to reality, its death vigil," Rosenstock-Huessy said. It is the modes of irreducible experience that must be recognized as the vital sources of change. The advancement of life requires new creations, new orientations, new revelations that are not reachable with critical analysis and objectivity.

And then we hear a Rosenstock-Huessy *cri de coeur*, one of his messages to academe which one day, I believe, will find its audience: "If only the objectivists, critics, and analysts were willing to admit they are supplementary latecomers! They could then become useful members of the human race again. As retrospective contributors they are always welcome. But they have wanted to pretend to us that their experience of time as retrospective is the first and only true and scientific one," which is untenable. Time as seen in this classroom-type thinking survives only as evidence of what came before and is now dead. "These analysts would have nothing to analyze if a glorious world were not previously created for them. Yet their own mode of thinking excludes all the other modes of time," which are the fount of progressive change. In other words, grace is at the center, but it slips through the net of "scientific" inspection.

Charles David Axelrod in *Studies in Intellectual Breakthrough* describes his purpose as studying the process of a breakthrough coming into being, as distinguished from recognition of the completed achievement. This is quite like Rosenstock-Huessy's aim. Axelrod refers to breakthroughs as a sociological question, the tension between the individual and the group, and how society makes room for breakthroughs. His book is in part an attack on Thomas Kuhn, who, according to Axelrod, is interested only in the results of a breakthrough but dismisses the question of origins because origins are inscrutable. This is, of course, the very notion that Rosenstock-Huessy is also opposing: What is not subject to validation in accordance with the certifiable method of determining the truth is to be ignored or avoided. Scientific speech uses its authority and prestige to censor and control, Axelrod argues. "It takes as its mandate the authority to rule on the legitimacy of other speakers." Hence a breakthrough is always difficult.[31]

Rosenstock-Huessy's description consciously overrode Freud's theories of psychological operation, with the functions of ego, superego, id, and external reality in never-ending contention. In a characteristic

31. Axelrod, *Studies in Intellectual Breakthrough*, 12, 22.

inversion, Rosenstock-Huessy jabbed that Freud's picture of personal experience is inadequate to capture the shape of his very own life, or the life of any person who makes a mark in history. This is a tactic of reversal that Rosenstock-Huessy employed often, demonstrating that a writer blindly saws off the branch on which he sits. "There is actually no place in Freud's system of reference for Sigmund Freud's own lifetime achievement," Rosenstock-Huessy wrote. "The same holds, by the way, for many other secular minds, for Schopenhauer, for Marx, for Nietzsche. In the worlds they envisioned, there was no place for them as creators, as authors, as commanded, i.e., as named 'thous.' . . . In a classless society an intellectual with his head in the clouds like Marx would be intolerable." Rosenstock-Huessy in general was preoccupied by the problem of how to reproduce men and women who have the virtues we deeply value and that we know are needed in a healthy society.[32]

Freud's life, we are asked to believe, illustrates the higher law of grammatical progression that Rosenstock-Huessy discovered and that he believed was his most important contribution to thought. Its implications are many and cannot be developed here. Suffice it to say, Rosenstock-Huessy devoted his life to resurrecting the vital, primary role in all human affairs of the imperative mood or the command, that is, the elementary phenomenon of being addressed, or spoken to, with the expectation that some action will follow. At the beginning, the whole person is called, which is to say, the soul is addressed, and the soul responds when it is *named*: "Sigmund, go forth!"

From infancy the child is called into life with the parents' countless orders: eat, go to sleep, don't tell lies, help your mother, etc., and orders remain indispensable in adulthood when we all crave knowing what it is we should do, what our mission should be: marry this man or this woman; make this business profitable; lead this group; become a monk in service to God; preach the new gospel of scientific investigation à la Paracelsus, or the influence of repressed sexuality on human behavior à la Freud; protect the environment at all cost. The source of the command may be very humble in origin and often appears to be no more than what we tell ourselves, perhaps reinforced by a friend. But importantly and essentially these imperative moments are not predictable and are not reducible to anything other than the spoken, or written, word: black ink on a page, pixels on a screen, or the material breath of utterance, perhaps

32. Rosenstock-Huessy, *Out of Revolution*, 73–90. Rosenstock-Huessy explicitly argued that God is waiting for humanity to continue His work. See chapter 12, below.

mentally recreated when we address ourselves. It can well be said, the spirit bloweth where it listeth. We are moved by the spirit (what else to call it?), and sometimes in response to its commanding intervention we choose a calling or a partner or a direction, and our life is changed forever, and maybe along with it the human environment.

The jocular saying, "Love makes the world go 'round" is wholly true if broadened a little. The moral command to love others is an imperative and being in love is an overwhelming series of imperatives. The imperative, then, makes the world go 'round and shapes the saga of creative individual lives from birth to death.[33] We can imitate Rosenstock-Huessy and quote Browning's "Paracelsus" once again: "Dear Festus," Paracelsus says, "hear me. What is it you wish? / That I should lay aside my heart's pursuit, / Abandon the sole ends for which I live. / Reject God's great commission—and so die!" (ll. 142–45). "I profess no other share / In the selection of my lot, than in / My ready answer to the will of God, / Who summons me to be his organ." (ll. 303–6).[34]

All of this makes sense most fully when it is put in the context of Rosenstock-Huessy's extensive writing on the fundamental role of speech as the connective tissue of human community in all its forms, past and future, from the family, to the nation, to the planetary realm. To sum up, if one accepts the premise that change for the better—and humankind is always in need of change for the better—depends upon individual initiative, including the very smallest and most isolated of actions and sacrifices, which was a fundamental conviction of Rosenstock- Huessy's, then it is good to know from what experiences, what non-mechanical origins, such initiatives may spring. It is also important to know how a misguided psychology, or the social sciences in general, when they are obsessed with measurement as a criterion for knowledge, may fail to understand, or worse, may impede human growth and development.[35] One thinks here of the so-called Humanistic Psychology movement, exemplified by Abraham H. Maslow, which grew out of dissatisfaction both with psychoanalysis because it is concerned mostly with pathology and with behavioristic theories because they are reductionist. Maslow, a prolific author, pioneered in studying the psychology of healthy, achieving people. He writes, "I want to demonstrate that spiritual values have naturalistic

33. Kroesen, *Planetary Responsibilities,* called to my attention the overlap in our common understanding of revelation, grace, inspiration, conversion, and love.

34. Browning, "Paracelsus," 121,127.

35. See Muller, *Tyranny of Metrics.*

meaning, that they are not the exclusive possession of organized churches, that they do not need supernatural concepts to validate them, that they are well within the jurisdiction of a suitably enlarged science."[36] This is a well-meaning attack on the limitations of a "scientific" psychology, but Maslow's concept of an "enlarged science" attempts simply to objectify spirituality along with Pavlovian salivation. Rosenstock-Huessy's point is that objectification is itself the problem, not simply, let's say, materialism. Maslow wants to change the practice of science; Rosenstock-Huessy wants to segregate it as but one valuable manner of engaging with reality and restrict it to its proper domain. "Our times," Rosenstock-Huessy wrote, "saturated with natural science as they are, ruin the very condition of a prosperous natural science by carrying over to subjects the rules that apply to objects only."

On the one hand, we are given hope, because we have faith that the spirit lives, that it leaps over borders and boundaries of every kind—geographical, racial, ethnic, social, and economic—and over generations, indeed over millennia. On the other hand, it is discouragingly fragile and tenuous in the face of the great engines of this fallen world, such as amoral corporate power; hypocrisy and self-interest in the realm of politics; the double-edged sword of a triumphant institutionalized science; the careerism of the academic brotherhood and sisterhood, who embrace the latest intellectual fashion heedless of its irresponsibility with regard to the broader educational mission; commercial capitalism, as in the world of entertainment and advertising, that inevitably panders to the lowest taste in the hunger for attention and profits, and that exploits and cheapens many things of value. Even the spirit itself can be an enemy, emerging in counterfeit guises in the shape of false prophets and as demagoguery in multiple forms. Satan also may issue imperatives.

What does Rosenstock-Huessy offer in the face of such challenges? He certainly had no utopian illusions. He was too alert to human failings for that. Confining my response to this very large question simply to the study of biography, here is what I note. Many failures of reform by individual initiative, or apparent failures, occur because the timing was wrong. The seed may yet sprout. We have to learn to wait ("Thy will be done") but not necessarily without continuing to nurture a cause that deserves to live and spread. Most vast "programs" for improvement are, by their very nature, doomed to fail or to run thin. Rosenstock-Huessy

36. Maslow, *Religions, Values, and Peak-Experiences*, 3.

distrusted any project with large beginnings. Let's invest millions of dollars to promote, let's say, "leadership," or "innovation," or "ethics." Such efforts are not wrong in themselves, but their advocates can be deluded by the notion that money and size are the great determinants of fundamental change, with or without inspiration and individual sacrifice.[37] None of the examples I have given above of significant lives includes the sacrifice of one's life, that is, martyrdom for a cause. Rosenstock-Huessy believed that the only causes the world will ever take seriously are those for which someone is willing to die. Real change is no light matter. He also believed that any drive for improvement that is not sustained for at least three generations will not leave a permanent mark.

The study of biography may thus give us one idea of how humankind advances. Leaving aside the misguided assumption that any new technology represents human "progress," Rosenstock-Huessy saw progressive change, great or small, as possible only through the gifts of the spirit to individuals—inspiration, or revelation, followed by sacrifice, suffering, and fellowship. One need not attribute to this paradigm a "religious" or transcendental meaning. But clearly religion world-wide, as *practice*, not doctrine, has lessons that may be generalized in all realms of human endeavor.

AFTERWORD: BIOGRAPHY AS THEOLOGY

I hope the reader will forgive me if I take the liberty of critiquing my own work and mounting some defenses as well. First, I admit I described a pattern that even without Rosenstock-Huessy's emphasis and terminology seems pretty obvious or self-evident. Take some great achiever in history—maybe a reformer, or an inventor, or an artist—and in their story we can often detect a sequence, from the original idea or insight, the struggle by this person to convince others of its truth or importance, the winning-over of converts or followers or collaborators, and then finally, after the fact, the admiring biography or eulogy. Recognizing such a pattern is hardly earthshaking. Moreover, it applies, I am guessing, to only a minority of great men or women. Some heroes, in the broadest sense of

37. See Rosenstock-Huessy, *Planetary Service*. A much-heralded contemporary example of the benefits that may spring from one man's determined initiative is Paul Farmer's medical and health project in Haiti, described in the best-selling work by Tracy Kidder, *Mountains Beyond Mountains*.

that word, gain easy or accidental recognition of their genius and contributions, it would seem, and the pattern is condensed.

But leaving aside the applicability of this elementary picture of how change in the world is effected, with Rosenstock-Huessy we move to a different, more abstract level, namely the argument that such biographical patterns reveal the impregnation of all human culture with a kind of code, the code of grammar. The common words we use describing a sequence from idea or insight, to the struggle to convince others, to the winning over of comrades-in-arms, to the story-telling about the person after the fact, masks this underlying code. The discovery of this code may make us uneasy, it is such a broad claim. Is it true that the sequence from the second person singular (you); to first person singular (I); to first person plural (we); to the "they" employed in objective narrative is so embedded in both the psyche and society that the inversion or distortion of the sequence always spells trouble for the individual or for society. We are inclined to be a bit skeptical until we see the theory tested. And if it is true, one may rightly ask: So what? We need to understand what the implications are of this new law.

What does it mean that we must be spoken to, addressed in some fashion, before we are impelled to act, if we are to act lawfully? One implication, perhaps, is that there should be an inherent reticence, a grasp of our dependence in the world, humility at the beginning until we are called, before we are emboldened to speak to others in the first person and say, "I know what we must do, where we must go." That is one example of how the grammatical sequence may be instructive. "God can never communicate something to me as long as I think of myself as an I," Rosenstock-Huessy wrote. "God recognizes me only as a you." [38]. Another consequence of accepting this grammatical law is that it gives the lie to all scientific claims of predictability in human affairs. The emergence of the new, of change, of a possible better future, dependent as it is on the word, spoken or written or internal, is always mysterious, but it must be coveted, encouraged, and protected against those who would reduce it to what is measurable, a mere statistic, as compared to unique inspiration. Robert Frost captured this idea beautifully in this excerpt from his poem "Kitty Hawk":

38. *Die Sprache des Menschengeschlechts*, I:105.

"But God's own descent
Into flesh was meant
As a demonstration
That the supreme merit
Lay in risking spirit
In substantiation.
Spirit enters flesh
And for all its worth
Changes into earth
In birth after birth
Ever fresh and fresh . . . ."

Rosenstock-Huessy takes us further still, beyond the sequence of grammatical persons to the sequence in moods. We begin with the imperative mood, when we are first commissioned; move from there to the subjunctive or conditional mood, when the outcome of our mission is uncertain; and the sequence is concluded at the fourth stage with the indicative mood, when what has happened is described in a factual narrative and is essentially dead information. The third stage, the formation of a group or a movement, does not have distinctive mood, but it is to some degree an extension of the conditional.

Thus far we have two layers, grammatical persons and grammatical moods. But there is more, a demonstration of how all events are impaled on the axes of time and space. That argument, too, at first may seem simple and obvious. Do we have to be told that everything happens in a particular place at a particular time, at least at the everyday level. We can be extremely precise about this, with GPS coordinates and an atomic clock. Yet what happens in ordinary human life is far too subtle for an atomic clock to measure, and a GPS device would be wholly inadequate, for example, for telling us who at any given moment is, let's say, truly a member of the Roman Catholic church, that is, inside the boundaries of faith, and who is outside the line, a condition that may shift over time. When is the church, for any given person, "we" and when "they"? When am I a member of a group and when an outsider? With regard to time, what constitutes the "present"? The present second, the present year, the present century? "Present" is a human construction, Rosenstock-Huessy emphasized. When I have a life-changing insight, when I commit myself to propagating a new notion that I believe will make a better world, everything else around me takes second place. For the present, I say, I am going to dedicate myself to this purpose, and that "for the present" can end up being a very long time indeed, even decades.

To make such time, or such times, real to us, Rosenstock-Huessy had to create a new terminology. So neglected has our attention to living in time been that the vocabulary of time is underdeveloped. He spoke of periods when we are "prejects," that is, governed by our vision of the future, and "trajects," that is, governed or held back by the pull of the past. These terms are analogous to the spatial terms of "subject" and "object." As subjects we live inwardly, we are subjective or personal in our judgments and must be seen as a man or woman with an individual will, an ego, as contrasted to being treated as an object, when we are poked by a doctor or nurse, or are a mere statistic in a demographic study. Objects are outside of us, but we ourselves may be objectified, as everyone has experienced. To use the currently fashionable term, "the other," we can torment the other as an object not worthy of address as a full person, or we can regard the other as a subject, who must be addressed not as an "it" but as a dignified "you," or even in the antiquarian mode, "thou."

Our tale has now been framed in two ways as a grammatical sequence: of persons and of moods. And we have seen it as an existential event, like all events suspended in personal realms of time and space. These alternatives to the standard indicative narrative form of truth enable us to understand more deeply what moves the world and what must be treasured and cultivated although it cannot be studied objectively. In other words, Rosenstock-Huessy wants us to look at what is truly essential in human society, what is the sine qua non, that without which we would be in hell. It is not air conditioning, or automobiles, or airplanes, or smart phones, or the gross domestic product that make life redeemable, not even modern medicine, or community churches, but the miracle of articulated speech, the open possibility of address and response, that underlies it all.

5

Soul, Body, Spirit

[The work below is an excerpt from *Practical Knowledge of the Soul* (1988, 2015), which is a translation by Mark Huessy and Freya von Moltke of Rosenstock-Huessy's *Angewandte Seelenkunde* (1924). The section of *Practical Knowledge* extracted here, although originally written as prose in a series of normal paragraphs, struck me as being sheer poetry, and I have re-formatted it accordingly. Not a word has been changed from the original, nor any punctuation, just the line breaks. "Soul" and "spirit" were words that Rosenstock used often in his writing and speaking, and the uninitiated reader might assume that their meaning for him was wrapped in supernatural mystification as commonly found in religious diction and thereby easily dismissed by the scientific-minded. In fact, he is clear and concrete here to the point that both terms refer to undeniable daily realities for which we have few other adequate words. Understanding the meaning of soul and spirit for Rosenstock-Huessy is basic to grasping his thought as a whole.]

Everything about men and women
That has to do with
The total duration and unity
Of their existence
Belongs to the soul.

Destiny, profession, marriage,
Children, honor, fame,
Disappointment, suffering, sacrifice,
Personal names—
All these things are given meaning
From the fact that they
All belong to one united line,
One life story.

One's bodily, material needs, on the other hand,
Start with daily bread
And with daily requirements
Of shelter, clothing, and urges.
Looked at from the material point of view,
Marriage is only an expansion of sex
    and reproductive urges;
Professions are only an expanded concern
    for daily bread;
And so forth.

And yet, an immense difference remains.
No matter how many daily wages
    are added together,
They will not equal the course of a life;
No matter how many sexual acts,
They will not equal a marriage.

So for men and women,
The material things about them
Are summed up in their concern
For units of time shorter than the
Span of their own lives.

This explains the immense importance
Material things have for people without
Real destiny in their lives,
For the proletariat and all other
People who have fallen prey to daily life.
It also explains the limits of material concerns,
Which remain passing in comparison
With the course of a whole life.

The powers and needs of the spirit,
    by contrast,
Go above and beyond the time limits of souls.
We call only those things spiritual
That are destined and appropriate for
More than one soul. . . .
We should understand all matters of the spirit
As an inherited succession of souls.
The spirit usually takes hold of more
Than one person.
When it does move one person,
As in the case of a genius,
Then it does so only in order to reach
    others through him.

Spirit is a power of mankind,
The soul a power of man or woman,
The body a power of nature in man.

The specific essence of the soul
Has to do with times and tenses.
Time spans of the spirit
Are longer than those of the soul,
And time spans of the body
Are shorter than those of the soul.
An individual man neither has spirit
Nor is spirit, as little as he is just a body.
Rather the spirit has the man,
And the man, in turn, has
A body, many changing bodies.

A person remains inspired
    only insofar as, and as long as,
He finds himself within a structure
    that reaches out beyond him, and
Only as long as he lives and acts
    on the basis of it.
Matters of the spirit are
Above the human level; in fact,
They transcend everything already organized.

For although every corporation, every club,
Every country, and every profession
Has "its own" spirit to which the members
are subject,
Still, all of these collective groups
Are themselves subject to
The One Spirit.

Most of the spirit that touches and captures
An individual man is this kind of
Middle-level spirit,
Not *the* spirit, but a kind of spirit
Vis-à-vis an individual.

Because our souls
Tend not to be up to
The spirit first-hand,
The spirit that typically seizes us individuals
Tends to be this kind of
Second-, third-, or fourth-hand spirit,
The spirit of derivative collective personalities.

Yet even these third-hand derivations have to
Transcend the individual, or
They cease being part of the spirit and
At that moment their spiritual power
is extinguished. . . .
The stronger the souls of a people,
The more directly they can bear spirit.

It is the weakness of our souls that leads us nowadays
To dress up the oldest spiritual white elephants
in the world with pathetic seriousness.
Not being up to original life,
These weakened souls fall prey
To the derivatives,
To the "isms" instead of the "doms,"
To the spirits instead of the spirit,
To superstition instead of faith.

But offshoots of the spirit
Should exercise power over our souls
Only as long as they retain the strength
Of the original spirit
From which they are descended,
The strength to pull us beyond ourselves.

A person who cannot think
Beyond his own advantage
Has been abandoned by the spirit.
A family or a nation which cannot
    think beyond its own advantage
Has been abandoned by God and by the spirit,
For the power of the future has slid away
    from it,
The power which could have lifted them
Beyond the advantages and prejudices
They have had hitherto.

In the life of the spirit,
Only the spirit itself is unchangeable.
Everything it grasps, must change.
So all individuals or communities which
Want to remain unchanged and unchangeable
Are putting themselves on
The same level as the spirit,
    which is presumptuous.

The soul to be inspired
Should remain changing.
Obedience to the appeals of the spirit
Is the life of the soul.

6

Heritage vs. History

Eugen Rosenstock-Huessy as "The Physician of Memory"

[This essay was originally published in the journal *The European Legacy* 24, no. 5 (2019) 511–36. I have made a few small revisions in this version.]

1

IN DECEMBER 1934, NOT even two years after he had emigrated to the United States, Rosenstock-Huessy presented a paper at the annual meeting of the American Historical Association (AHA) in Washington, D.C., entitled "The Predicament of History." A few months later the paper was published in the *Journal of Philosophy.* [1] I cannot be precise about what provoked Rosenstock-Huessy to write this admonitory piece except to note that if he was recognized at all in scholarly circles it was as a historian; so to debut in the United States from his temporary perch at Harvard University with a commentary on historiography made sense.

A medievalist and legal historian by training, Rosenstock-Huessy all of his life retained an interest in the mission of the academic discipline of history, although after the publication of *Out of Revolution: Autobiography of Western Man* in 1938, he never again turned his hand to writing

1. Rosenstock-Huessy, "Predicament of History," *Journal of Philosophy.*

history as it is usually practiced. His later work is suffused with an astonishing breadth of historical knowledge, but it is knowledge integrated into his writing on sociology, economics, language, and science. Even his courses on "Universal History" at Dartmouth College and later at Santa Cruz, California, do not fit easily into the conventional form of academic discourse called "history."[2]

"The Predicament of History" deals with a problem that has much engaged philosophically-minded historians in recent decades: the opposition between received tradition, collective memory, or heritage, on the one side, and critical or "scientific" history as practiced by the academic guild, on the other. Rosenstock-Huessy did not use the word "heritage" nor did he advert to the philosophical underpinnings of his reasoning, but he could not have seen into the problem as deeply as he did without the application of his broader thought about society, language, and the place of the temporal in understanding Man and society. It remains to be determined whether what he had to offer on this subject brings anything new to the table in 2022.

To begin with a not too distant example of the contention between heritage and history, ten years ago in the *New York Review of Books* (January 13, 2011) the eminent American historian Gordon Wood was disturbed by the condescending attitude of the historian Jill Lepore toward members of the populist "Tea Party" movement, who were in the habit of portraying America's revolutionary past uncritically. Tea Party leaders casually invoked "history" without recourse to the tools academic historians use to separate truth from fiction. In his review of Lepore's *The Whites of Their Eyes: The Tea Party's Revolution and the Battle Over American History* (2010), Wood spoke in defense of "popular memory," citing the perennial need of people to gain reassurance from stories about the past that reinforce their political and social values. Professor Lepore, according to Wood, verged on "contempt for the attempts of ordinary citizens to find some immediate and emotional meaning in the [American] Revolution." There can be no doubt that legends or myths or moral tales by the hundreds enshrine national or ethnic values all over the globe, while at the same time there is no denying that they mask and cover up the often contrary mixed truth of what actually happened. "Certainly Lepore is correct in believing that historians have a professional obligation to dispel myths and legends," Wood wrote, but he rebuked her

2. For Rosenstock-Huessy's recorded lectures on universal history, see www.ERHFund.org/online-lecture-library.

as an "expert at mocking" and for insensitivity to the value of "collective memory." "Heritage no less than history is essential to knowing and acting," Wood proposed, quoting David Lowenthal's *Possessed by the Past*. "By means of it we tell ourselves who we are, where we come from, and to what we belong."[3]

Most individuals assembling their autobiography, whether in their head or on paper, will sanitize it, perhaps glorifying their achievements a bit and somehow failing to recollect the most shameful moments. It is no different with national or ethnic histories. The process of historical rectification can be extremely painful, though necessary, yet we want to come out of it with some quotient of self-respect. The professional historian who has devoted years to meticulous research and regards absolute accuracy as essential to historical narrative finds it hard to tolerate "fictions" about the past. He is no different in this respect from the natural scientist who reacts with dismay when a layman asserts, for example, that there has been no evolution of species over time. When there is overwhelming evidence behind a particular truth, it is hard for the specialist to be patient in the face of nonsense. These issues become especially acute in the United States when committees at one level or another—national, state, or local—attempt to establish curriculum standards for the teaching of history in public schools. Textbook publishers struggle to satisfy diverse interests—in one corner the school boards, made up of local citizens, who tend to be traditional in their views, and in the other those concerned about doing justice to the history of women, for example, or the history of African-Americans, Native Americans, and the laboring poor. The so-called master narrative of the history of the United States, still operative a century ago, incorporated little of such material, and distortions for the sake of patriotism were rife. Inculcating pride in country and fulfilling other ends deemed socially beneficial were the overriding concerns. The objections raised to a work like Charles Beard's *An Economic Interpretation of the American Constitution*, published in 1913, which "exposed" the upper-class financial interests of the Founding Fathers, were a foretaste of the battle in the second half of the twentieth century and beyond, between popular sentiments deifying the Fathers and the historiographical methods of the professionals.

3. Wood addressed the same heritage vs. history question years earlier in a review of Pauline Maier's *American Scripture* (*New York Review of Books*, August 14, 1997), reprinted in Wood, *Purpose of the Past*, 180–95.

Within academe there are rewards for seeing the past freshly and debunking prevailing unexamined views. Historians strive to be original in their interpretations, for better or worse. University instructors often take positive delight in disabusing college freshmen of the myth-laced historical knowledge they bring from home or high school, although the high schools, too, have become active participants in the trouncing of traditional narratives. The celebrated historian William H. McNeill, in a presidential address to the American Historical Association in 1985, stated bluntly: "Challenging prevailing myths without regard for the costs arising from the disintegration of belief . . . became professors' special calling."[4]

In the United States, it is not just the historiography of the founding era where such controversies abound. More than a half-century after the events, we encounter questioning by serious historians of numerous unexamined assumptions in the standard narrative about the so-called good war of the twentieth century, the war against the Axis. It is to be expected, and significant, that such questioning began in earnest only after the generation of Americans with living memories of the war had mostly passed away. In grammatical terms, there is a considerable difference between the epic recounting of what "we" did and the same story told with detachment, after the fact, of what "they" did.[5] Is one of these narratives preferable to the other and on what grounds? How can they coexist, the first-hand recollected personal testimony versus the historians' broader examination, from a distance, of what occurred? Is one more real than the other? Such questions are of the highest importance because society cannot do without *both* scientific investigation to determine unbiased truth and such sentiments as love of country and a positive sense of national identity. For solidarity the people of the United States, with no millennia-old unifying ethnic identity, are particularly dependent upon abstract shared faiths and the emulation of heroes. Yet sometimes the differences between these two—science and sentiment, or history and heritage—are so profound that they provoke extremes: on the popular

4. William H. McNeil, *Mythistory*, 32. In a series of lectures at the University of California at Santa Cruz in 1967, Rosenstock-Huessy expressed dismay at the constant search by historians and others for ulterior motives behind the actions of historical figures, reducing all of them to the level of mere "propagandists."

5. On Rosenstock-Huessy's grammatical analysis, see his "In Defense of the Grammatical Method" and "Grammar as Social Science" in *Speech and Reality*. See also Fiering, "Structure of Significant Lives," chapter 4, above.

side, anti-intellectualism and fundamentalism, and on the side of the professionals, sometimes divisive contempt for the ill-informed.[6] We are in need of a comprehensive understanding that can put both sides in proper perspective and perhaps balance them, or at least explain how both sides may be integrated into a larger framework.

Some of these issues were brilliantly addressed in a series of lectures by the late Columbia University professor Yosef Hayim Yerushalmi, published as *Zakhor: Jewish History and Jewish Memory* (1982). It is a work of remarkable insight and has generated much excellent commentary. The Jews serve as the perfect case study of the point, made by Yerushalmi, that "meaning in history," "memory of the past," and "the writing of history" cannot be equated. The book revolves around the seemingly paradoxical fact that the Jews, a people assumed to be immersed in their past, in fact almost never tried to write their own history in the eighteen hundred years that elapsed from the time of Josephus in ca. AD 70 to their emancipation in Europe in the aftermath of the French Revolution. The rich, providential history told uniquely in the Bible sufficed for an understanding of all historical processes, principally of God's way with the world. "Scientific" curiosity about details of the past and the quest for the novelty of discovery were not operative motives.

There was certainly no lack of intellectual energy and learning amidst the Jews in this interregnum—think of the subtlety of Talmudic commentary or of Jewish participation in science and philosophy in Spain in the Middle Ages—but the example of Josephus, or of Thucydides for that matter, carried no weight. "Although Judaism throughout the ages was absorbed with the meaning of history," Yerushalmi writes, "historiography itself played at best an ancillary role among the Jews, and often no role at all; and concomitantly, that while memory of the past was always a central component of Jewish experience, the historian was not its primary custodian." "The Jews . . . have the reputation of being at once the most historically oriented of peoples and as possessing the longest and most

6. Lowenthal's *Possessed by the Past* is a comprehensive, detailed, almost exhaustive, work. "Heritage" in Lowenthal's definition is concocted, inauthentic, and often commercially packaged history. One could even speak of a heritage industry. He keeps that concept distinct from more grounded "tradition, memory, myth, and memoirs," as well as from scientific history. I am using "heritage" more loosely and broadly, referring to the many modes of representing or receiving the past that are distinct from "scientific" or critical history.

tenacious of memories. Yet such accolades can be profoundly true or completely false, depending upon what one means by 'history' or 'memory.'"[7]

Although since the late nineteenth century Jewish history (along with that of many other peoples and eras) has been massively studied, making up for lost time, Yerushalmi raises the question of whether such detached scholarship can ever substitute for the living presence of the past in the culture of a people. The ancient past was (and is) preserved in Jewish culture not only through a number of well-known commemorative holidays, such as Passover celebrating the exodus from Egypt, but also in rituals and in the liturgy of the synagogue. "The meaning of history is explored more directly and more deeply in the prophets than in actual historical narratives; the collective memory is transmitted more actively through ritual than through chronicle." Perhaps it can truly be said that commemorative observance of a past event is sufficient to the degree that it preserves "the essential memory," although it may fail to preserve the historical details.[8]

What, after all, is the professional study of history for? To keep the past alive and available in order to better grasp the workings of the world? To bring some comprehensible order to the seeming chaos of past events? To hone critical intellectual skills, regardless of the substance? To provide content for dissertations in the autonomous realm of a humanities discipline? That is a far from exhaustive list of the multiple purposes of history. But to undercut more radically the sovereignty of the academicians, listen, for example, to Hayden White:

> The professionals may own "history," insofar as by the term "history" they mean that aspect of the past which is studied in the way they study it and write about it. But professional historians do not own the past, and they have no exclusive claim over the study of the way in which the past and the present may be brought together in a comprehensive vision of historical reality.[9]

Yerushalmi mentions that in each weekly synagogue service a section of the Pentateuchal narratives is read aloud in sequence beginning with Genesis, together with the weekly lesson from the prophets, such that in the course of a year all of these biblical books have been read in

7. Yerushalmi, *Zakhor*, xiv.

8. Yerushalmi, *Zakhor,* 15, 51. Cf. McNeil, *Mythistory*, 94: "Who besides ourselves really cares for the details."

9. White, *Fiction of Narrative*, x.

entirety. And then immediately upon completion, the cycle begins again. The comparison is weak, but a similar drive to keep the past alive through active participation in the present is observed in the U.S. Senate. Since 1888, George Washington's Farewell Address of 1796 has been read aloud every year in that chamber on February 22, the first president's birthday. The original 1862 petition that launched this tradition asked the Congressional body in those "perilous times" to "recur back to the days, the times, and the doings of Washington and the patriots of the Revolution, who founded the government under which we live."[10] Not far different, the countless reprintings and free distribution of the Declaration of Independence and the Constitution in a pocket-size edition authorized by Congress is a means of infusing the present (and the future) with this country's scriptures, without the mediation of historiography. And quite amazingly, on January 6, 2011, according to the *New York Times*, for the first time in the history of the Congress, apparently in response to Tea Party pressure, the Constitution was read aloud from beginning to end in the House of Representatives, sentence by sentence (or nearly so), with members taking turns over a period of ninety minutes. Such rituals are asking participants not just to know, but to feel, that is, to be subjective or immersed, not objective or detached, and to keep the faith. As Yerushalmi writes, "collective memory" should not be thought of as merely a metaphor or some vague Jungian archetype. If it is to exist at all, it is as "a social reality transmitted and sustained through the conscious efforts and institutions of the group."[11]

All of this raises the question of the proper role of the historian vis-à-vis popular observances, rituals, re-enactments, traditions, monuments, political speeches, and especially in the past one hundred years, film, none of which, alas, may reflect the latest scholarly research. Needless to say, in a free society it is hard to assign, let alone mandate, a "proper" role for anyone. Still, although we all genuflect to the authority of any form of supposed scientific knowledge, that authority is not unbounded.

10. *Wikipedia* has an article on this Senate tradition, but my attention was initially drawn to this annual event by a reference in Eugen Rosenstock-Huessy, *Out of Revolution*.

11. Yerushalmi, *Zakhor*, xv. The reading of the Constitution in Congress was not politically neutral. To avoid embarrassment to "originalists" or textualists certain passages now considered obsolete or politically unpalatable were omitted. One thinks here of Eric Hobsbawm's concept of an "invented tradition," motivated by the desire to establish continuity with a particular segment of the past. See Hobsbawm and Ranger, eds., *The Invention of Tradition*.

Society tries to protect itself against excesses, including the gratuitous undermining of traditions considered beneficial. Historians have always had responsibilities. Yerushalmi observes that the modern effort beginning in the nineteenth century by trained historians to reconstruct the Jewish past came at a time that witnessed "a sharp break in the continuity of Jewish living and hence also an ever-growing decay of Jewish group memory. . . . For the first time, history, not a sacred text, becomes the arbiter of Judaism." Yet, and here's the nub:

> To the degree that this historiography is indeed "modern" and demands to be taken seriously, it must at least functionally repudiate premises that were basic to all Jewish conceptions of history in the past. In effect, it must stand in sharp opposition to its own subject matter, not on this or that detail, but concerning the vital core: the belief that divine providence is not only an ultimate but an active causal factor in Jewish history, and the related belief in the uniqueness of Jewish history itself.[12]

Jewish history has become "divorced from Jewish collective memory and, in crucial respects, thoroughly at odds with it." And this fact, Yerushalmi notes, "reflects a universal and ever-growing modern dichotomy. The traditions and memories of many peoples are in disarray."[13]

For his brief discussion of what remedies are possible for such disarray, Yerushalmi reached back fifty years to Rosenstock-Huessy's injunction to the historian, first in the "Predicament of History" article of 1934 and restated in his seven-hundred-page *Out of Revolution: Autobiography of Western Man*. What is the duty or the task of the historian, Rosenstock-Huessy asked, not at all thinking of Jewish history in particular? Tradition cannot be abandoned, he said, but it must be "corrected and purified, enlarged and unified memory." The historian, according to

12. Yerushalmi, *Zakhor*, 86–89. Cf. Rosenstock-Huessy in *Out of Revolution* on a similar point: In the nineteenth century "For the first time in the history of the world, the values cherished by a child's parents [and aunts, uncles, grandparents, etc., Rosenstock-Huessy says] became less noticeable in its education than the traditions created by its schoolmaster's textbooks." "Modern man no longer trusts in aunts and grandmothers; they, like old furniture, became the outfit of museums. He does trust in textbooks." Rosenstock-Huessy speaks of the "catechizing power" of textbooks (689–90). There has always been an underlying providential theme in standard U.S. history, and similar beliefs are found in other national ideologies. Its equivalent today in the United States may be the belief that the U. S. is "exceptional" among nations and has a special, beneficial role to play in the history of mankind.

13. Yerushalmi, *Zakhor*, 93.

Rosenstock-Huessy, "is the physician of memory. It is his honor to heal wounds, genuine wounds. As a physician must act, regardless of medical theories, because his patient is ill, so the historian must act under a moral pressure to restore a nation's memory, or that of mankind."[14]

Although Yerushalmi quotes this advice, he is skeptical of its practicality, at least with reference to Jewish history: "Those who would demand of the historian that he be the restorer of Jewish memory attribute to him powers that he may not possess." "Intrinsically, modern Jewish historiography cannot replace an eroded group memory which . . . never depended on historians in the first place. . . . Ultimately Jewish memory cannot be 'healed' unless the group itself finds healing. . . . For the wounds inflicted upon Jewish life by the disintegrative blows of the last two hundred years the historian seems at best a pathologist, hardly a physician." We need, he says, "more modest and sober expectations" of the historian, acting "within his proper sphere, so to speak." And he emphasizes the depth of the conflict: "Memory and modern historiography stand, by their very nature, in radically different relations to the past."[15]

It is impossible to say how many people in 1934 were paying attention to this "predicament," but we do know that Samuel Eliot Morison, fifteen years later in his well-known 1950 presidential address to the American Historical Association "Faith of a Historian," quoted Rosenstock-Huessy's article substantially. "A historian owes respect to tradition and folk memory," Morison said, and continued:

> "History is corrected and purified tradition, enlarged and analyzed memory." Rosenstock-Huessy, in an address before

14. Rosenstock-Huessy, *Out of Revolution*, 696, in which he more or less incorporated "The Predicament of History."

15. Yerushalmi, *Zakhor*, 94. It is not just orthodox Jewish historians writing Jewish history and trained in the secular, "scientific" historiographical method who face this dilemma. Historians of any faith may have to struggle with the problem. Consider, for example, professional historians of the Mormon faith writing Mormon history. See Richard Bushman on the history of the Mormon church and on Joseph Smith, at https://wheatandtares.org/2015/07/21/richard-bushman-on-mormonism/. The subject of heritage and history is not far different from the subject of faith and history. Not all modern historians have worried about this conflict. For J. H. Plumb, writing in 1970, very little of the inherited past has value: "The past is always a created ideology with a purpose, designed to control individuals, or motivate societies, or inspire classes. Nothing has been so corruptly used as concepts of the past. The future of history and historians is to cleanse the story of mankind from those deceiving visions of a purposeful past. . . . The past has only served the few; perhaps history may serve the multitude." (Plumb, *Death of the Past*, 17).

> this Association in 1934 from which this dictum is quoted, warned our profession that we were losing our hold on the public through wanton and unnecessary flouting of tradition. He meant not only the "debunkers" but the historians who embraced dialectical materialism as an easy explanation of past reality—which saved them a great deal of painful thought.

Although it is less cogent today than fifteen years ago, Morison continued, "I wish to repeat Rosenstock-Huessy's warning—historians, deal gently with your people's traditions! If you feel the urge to pull something apart, try your hand on a myth rather than a tradition."[16]

It is striking that thirty-five years later, in December 1985, William H. McNeill, also in an American Historical Association presidential address, expressed the same concern: "We cannot afford to reject collective self-flattery as silly, contemptible error. Myths are, after all, often self-validating. A nation or any other human group that knows how to behave in crisis situations because it has inherited a heroic historiographical tradition that tells how ancestors resisted their enemies successfully is more likely to act together effectively than a group lacking such a tradition. . . . A corrosive version of history that emphasizes all the recurrent discrepancies between ideal and reality in a given group's behavior makes it harder for members of the group in question to act cohesively and in good conscience. That sort of history is very costly indeed."[17]

In Rosenstock-Huessy's telling, the "emancipation of history from its service to real memory" had two causes. First, in the nineteenth century, liturgy, prayer, and ritual were practically dying out as a consequence of the Industrial Revolution, the weakening of the church, and the

16. For AHA presidential addresses, see the Association's website. From 1933 to 1935 Morison and Rosenstock-Huessy were colleagues at Harvard. Morison was possibly reminded of Rosenstock-Huessy's "Predicament" by Page Smith, his research assistant in 1949–50, who earlier was a devoted student of Rosenstock-Huessy's at Dartmouth College. Morison and Rosenstock-Huessy clearly had similar sympathies with regard to historical writing. Rosenstock-Huessy cited with approval Morison's remark that Stephen Vincent Benét's epic poem *John Brown's Body* (1928) was the best history of the Civil War. Disentangling "myth" and "tradition" as Morison urged may not be a simple task in itself, and Morison does not help much. "The Predicament of History" also had some influence on Paul Tillich as Christian Roy relates in "Interpretations of History" in *Paul Tillich im Exil*, 103–24.

17. McNeill's AHA presidential address was later incorporated into a collection of essays, *Mythistory and Other Essays*. The presidential address alone may be found at this URL: *https://www.historians.org/about-aha-and-membership/aha-history-and-archives/presidential-addresses/william-h-mcneill*

erosion of immemorial folk traditions, caused, one might say, by widespread deracination. Society was losing part of its "temporal balance," an essential good in Rosenstock-Huessy's eyes, which depends upon the persistence of a remembered past along with an envisioned future. This disequilibrium was countered by looking to formal historical writing as an evocation of the past, although such a recovery was obviously not the same as the continuation of the past in the form of rituals, monuments, commemorations, and the holidays on a patriotic or church calendar. The Romantic historians, such as George Bancroft in the United States, Thomas Macaulay in England, and François Guizot in France, tried to provide a remedy for the decline of tradition. But that was an emergency measure at a moment when the historian seemed to be the only available protector of tradition. The measure was not adequate, but it is "only fair to say," Rosenstock-Huessy wrote, that the Romantic historians "partially rescued memory in a period of forgetfulness and destruction of tradition." The predicament of modern history, then, in his words, "arises from its no longer being in harmony with the memories and traditions of any clearly defined group."[18] In a splintered society the question arises, whose memory is to be treasured?

The second, and long running, factor behind the fissure was—in the spirit of the Enlightenment—the divorce of history from all the "nonliterary forms of tradition." Inexorably historians began to define themselves as practitioners of an "objective" *written* science, modeled on the natural sciences. In consequence, the reliance on historiography had exactly the opposite effect of what was intended: it undermined rather than reinforced tradition. Toward the end of the nineteenth century, the writing of history accompanied the "triumphal march of the natural sciences, those clearest outposts of our outward tendencies." It could not hope to maintain the full temporal balance because it remained enclosed in the general field of prose. Historiography in our time is a "subspecies in the sphere of prose," and prose is "always analytic, dissecting, aggressive."[19]

> It is no mere guess when we assume that the health of an individual and the wealth of nations may depend on a balance between prose, poetry, ritual, and imperative. This can be

18. Rosenstock-Huessy, "Predicament," 98. Plumb, *The Death of the Past*, 14, explains the decline of tradition in the nineteenth century: "Industrial society, unlike the commercial, craft and agrarian societies which it replaces, does not need the past. Its intellectual and emotional orientation is towards change rather than conservation."

19. Rosenstock-Huessy, *Out of Revolution*, 689–98, and *Speech and Reality*, 79–97.

> expressed grammatically by saying that any individual or group must remain capable of shifting freely and at the becks of fate from the subjective "I" to the objective "it," and further to the listening "thou"and to the remembering "we."[20]

Most historians, Rosenstock-Huessy believed, do not fully recognize that their work, although modeled on the scientific approach to nature, does not deal with a neutral or mute animal kingdom but with territory that "mankind has previously conquered, by action, discovery, sacrifice, emotion. The historian's facts are not facts in the common sense of that abused word. His facts are man's experiences." Human history is a speaking past, whereas the very definition of "nature" in Rosenstock-Huessy's thought is precisely that, in contrast to humanity, it cannot speak or listen. The past, in other words, is not analogous to a cadaver waiting to be dissected.[21]

In their vanity, Rosenstock-Huessy wrote, professional historians wrangle over the importance or unimportance of this or that event, and even presume to believe, rather arrogantly, that their efforts at periodization are definitive. "The process of commemorating is underway," however, "long before the critic argues about the importance or unimportance of an event. Gettysburg, Saratoga, Yorktown, Marathon, are not facts, but creations of a nation's memory." "Man is a name-giving animal. . . . Conscious experience is the presupposition for a new name." Neither historiography nor any other "science" is capable of producing enduring,

20. Rosenstock-Huessy, *Speech and Reality*, 85. Rosenstock-Huessy failed to make clear in this compressed statement the parallelism intended: prose is the objective "it"; poetry is the subjective "I"; ritual the *trajective* "we"; the imperative is the *prejective* "thou." In "Between Memory and History," 9–15, Pierre Nora refers to the end of the nineteenth century when "the decisive blow to *traditional balances* was felt—in particular the disintegration of the rural world" (emphasis added; cf. Rosenstock-Huessy's "temporal balance"). Pierre Nora speaks of the "memory-nation" created by the nineteenth-century nationalist historians, as "the last incarnation of the unification of memory and history." "Memory installs remembrance within the sacred; *history, always prosaic*, releases it again" (9–15; emphasis added; cf. Rosenstock-Huessy, "history is a subspecies in the sphere of prose"). Many of Nora's assertions echo Rosenstock-Huessy's analysis. I do not know whether Nora acknowledged any influence from Rosenstock-Huessy.

21. Rosenstock-Huessy, *Out of Revolution*, 693. See the section "History vs. Science" in *Speech and Reality*, 109–14. On the sharp differences between the writing of good history and the practice of good natural science, it is hard to imagine a more definitive analysis than that provided by Isaiah Berlin's "History and Theory," 1–31. In *The Linguistics of History*, 75, Harris notes that the historian's account can never be wholly verifiable, which is a principle in science. At best, it is credible or probable.

instantly recognizable names. "The work of research is unable to create names." The scholar proceeds by concepts, definitions, and mere corrections of names.

"The memories of an individual or a group are not built up by science. They are a process of selection by the group which goes through a decisive experience of victory or defeat. Memory differs in its working from literature or science. . . . It is not an effort of the intellect. The whole being of the nation is at stake in a great event."[22] "The new name is . . . the minimum requirement for the assimilation of an overwhelming experience," Rosenstock-Huessy wrote. "Monuments are built, ceremonies are devised, to keep the memory awake" and to help to integrate it. "The periods of history are products of this creative process." They are "expressions of group morale, and not in the least the outcome of scientific research. . . . The climax is reached when an event is incorporated into the calendar as a recurrent date. Memory is fixed by the calendar of a group or a nation."[23]

In fact, the scholar ultimately *depends* upon existing group traditions, "for otherwise history cannot demonstrate that its conceptions are rooted in empirical reality. If [scientific] history were the only human activity for representing the past," Rosenstock-Huessy stressed, "it would remain arbitrary and would have no means of distinguishing itself from mythology." The fallacy that history concerns "facts" no different from those established by the biologist is illustrated here. There are obviously billions of facts in the past from which to choose. The historian who

22. "Predicament," 93–95.

23. Rosenstock-Huessy, *Out of Revolution*, 694. Cf. Wood, *Purpose of the Past*, 276: "History is much more powerful than the historians who would reform it"; cf. also Carl Becker, "Everyman His Own Historian," 221–36: "Mr. Everyman is stronger than we are. . . . We do not impose our version of the human story on Mr. Everyman; in the end it is rather Mr. Everyman who imposes his version on us." It is ludicrous when a coterie of historians focused on a particular research agenda declares the need for reframing whole epochs. See, e.g., Cayton, "Not the Fragments but the Whole," 513–26, calling for a "revolution" in the writing of the history of eighteenth-century North America in favor of the Indians' story and Indian voices. Cayton recommends that we "engage the general problems of periodization and perspective . . . in the making of our histories. . . . We have to consider not just the words we choose to describe Indians and their behavior but the ones *we choose* to organize *periods of time*, such as the American Revolution and the early Republic" (my emphasis). In this recommendation, the Revolution becomes an ordinary period of time, like any other, but where would Cayton be without that Revolution, the legacy of which sustains him? The commemoration of July 4th was not the choice of a group of academics.

respects popular memory knows that he is dealing with a past already filtered through human experience, which is his defense against merely arbitrary "research." Without that basis for defining what really matters, he will turn to some abstract scheme or ideology, some structural mantle, let us say Marxism, in order not to lose himself in the ocean of facts, and indeed to justify his endeavors.[24] Periodization must be responsive to the reality of public experience, and not be based on "new documents found in the archives of Erewhon."[25]

We hear in this critique a call for humility and deference in the practice of the historian, since any historian is always and only a latecomer to the events of the past. "Only a few events," as Rosenstock-Huessy writes, "can become holidays, names, or monuments." Traditions are based on a highly selective process, and "memory is tyrannical. It represses and excludes, it exalts and prefers."[26] It may be unfair, Rosenstock-Huessy says, but it is real. "Memory" here is the middle realm between real time actions of particular people in the past and the later prosaic work of professional historians constructing from documents and artifacts a narrative about what happened. This vast intermediate realm of collective impressions is passed on in multiple forms over indeterminate lengths of time by the "onlookers," to use Roy Harris's term: "The onlookers, too, make history, as do their descendants. They constitute by far the largest body of history-makers" by their anniversary parades, erection of statues, likenesses on coins, period dramas, and so forth.[27]

24. Rosenstock-Huessy, "Predicament," 100. Yerushalmi, in *Zakhor*, 100, makes the same point, perhaps influenced by Rosenstock-Huessy: "What historians choose to study and write about is obviously part of the problem. The notion that everything in the past is worth knowing 'for its own sake' is a mythology of modern historians, as is the lingering suspicion that a conscious responsibility toward the living concerns of the group must result in history that is somehow less scholarly or 'scientific.' Both stances lead not to science, but to antiquarianism." Cf. Nora, "Between Memory and History," 13–14: "the gigantic and breathtaking storehouse of a material stock of what it would be impossible for us to remember," "the veneration of the trace," is a symptom of the decline of authentic memory. "Even as traditional memory disappears, we feel obliged assiduously to collect remains, testimonies, documents, images, speeches, any visible signs of what has been, as if this burgeoning dossier were to be called upon to furnish some proof to who knows what tribunal of history."

25. Rosenstock-Huessy, *Out of Revolution*, 691.

26. Rosenstock-Huessy, "Predicament," 95.

27. Harris, *Linguistics of History*, 171–73. Lowenthal, *Past is a Foreign Country*, 185: "The past surrounds and saturates us; every scene, every statement, every action retains residual content from earlier times".

The necessary detachment or objectivity of the scientific historian comes into play when he or she respectfully corrects the biases and prejudices of the tyranny of memory. "The historian regenerates the great moments of history and disentangles them from the mist of particularity." The historian who has a moral or religious standpoint that propels him to do justice to the past (*nota bene*, it is not the objectivity of the scientific method that provides this motivation) rightly combats the entrenched prejudices of only one side: "He will see the relative right of the Carthaginians or the Loyalists, and he will therefore not be at home in the primitive temple of tribal worship."[28]

The pursuit of historical and antiquarian research is a pleasurable and innocent vocation for many people and deserving of encouragement. In fact, we never know when seemingly random antiquarian knowledge may overnight become useful knowledge. Rosenstock-Huessy held, however, as he wrote in *Out of Revolution*, that three purposes only give historical research a serious and vital mission in the world: (1) to do justice to the past, which may involve recovery of what of importance has been ignored, misjudged, or slandered; (2) to heal wounds by reconciling the opposing sides in past conflicts through reportage that overcomes the biases of each side; and (3) to salvage from the past that which must be known for the sake of the future, which is an ever evolving demand depending upon the urgency of the special understanding that is needed to help mankind move forward: "History-writing cannot replace the memories of the layman. It is the birthright of man to build up a memory and to have faith in the future. . . . It is the privilege of the historian to unify dualistic memory; and for this healing capacity he must be made independent in his research." Or as he put it in "The Predicament of History": "History is safe if it remains what practically it always was: the *restoration of memory*. As tradition restored, memory regenerated, history regains its quality of an empirical science. All history corrects and restores a corrupt memory. In order to do so, it must be able to depend on the existence of primary memories and traditions."[29]

28. Rosenstock-Huessy, "Predicament," 97. Bernard Bailyn's chapter "The Losers" in *Sometimes an Art*, documents how in the course of two centuries historical treatment of the Loyalists gradually achieved a fairer and more accurate portrayal, subsequent to the initial obliteration they suffered in Patriot accounts of the American Revolution.

29. Rosenstock-Huessy, *Out of Revolution*, 697. Rosenstock-Huessy, "Predicament," 100.

Yet Rosenstock-Huessy warned, as did Pierre Nora fifty years later, that even the ways of building up traditions, once seemingly instinctive, now require study. "Remembrance is a social and individual capacity which has to be nourished by appropriate conditions. Modern man seems no longer to register experience without special training." It cannot be assumed that historical memory is automatically gathered and stored. What Rosenstock-Huessy called the "trajective" vector in life is undernourished.[30] There was a time when the public schools, beginning with the earliest years, were vital keepers of national traditions by enacting traditional stories. I do not know if this is still the case in the United States.[31] Children probably no longer dress up as Pilgrims and Indians in school rituals as an educational complement to the Thanksgiving feast at home? What story is told that provides "meaning" to the Thanksgiving holiday? It is hard to overestimate the damaging effect on tradition in the United States caused by the merging of commemorative historical holidays into abstractions lacking in specific reference to the past. The compression of the long-observed birthdays of Washington and Lincoln on February 22 and February 12, respectively, into a single generic Monday holiday called "President's Day," has no historic resonance whatsoever. Not all U.S. presidents are worthy of remembrance. The calendar itself, then, is on the way to losing its historicity. Holidays do come and go over time, and are highly indicative of public sentiment, a subject about which Rosenstock-Huessy wrote at length. He particularly emphasized that no historian per se can create a holiday or diminish one.

Rosenstock-Huessy's recommendations are not at all the same as the solution to the heritage vs. history problem that we often hear proposed: that scholars should write more appealingly for the general public as a means of weaning it from inherited popular mythology. According to this view, if academic books were more accessible to laymen, they would displace the myths clung to in popular memory. One cannot quarrel with advocacy for more readable writing in all realms of culture, but this proposal seems to have as its aim the elimination, not the reinforcement, of the organic transmission of beliefs and traditions. Rosenstock-Huessy was arguing that any tack that depletes the authentic emergence of popular memory deprives the historian of engagement with what is truly important

30. Rosenstock-Huessy, "Predicament," 100.

31. Rosenstock-Huessy, *The Christian Future*, 99: "To omit the legendary form of truth is to suppress truth." Santa Claus is appropriate for children, so that "they may understand the workings of the Spirit among us."

in the inheritance from the past, leaving him open to getting mired in trivial topics: "The true function of history must be recovered. The important facts, experienced, remembered, and created into traditions and instincts, must once more become the foundation of historical research."[32]

2

The kind of scholar Rosenstock-Huessy described may be called the "listening historian." Much of his philosophical work focused on the nature of dialogue, the interaction of listener and speaker. In the 1920s, he and the most famous theorist of dialogue in the twentieth century, Martin Buber, were collaborators on the path-breaking journal *Die Kreatur* (published in Berlin) and remained friends for life. Rosenstock-Huessy, although much less known today, went further than Buber in elaborating on the reciprocity and implications of speaking and listening. "When I sing and my listener is an effete aesthetic critic, he will abuse me for my innocent song which he takes to be a case for scientific analysis, perhaps as a mere critic. Instead of singing with me, he dissects my singing."[33] The listening historian, on the contrary, knows when empathy, not detached science, is needed, that is, the ability to share the received experience. "I am unable to stare at history like a spectacle to be contemplated from a box," Rosenstock-Huessy wrote. "The world's history is our own history.

32. Rosenstock-Huessy, "Predicament," 100. Regarding the failure of collective memory, see Nora "Between Memory and History," 7–9, on the project in France: "We have seen the end of societies that had long assured the transmission and conservation of collectively remembered values, whether through churches or schools, the family or the state." "The 'acceleration of [scientific] history', then, confronts us with the brutal realization of the difference between real memory—social and unviolated . . . —and history, which is how our hopelessly forgetful modern societies, propelled by changes, organize the past." "Memory and history, far from being synonymous, now appear to be in fundamental opposition". "Memory installs remembrance within the sacred; history, always prosaic, releases it again." "History is perpetually suspicious of memory, and its true mission is to suppress and destroy it."

33. Rosenstock-Huessy, "Listener's Tract," 134–54, and see chapter 8, below. Rosenstock-Huessy comments on Buber briefly in *Judaism Despite Christianity*, 69–70. This work was re-issued in 2011 by the University of Chicago Press, with new introductory material. Cf. the comments of the historian Page Smith, a student of Rosenstock-Huessy's at Dartmouth College in the 1930s, in "On Writing History," 59: "I suppose that if I have one basic article of faith about the process of writing history it is this: *Listen to the voices of the past*, their precise tones and accents, and try to enter sympathetically into their hopes and visions." See also, Smith's *The Historian and History* and *Killing the Spirit*.

If it were but a world's history, its facts would be endless, the selection of its millions of dates would be undertaken in vain; it would be nothing but a hopeless library of dust."[34]

But the historian's work is not only to salvage. He must as often be "the grave-digger of our memories as their restorer. His work tests the duration of living memory, strengthens the rising, and buries the withered." Yerulshalmi echoed this thought: "Myth and memory condition action. There are myths that are life-sustaining and deserve to be reinterpreted for our age. There are some that lead astray and must be redefined. Others are dangerous and must be exposed."[35] Rosenstock-Huessy tried to bridge the chasm between popular memory and scientific history by proposing that historians rethink the foundations of their craft, and in particular by giving up any modeling after natural science. Today, eighty years later, historians are far less wedded to models from the natural sciences with regard to method and aims. History seen partly, or even predominantly, as a literary art, as distinguished from a social science, has had no lack of exponents, and there have been radical theorists intent on entirely blurring the line between history and fiction. Although history as a discipline is extremely accommodating to a wide variety of approaches and methods, more than ever its practitioners have had to defend its boundaries against those who would altogether dismiss the very goal of objectivity as chimerical, leaving aside the difficulty of its application.[36] The essential problem for our time, however, is not the validity of objectivity as a standard of truth, but the failure to realize the limitations of that one standard in a comprehensive picture of mankind's engagement with the world including the past; the essential problem is

34. Rosenstock-Huessy, *Out of Revolution*, 7.

35. Rosenstock-Huessy, *Out of Revolution*, 698; Yerushalmi, *Zakhor*, 98. In the United States at this very moment there is a vigorous effort by professional historians to expose and finally bury the persistent myth that the Southern Confederacy in the Civil War was a "noble cause," which masks the truth that the goal of the attempted secession was to protect a patriarchal, racist, slave society.

36. Peter Novick's *That Noble Dream* is a masterly treatment of the concept of objectivity and the skepticism towards it in historiography. In *Linguistics of History* , 122, Harris attacks writers such as Roland Barthes, who see the Western tradition of historiography as less a search for truth about the past than "an effort to present partisan versions of the truth; and this in turn casts cumulative doubt on whether there is any objective truth to be reported."

the over-extension of the "science" faith into realms where it is inapplicable and in fact misses the truth.[37]

Rather than objectifying the past in the search for truth, and seeking detachment, which is bound to be destructive of collective memory, Rosenstock-Huessy called for a profession that would identify with what they hear. The historian by listening to the voices of human experience enters into dialogue with the past. The relation of speakers and listeners is never "objective," since true listeners must run the risk of being changed by what is said. It was not just a rhetorical flourish that Rosenstock-Huessy subtitled *Out of Revolution*, which is a history of Europe over the past one thousand years, *Autobiography of Western Man*. By describing it as autobiography he wanted to emphasize that not only was he not a hypothetical observer of Western civilization from another planet but was indelibly the direct product of those centuries and was thus incapable of writing it without that precise inheritance sustaining him. Every word in the book implicated him not only in the past but also in the future of the West. The past the historian is writing about is part of who he is; he can repudiate that past, or rejoice in it, but he cannot pretend it has nothing to do with him, lest he also fail to take responsibility for the future.

In 1938 another work was published on the European revolutions, far more recognized than Rosenstock-Huessy's, though much inferior: Crane Brinton's *Anatomy of Revolution*. In his review of the book the following year in the *American Historical Review*, Rosenstock-Huessy wrote:

> To me the meaning of revolutions does not disclose itself to the man who thinks that he himself moves outside of their orbit. . . . Do not the authors [i.e., Brinton and Roger Bigelow Merriman whose *Six Contemporaneous Revolutions* (1938) is assessed in the same review] owe their own chairs of history to the English, the French, and the American revolutions? Yet, responsibility for the future of social evolution is excluded from their patterns of scientific thinking. . . . The books testify to J. Benda's *Trahison des Clercs*. The academic scientists have imperiled

37. It is impossible to discuss here the complex issues that have arisen in the past half-century as a result of the skepticism generated by the strengthened recognition that the historian does not hold up to the past a magic mirror that reflects unerringly its story and meaning. The only mirror available is a woven fabric of words that as often deceives as it reveals and is always imperfect. Cf. Paul Ricoeur, *Memory, History, Forgetting*, 256. There is no better work on this subject than Harris, *Linguistics of History*.

> our intellectual freedom. They have watched society instead of watching out for it.[38]

Trying to connect with vital human experience is one way historians can transcend the arbitrary and the insignificant and be of service to communities about their past. They must distinguish sharply between merely recurrent and cyclical events, such as the processes of nature, which have no historical meaning precisely because in themselves they create no milestones, no singular high moments, and events that change everything monumentally and forever. Rosenstock-Huessy called for a concentration on events that are "once and for all," events from which there is no going back. So-called everyday life, for example, as a historical subject has its fascinations, but it tells us little about how mankind, or any part of mankind, got to where it is today. To fulfill its central mission, at least some members of the profession must focus on those events that have made a profound, irreversible difference in the progress of humanity. Such moments usually leave their mark at the time with an indelible name. The historian can recover them and present them in a balanced fashion. Implicit in this thought is the argument that the recounting of lesser events ultimately must justify itself by connecting to the highest moments in history and to the human story as a whole, the universal history of mankind.[39]

The splintering of academic historical writing into what would appear to be endless self-sustaining bits and pieces is sometimes the result of nothing more elevated than the professor's boredom with the well-known and important facts. The poor teachers, Rosenstock-Huessy

38. *American Historical Review,* 44 (July 1939) 882–84.

39. As Rosenstock-Huessy writes in *The Christian Future,* 72: "Purely secular histories never achieve unity. They offer us hundreds of familiar fragments—the history of art, or of economics, or of America, or of the modern theater—but the meaning of all these partial histories will vanish at once if their author cannot connect his story with the more comprehensive one which transcends it." "The hierarchy of importance is unknown in the academic community; the unpaid laundry bills of Walt Whitman may be given as much importance as his 'Ode for Lincoln'. . . . We who, under the influence of science and techniques, are so accustomed to speak of the proper order of things must reeducate ourselves to the proper order of topics to think about." (236). Cf. White's essay, "Guilty of History?" See also McNeil, *Mythistory,* 17, 36: "The moral duty of the historical profession in our time" is "to develop an ecumenical history, with plenty of room for human diversity in all its complexity." The resistance to this vision, this shying away from the large picture, is accounted for by a "residual faith that truth somehow resides in original documents." "The larger patterns of the past . . . cannot be discovered by consulting documentary sources."

wrote, "do their utmost to find some new nuance while teaching the same material year after year. In their despair, they may force their students to read Shakespeare's *Titus Andronicus* instead of *Hamlet*. This does not alter the fact that Shakespeare is read in colleges because he wrote *Hamlet* and despite the fact that he wrote *Titus Andronicus*."[40] By analogy, the history of the Indian tribes of North America becomes "important" because of their interaction with the British and French empires and with the origin and development of the United States, including the history of abuse by the dominant power, wherein the work of the historian can be redemptive. If not for the central, world-changing creation of the United States, the history of the tribes would still be interesting and worth studying but only on the quasi-religious (i.e., Christian) grounds that all souls deserve recognition and recounting. There are thousands of indigenous tribes all over the globe, and have been for millennia, that are largely neglected because their history has not intersected with decisive events in the history of mankind. Some may argue, taking a historicist or relativist position, that there is no central story. But such an argument is tantamount to cutting off the branch on which they are sitting. It belies their own existence. Would these polemicists be in their comfortable offices, protected by their institutions and U.S. laws, without the formation of the United States—not to mention broader forces and foundations, such as Christianity and Western development as a whole?[41]

At the same time, we can agree with Von Ranke that "God, existing in no particular time, gazes over the whole historic humanity in its totality and finds them all equally valuable. . . . From God's point of view all the generations of mankind have equal rights, and this is the way, too, the historian must regard them." Beyond this humane doctrine, from which humankind may deviate only at its peril, it needs to be acknowledged, too, that we never know what events may be hidden in the recesses of the past that at the moment seem minor, the importance of which is yet to be revealed. As David Bade pointed out to me in a private communication, that surely is one of the lessons of the Christian gospel, of news that is not

40. Rosenstock-Huessy, "Letters to Cynthia," an unpublished series of letters written over a period of a year to Cynthia Harris, a college student at Radcliffe. They touch on a wide range of subjects, especially the history of ancient Egypt and the formulation of a universal history. See *Miscellanea*, below.

41. See Headley, "Multiculturalism Reconsidered."

news until it becomes news. Ranke's message, however, should be seen not as a historiographical strategy but as a call for humility.[42]

Since the 1930s historical practices have taken many different creative turns. The number of academic historians has vastly multiplied, with a concomitant search for novel dissertation topics. To earn a doctoral degree, one must prove oneself to be a qualified practitioner of approved professional methods, and one must adhere to the codes of the guild. Generally speaking, the area or substance of one's research within the larger "fields" is not the dominant consideration. Published journal articles can be on matters of relatively little significance, although in the larger scheme of things as a result of these efforts there is an incremental gain in the understanding or information available on any given topic. While these writings showcase journeymen exercising their craft, there is gratification in the thought that substantively we know more than we did ten years ago about this or that. And with the ease of online retrieval, an incalculable amount of relatively arcane, pedestrian scholarly work provides fertile ground for both insignificant findings and towering achievements. Great intellectual work flourishes in a context of widespread learning upon which genius feeds. Superb works of history rest on a foundation of thousands of publications that are merely accomplished and yet set a standard beneath which no acceptable book or journal article can fall.

The diversity of approaches to history is far greater than it was several generations back. Rosenstock-Huessy could claim in "The Predicament of History" (although his own writing does not wholly bear out this statement): "History deals solely with conscious experiences." Yet it is not uncommon now for historians, successfully borrowing methodologies from the social sciences, to assemble vast amounts of social, economic, and demographic data and from that aggregate arrive at convincing conclusions about forces in the past that were not part of the consciousness of anyone alive at the time. Bernard Bailyn has spoken of the difference between "manifest" history, events that people of the time are conscious of, and "latent" history, essentially systemic processes that may not be visible until years later when the data is aggregated. The latent history that is then revealed can easily undermine settled myths about what happened and why.[43] The distinction between manifest and latent parallels that be-

42. Von Ranke, *The Secret of World History*, 157–60.

43. Bailyn, *On the Teaching and Writing of History*, 35, and explicated more fully in *Sometimes an Art*, 53–79. Wood, *Purpose of the Past* is a goldmine on the trends,

tween memory and critical history, the latter of which in the twentieth century became "emancipated" from memory, to use Paul Ricoeur's phrasing, in which "chronology owes nothing to remembering." History in the latter case deals with "what was not an object of apprehension on the part of contemporaries." The notion of "source" becomes "freed entirely from that of testimony" and a past is "constructed that no one is able to remember."[44]

At the other extreme, we have microhistories and ethnographic histories, which usually involve a great deal of close listening to what a particular past reveals of itself, although it may be questioned whether what is found has enduring implications beyond the exposure of everyday life. Historical writing at that level can be deeply revealing, approximating the skill of the anthropologist or the novelist. It is certainly not to be disparaged, especially insofar as it effectively differentiates the past and the present, always a desideratum. Still, a fundamental mission of the historian is neglected in the process. While the satisfaction of curiosity has its place, it is not the noblest of historiographical goals. At the same time, history as moral object lesson is never unwelcome.

There has also been a strong drive in the past half-century to try to recapture the history of those without a recorded voice, as distinguished from the visible and vocal histories left by so-called "great white men." This is a worthy ambition as long as it is not simply another form of relativism, which refuses to rank anything on the basis of importance or significance. Everyone it seems, even relativists, readily describes some events as "historic," which means that the event is one that effected permanent change. Yet clearly, very little of the mundane totality of things that happened in the course of time is historic. We know the difference, ultimately, from the collective popular response, such as occurred in the United States following the destruction of the World Trade towers in New York on September 11, 2001, from which the enduring historical name "9/11" emerged.

Historians have the luxury of dwelling in unlimited realms of the past, addressing inconsequential problems, surrounded figuratively by like-minded colleagues, sometimes under the illusion that what they are

fashions, and byways of professional historiography in America since the 1960s. See also Roger Chartier, "History, Time, and Space," in *Republics of Letters*, 1–13.

44. Ricoeur, *Memory, History, Forgetting*, 387. In some of the quotations Ricoeur is himself quoting from an article by Krzysztof Pomian, "De l'histoire, partie de la mémoire, à la mémoire, objet d'histoire."

doing is of great moment. With regard to addressing certain historical "problems" it's a closed autonomous enterprise, a kind of free-floating bubble, often with its own lingo and a short lifetime, more or less detached from the real world and thus becoming a species of play. The analogy in journalism is sports news: fascinating, exciting, competitive, with stars and washouts, surviving in an artificial framework outside of what is driving the world forward or backward at any given time. As in sports, historians engaged in this play may demonstrate the mastery of various skills such as keen writing style, powerful argumentation, gifted assembling of buried evidence, a capacity for deep inquiry, but all of this effort is still as evanescent as yesterday's basketball game because the substance of what is debated is not "worthy of public remembrance," to borrow a phrase from Roy Harris.[45] I am not arguing that society should cease to support seemingly inconsequential historical research and writing. The skills involved, like athletic skills, are beneficial. The alleged impracticality of humanities research is false. We need citizens who can think critically, argue forcefully, and function as teachers cultivating these skills in the young. Like physical fitness, mental fitness should be encouraged. What is needed only is a sense of proportion.

Whatever the divergences in topic or substance, the majority of scholarly journal articles and books generated today by the Ph.D. mill are of high quality technically, but at the same time, the majority are also lacking in significance because the topics do not draw deeply from what has shaped mankind decisively and permanently. They are not echoing voices from the past and restoring memory. The production of academic history is engrossing and intriguing to those immersed in particular historical questions, but most of this work is not compelling to a broader audience, let alone to students in the classroom, and sometimes it undermines the legacies people live by, with little in the content to redeem that demolition.[46]

Having said that, it is illustrative of my argument that the second half of the twentieth century was a time of indisputable achievement in rectifying some of the worst biases of past historiography and bringing

45. Harris, *Linguistics of History*, 171–73.

46. The unearthing of sources, both archival and archaeological, along with the nearly axiomatic opinion that *everything* must be preserved for posterity, has meant that the newly formed armies of trained and untrained historians can easily find material to study. Lowenthal, *Possessed*, describes the huge glut of information descended from the past, "the dogmatic preservation of which is the correlative of the anxious superstition, if that word is apt, that everything deserves to be documented."

to the fore huge areas of quite nontrivial human experience that had been largely ignored or avoided. To mention three outstanding examples: the history of modern slavery and in particular of the slave trade to the Americas from Africa was not just transformed, it was comprehensively and magnificently rescued from near oblivion. To a lesser degree, the same might be said of the study of the role of women in human affairs and of the entwined history of Native Americans with the European interlopers. It is notable, with reference to Rosenstock-Huessy's criteria, that all of these historiographical efforts were connected to passionate demands in the present with an eye to the future. The advent of a reinvigorated Black history was inseparable from the Civil Rights revolution. Similarly, the revival of feminism after World War II included a demand for a new history that did not overlook the role of women, so demonstrably present in the course of that worldwide struggle. These are examples of scholars restoring crucial elements of the past that were unjustly ignored, yet not altogether unremembered. This is the physician at work who makes harmony in the future possible by means of intellectual restitution.

Rosenstock-Huessy often remarked that contrary to common opinion, the past does not *cause* the present and the future, like a concatenation of colliding dominoes. Historians strive to create that retrospective illusion in the midst of the inescapable contingency of human affairs. We inveterately look for explanatory causes. But it is the future—human aspirations, ideals, dreams, needs, visions—that determines both what occurred and what is retrieved from the past. We repeatedly create a new past to serve a new future, which requires listening. Man has the freedom at any time to opt for a new future, albeit sometimes only with great sacrifice, often mortal, such as in true revolutions. The capacity of human beings at all times to make spontaneous choices, defying the expected, undermines the supposed explanatory power of alleged prior causal chains. The "past" doesn't cause the "present," Rosenstock-Huessy insisted, and the "future" is not anticipated by the present. The present, an elastic human invention, is the pressure point where past and future converge and hold us in suspension. It is always a moment of choice. The historian Michael Ermarth in an essay on Rosenstock-Huessy took note of some of these ideas: "Insofar as life and history have meaning," according to Rosenstock-Huessy, "they must be led or inspired from ahead, neither caused nor causally driven from behind. . . . History transpires much more as a process of half-conscious proleptic expectancy than of closed determinist causation. 'All the revolutions of Europe share this same heroic rallying of past and future against a rotten present.' If not condemned totally on all counts as a completely 'rotten present,' the present age of mass collective modernity was judged by Rosenstock-Huessy to be overripe for its own overcoming."[47]

3

Rosenstock-Huessy began his career in Germany as a historian of medieval law, as noted, teaching at Leipzig and Breslau. But the disillusioning trauma to Western civilization of the Great War—he served as an officer in the German army on the western front—led to his abandonment of conventional academic intellectual procedures (although he taught at Dartmouth College from 1935 to 1957) and to his emergence as an unclassifiable "social philosopher," for lack of a better descriptive term. He was deeply engaged in the study of the ramifications of the uniquely human capacity for definitive speech and in the study of the consciousness of the elements of speech that are formalized in grammar. His exploration of grammar unexpectedly serves as a key to understanding human society and its history.[48] Thus his writings on history, memory, science, tradition, ritual, and a myriad of other subjects are all informed by the basic structure of human experience revealed by grammar, namely, the perpetual embeddedness of human beings within space and time axes. This "cross of reality," as he called it, was not merely a theory but an empirical fact that describes human experience at the most elementary level.[49] Most impor-

47. Ermarth, "From Here to Eternity," 309–10, is an excellent exposition of Rosenstock-Huessy's philosophy of history, as distinguished from his critique of present-day professional historiography. Rosenstock-Huessy, *Out of Revolution*, 559: "For the modern historian the only facts that exist are facts of the past. Yet the facts of the past, for the living, would be of no importance whatever except for the facts of the future!" And Rosenstock-Huessy, *The Christian Future*, 87: "All living history connects the past with the future. But the mere past created by scientific history considers the past not as the corollary of our future, but as the cause of the present."

48. The following summary remarks are derived from numerous works by Rosenstock-Huessy, which, for the most part, I will not be citing individually. I have relied mostly on *The Origin of Speech* (1981), written ca. 1944; *Speech and Reality* (1970), a collection of essays going back to the 1930s; *The Christian Future* (1946); and the transcriptions of hours of classroom lectures from the 1950s and 1960s. Indispensable is Lise van der Molen's definitive bibliography, *A Guide to the Works of Eugen Rosenstock-Huessy*. For recent works regarding Rosenstock-Huessy's thought, see www. erhsociety.org/publications.

49. Bade, "*Respondeo etsi Mutabor*," 87–100, shows the resemblance between

tant here, the grammatical method also offers a means of accommodation with regard to the complex issue of heritage versus history.

In our contact with reality, we all live facing four fronts, two in space and two in time. Distinguishing between the inner and the outer, the inside and the outside, inward and outward, interior and exterior, and yes, subjective and objective, are our primary experiences of space. That all people distinguish between "us" and "them," "we" and "they," "I" and "it" encapsulates in grammar this phenomenon. The man who conscientiously served a business firm for many years and always spoke of it as "we," after he quits looks at his former coworkers as "they." Throughout life we deploy a moving, changing membrane within which we live, defining who or what is inside and who or what is outside, and thereby constructing the difference between the subjective and the objective, and the first person and the third person, singular or plural. These days we are asked sometimes to be citizens of the world, abandoning the frontiers of countries or homelands within which people live and by which they identify themselves. In such instances, "we" encompasses all of the planet's peoples, as in "We are the children of the world." Natural science necessarily objectifies what it deals with. All must be treated as dead "its" and mere things, even if they happen to be alive.

The distinction between subject and object is firmly entrenched in philosophical and common thinking. I am sometimes a subject, but I can also be objectified, that is, treated as someone not belonging, and made into a thing, or "the other." The subjective is internal, the objective external, which is a spatial division. Rosenstock-Huessy was incredulous, however, that the philosophical tradition has been so satisfied with the subject/object distinction, as though it encompassed all reality: "This division is taken to be the division of the world. Alas, the world would not survive this division if it were to be taken seriously." The attitude in which we face the outward world as a subject and write about it objectively is "merely one perfunctory and transient function or mood among other functions and moods."

What is massively left out is our orientation in time, which is far more intrinsic than the experience of space: "Man is peculiarly a temporal being," Rosenstock-Huessy wrote, "ever but an exile and a pilgrim in the world of space." There is the inner and the outer, but there are also the perpetual choices of future and past, between moving forward

Rosenstock-Huessy's writings about speech and the much later integrationist linguistics of Roy Harris.

or backward, time behind and time ahead of us. Our immersion in time is no less inescapable than our immersion in space and is revealed not only in the grammatical tenses of future and past but also in grammatical moods. The imperative calls us forward into the future—"Go forth!" "Save the earth!" "Make love not war!"—while the first-person plural that recounts what *we* went through back then, or what happened to us, is employed to connect us to the past as in the U. S. national anthem: "What so proudly we hailed at the twilight's last gleaming."[50]

The person called into action—"You, or Thou, go and help!"—is at that moment neither a subject nor an object. Rosenstock-Huessy designated such an addressee a "preject," finding a verbal equivalent in the temporal realm to the terms used with regard to space. In the prejective state, we give up our anchorage in the past and willingly attach ourselves to the future. In the opposite direction, the person allied with the past is at that moment a "traject." In the observance of rituals at all levels, beginning with the family, of ceremonies and traditions, including national or religious holidays, we are neither subjects nor objects, but trajects in the realm of time, not space. Dozens of minor rituals giving us the assurance of the past are so pervasive we normally take no notice of them as such. One may think such verbal coinages are oddities and little needed, but we are in life far more often prejects and trajects than we are subjects and objects. The bookish tradition of the past twenty-five hundred years has misled us, Rosenstock-Huessy argued, because the imperative is not found so much in books as it is in everyday spoken language, in the give and take of simple human interchange, beginning with parental orders to children, the commands that shape us as we grow up—"Go to sleep!" "Eat!" "Be nice!" It is found later in the classroom, directing students to their future, "Read this," "prepare that," and in the procedural manuals of science and technology.[51]

Similarly, ritual, "the powerful realization of the past," persists in countless ceremonies and traditions, spoken and enacted, conscious and unconscious. The use of quotations of every kind and formulaic language, the function of which is "to guard against the inroad of an uncertain

50. Rosenstock-Huessy is one of the great "time" thinkers since Henri Bergson. Two recent commentaries are Stünkel, "Nations as Times," 297–317, and Leithart, "The Social Articulation of Time in Eugen Rosenstock-Huessy," 197–219.

51. Fiering, "Structure of Significant Lives," (chapter 4, above) discusses the imperatives, sometimes called inspirations, that launch creative men or women into unique productive endeavors.

future," are found not only in obvious ecclesiastical forms and in much poetry but in all forms of legal practice. In the United States more than anyplace else, where tradition may appear to be most eroded, the lawyers, Rosenstock-Huessy observed, are the "priesthood" of the formulaic, as evidenced in what we have come to call "legalese." "Modern democracies find their most sacred ritual in parliamentary speech and procedure." At all sorts of meetings we hear: "Will anybody second?" "All in favor; the motion is carried," and so on. This shows the "tremendous power of the formula for binding society together." When radical political movements favoring so-called direct democracy reject parliamentary procedure, more of the past is thrown overboard than the practitioners may realize.

Three of these four fronts in life are associated with a grammatical mood. We have already noted the connection between the *prejective* state and the imperative mood. Similarly, the *subjective*, the internal, is associated with the subjunctive or optative mood, as we endlessly revolve in our minds "woulds," "coulds," and possibilities, and the subjective is where we inwardly experience emotions such as elation or depression as well as contingency. The *objective*, our attack on and mastery of the external or natural world and our implementation of all forms of scientific analysis, is expressed in the indicative mood and declarative sentences, the prosaic. Mankind's wondrous achievements in medical care, for example, and in the development of technology of all kinds, have so awed us that we are led to place enormous trust in objectivity and outward observation as the only basis of truth, with little attention given to the narrow limitations of this approach. Is truth to be expressed only in the analytic indicative, at the cost of ignoring or denigrating several other equally valid forms of encounter with reality? Finally, the *trajective*, our immersion in the reassuring stability of the past, has no precisely corresponding grammatical mood, but it is found in the reliance on participles and formulas, and in quotations, as noted, as well as in the languages of the law and religion and inherited ceremonies.

All of the above pertains to the individual, who must live constantly and permanently with the choices before him of electing a new future or holding onto the past, and in space remaining inside or outside of any particular group, whether it be a family or a political party. Like the shifting of gears in an automobile or the back and forth of the players in a string quartet, we embrace one or the other of these forms, perhaps in quick, perhaps in slow succession, instinctively aiming to maintain a temporal balance. No one, it must be emphasized, can erect a standpoint outside of these vectors, this cross, as the "observing objective" social scientist might try to do. Our personal health depends upon such equilibrium, as does the health of nation states and human society as a whole. Moving rashly forward, indifferent to vital ties, or conversely, being stuck in the past, unable to liberate oneself from existing bonds, are equally disastrous choices, as is the failure to differentiate between who is inside and who is outside, treason being an extreme example at the national level. Every family has a strong sense of the difference between what is private and what is public, which children early come to understand. Being unable to take a step into a new future, on the one hand, or recklessly abandoning all of our relations from the past, on the other, are both akin to sicknesses, just as being unable to differentiate between "we" and "they" in our social relations is a formula for personal disaster. We dare not objectify someone we love.[52]

The historian insensitively belittling a popular myth or disrespecting a dubious patriotic belief is breaking faith with the society that sustains him or her, that indeed makes the historian's work possible. The historian's "we" is usually the professional guild of his or her academic colleagues; collective memory is what "they," the public, relies on for understanding. The historian's credo of "objectivity," with pronouncements in the indicative mood deemed the sole source of truth, would disenable, for example, reliance on the messages in Christian hymns such as those that emboldened civil rights marchers in the 1960s, that helped make possible the creation of a new future. Reliance on "objectivity" may leave one unable to respond when the call comes to mobilize for a great cause, when detachment disastrously weakens attachment. The trusted "scientific" view of the world is, after all, Rosenstock-Huessy notes, no more than the *scientists'* professional, and necessarily limited, view of the world, which is but "a fraction of the whole truth":

> Society compensates for our individual inadequacies by division of labor. For example, teaching, ceremony, and ritual preserve our continuity with the past, and teachers, priests, and lawyers

52. Rosenstock-Huessy, *Christian Future*, 168–69: "No individual can move adequately in all four directions at once. Therefore life is perpetual decision: when to continue the past and when to change, and where to draw the line between the inner circle we speak to and the outer objects we merely speak of and try to manipulate. . . . Integration, living a complete and full life, is accordingly not some smooth 'adjustment' we can hope to achieve once and for all and then coast along with. . . . It is rather a constant achievement in the teeth of forces which tear us apart on the Cross of Reality."

> serve on this front for all of us. We build up social unanimity by playing, singing, talking together, sharing our moods and aspirations, and on this inner front poets, artists, and musicians are typical representatives. We win our living and protect our lives by learning to control natural forces and manipulating them for our ends in farming, industry and war; scientists, engineers, and soldiers typify the millions who fight for us on the outer front. Lastly, religious and political leaders, prophets and statesmen are responsible for initiating change and drawing society into its future.[53]

Where do historians fit in this scheme? Clearly, they work *both* on the outer front, in space, like engineers and scientists, and also, on the time vector, they station themselves in the past as responsible teachers, helping to anchor and stabilize society simply by the evocation of the past. That they have this dual conflicting role is their burden.

The task of the historian differs profoundly from that of the natural scientist not only in that the former must primarily listen while the latter must primarily look. The scientist struggles to discover hidden attributes of nature. Once his discovery is verified and confirmed, it becomes an indisputable fact. In the case of the historian, Rosenstock-Huessy argued, most of the time the basic facts of the past are known or are readily available. Unlike the scientist, the historian struggles not to establish a fact but to convince readers to connect with the past that has been evoked, to make them believe that what the historian has to tell them they must come to know. For the historian, the obdurate matter is "us," you and me, who are likely to be indifferent. For the scientist, the obdurate matter is a natural world that yields its secrets so reluctantly. As George Morgan summarized Rosenstock-Huessy's position: "Mere knowledge does not yield power over human affairs as it does over nature."[54]

The same space and time quadrilateral in which individuals are suspended is represented in macro terms in the nation state. In a healthy country, Rosenstock-Huessy observed, there is legislation, which always points to the future; sciences, which are always engaged in outward objective studies of many kinds; the arts, which are inward turning and produce subjective literature, painting, sculpture, cinematography, and music, with the capacity to unite a people in symbol and song; and there are ceremonies, re-enactments, and rituals manifest in holidays, and

53. Rosenstock-Huessy, *Christian Future*, 55, 169.

54. George Allen Morgan, *Speech and Society*, 72.

many observances— baptisms, graduations, funerals, weddings— that connect us to the past and provide fixity in the flux of time. Heritage, insofar as it reflects genuine tradition and memory, on the one side, and professional historiography, on the other, represent two fundamental forms of experience and expression, the trajective and the objective, both of which are necessary for social and psychological stability. They are more complementary than inimical.

Prof. Bernard Bailyn captures this complementarity eloquently in his essay "Considering the Slave Trade: History and Memory":

> The history of the slave trade is a critically assembled, intellectually grasped story of distant events, but the memory of it is immediately urgent, emotional, and unconstrained by the critical apparatus of scholarship. . . . Perhaps history and memory in the end may act usefully upon each other. . . . The passionate, timeless memory of the slave trade that tears at our conscience and shocks our sense of decency may be shaped, focused, and informed by the critical history we write, while the history we so carefully compose may be kept alive, made vivid and constantly relevant and urgent by the living memory we have of it.[55]

Modern historiography, whether it is dubbed "scientific" or not, is presented, like the physical sciences, in the prose of the indicative mood. "The world is round." "The hummingbird's heart beats twelve hundred times a minute." "The North won at the battle of Gettysburg." Abraham Lincoln's address at Gettysburg, however, was not an objective description of the battle or the war, although he began like a historian with a datum: "Four score and seven years ago . . . ." Only a dunce would deny that Lincoln spoke the essential truth of what happened, despite the absence of historical details. He uses the first-person plural: "We have come to dedicate . . ." thus uniting his listeners. He uses the imperative to define urgent tasks for the future: "It is for us the living . . . to be dedicated . . . to the unfinished work. . . ." He employs the root word "dedicate" in one form or another six times in an address that in total is under 300 words. All dedications are trajective; they are evoked for the purpose of ensuring that the lessons of the past will be represented in the future.

The child in school reciting the Gettysburg address is engaged in a ritual act of a different order than when that same child that very same day is asked in a history lesson to cite three reasons why the Civil War

55. Bailyn, "Considering the Slave Trade," in *Sometimes an Art*, 16–17.

occurred. The child is in an altogether different mode, too, when the class sings "The Battle Hymn of the Republic," let us hope with heart, minus analysis. That moment is one of subjective elation, as well as a ritual. And finally, perhaps, the classroom instruction related to the Civil War includes an inspiring verse from Whitman or Melville that envisions a future of peace and implores us with imperatives to work to bring it about, as in this example with powerful irony:

> Beat! beat! drums!—blow! bugles! blow!
> Make no parley—stop for no expostulation,
> Mind not the timid—mind not the weeper or prayer,
> Mind not the old man beseeching the young man,
> Let not the child's voice be heard, nor the mother's
> entreaties,
> Make even the trestles to shake the dead where they lie
> awaiting the hearses,
> So strong you thump O terrible drums—so loud you
> bugles blow.
> Whitman, "*Beat! Beat! Drums!*"

Scientific description and analysis, including scholarly history, is at best one-quarter of what is needed for wholeness in a person or in society.[56] It is a desperately needed quarter on which we are dependent if we are to manage our lives intelligently as individuals and as citizens. But because the historian is dealing most of the time with a living and expressive past, a speaking past, his striving for scientific objectivity must be checked lest he go astray and lose contact with the vitality of the legacy handed to him. Insofar as he is *spoken to* by the past, the listening historian is not a subject dealing with objects. He is a traject, locating himself in the past, writing for the future, a preservationist writing what he feels the future must know. The voices from the past that he hearkens to are not "objects" for detached study; they, too, are trajects, perhaps hoping to reach descendants. Collective memory, tradition, heritage, expressing itself in manifold ways, is not in opposition to the professional historian

56. When I admire a lily, I may do so as an evolutionary botanist, as a painter preparing for a still-life, as an inspired poet, as an ecological preservationist, as a marketer of bulbs and seeds, as a florist for a funeral, or as a spiritual teacher invoking the lilies of the field for moral guidance. Who is in possession of the *real* knowledge about the flower? No one, obviously; each has a distinctive truth to convey. As Harris writes in *Linguistics of History*, 49: "Poetry and history involve different uses of language. It is not that one of them pays attention to the truth while the other ignores it, but that the poet is concerned with a different level of truth from the historian.".

insofar as these forms of expression are not assertive about facts in measured declarative sentences, but are rather celebratory, emotional, inspiring, liturgical, memorializing, and unifying.

Thus, the historian straddles the line between scientific objectivity and trajective recovery, preservation, and restoration, using the signals of popular and collective memory as guideposts. Spatially he is a conquering warrior acutely analyzing the external world with the instruments of aggressive prose, and equally he should be the bearer or recipient of temporal communal memory, humbly purifying it as opposed to asserting that he is the sole source of truth. But can common ground be found between the practice of the professional historian and commercialized, ersatz, concocted, myth-ridden "heritage"? In the eighty years since Rosenstock-Huessy wrote the "Predicament of History," popular culture has been overwhelmed and dominated by a gigantic force hardly imagined a century ago, the capitalist entertainment industry. Those engaged in the segment of the entertainment industry that David Lowenthal calls "heritage" would readily acknowledge that their primary goal is to entertain and by that means make their productions profitable. Yet entertainment drawing on historical themes, such as period dramas, however inaccurate or even bogus, to be profitable must tap into public interest or concern. Hence, even the most audacious fabrication or distortion can be a clue for the listening historian.

7

"The Uni-versity [*sic*] of Logic, Language, Literature"

Eugen Rosenstock-Huessy at Dartmouth College, 1935

[I presented a version of this paper initially at the conference "EugenRosenstock-Huessy Then & Now" organized by M. Darroll Bryant at Renison University College/University of Waterloo, Waterloo, Ontario, June 19–22, 2014]

In the late fall of 1935, only a few months after he first arrived at Dartmouth College, a recent émigré from Nazi Germany, Professor Rosenstock-Huessy presented a paper to the campus Philosophy Club nominally on the subject of the underlying unity of philosophy, linguistics, and literature. Entitled "The Uni-versity [*sic*] of Logic, Language, Literature: A Program for Collaboration," it was a topic sure to be intriguing to his new colleagues, but it was also a bit misleading, for the text covers far more ground and cuts deeper than that declared theme indicates. There is also not much mention of collaboration in any practical sense.

Because of the circumstances of its presentation—a moment when Rosenstock-Huessy was consciously introducing himself to Dartmouth, several years before the publication in 1938 of his major book in English, *Out of Revolution*—it is deserving of close attention. Many topics of passionate interest to Rosenstock-Huessy but not normally associated with the unity of the disciplines are touched on, and there is a formidable display of erudition. The paper is thick with ideas, to the point that any commentary must be selective. I offer here little more than an explication of salient parts of this work with some of my ruminations.[1]

Coming to the United States in the fall of 1933, Rosenstock-Huessy first spent a contentious three semesters at Harvard before moving permanently to a professorship at Dartmouth. It would appear that the distinguished forty-seven-year-old genius from the old country, with two degrees from Heidelberg and professorial positions at Leipzig and Breslau behind him, wanted to be sure from the start that the college recognized not only his vast learning but, more than that, his penchant for radical reform. Indeed, only a few years later, Rosenstock-Huessy was leading a faculty seminar at Dartmouth on educational reform, but without lasting result, to my knowledge.

The title of the piece, as I have noted, hardly begins to capture its substance; no title could. The work has an underlying coherence, which I will try to bring out here, but on the surface it seems to lack logical development, which could discourage some listeners or readers. As is often the case in Rosenstock's work, the text is elliptical. His mind leaped, and the poor reader can only plod on behind, looking for footing. The essay introduces fresh ideas and repeatedly challenges the accepted wisdom, which most of Rosenstock-Huessy's writing did, but in this instance there seems to be no easy surface connection among the various topics addressed. Only at the deepest level do we see the intertwining of the roots of his argument. Some of Rosenstock-Huessy's most fundamental and original ideas are evident in this rich concoction, but they are presented with only the briefest elaboration, and as the essay moves along, with mounting attacks on the philosophical establishment, it becomes more

1. This paper by Rosenstock-Huessy is reprinted in *Speech and Reality*, 67–97. A typewritten version, perhaps properly designated the "original," was included in the microfilm of Rosenstock-Huessy's works, Reel 6, item 206. At the end of the original typescript in Rosenstock-Huessy's hand is written: "Address to the Philosophy Club late fall 1935." The membership of the Club, or who might have attended the lecture, is unknown to me. I am assuming that the speaker was addressing primarily faculty, not undergraduates. Dartmouth had no graduate students in the humanities. It is possible that information could be found about the context of this lecture in the archives of Dartmouth. The 1970 publication varies slightly here and there from the original, but there are no substantive differences. The numbers in parentheses in my explication refer to the page numbers of the reprint.

unconventional in its findings. Perhaps above all "The Uni-versity of Logic, Language, Literature" is about the nature of man (and, of course, woman), which is properly a precondition for any talk about the unity of the humanities. The disciplines become aspects of the whole man.

By my analysis, three central arguments are presented:

1. All people go through life both disclosing the truth they see and also much of the time hiding it. "Man is essentially concerned with disclosure and velation," he writes. What we know of reality we may reveal or declare, but at other times, for any number of reasons, we conceal or veil the truth. Dishonesty, or lying, in other words, is endemic. This is not so much a moral judgment for Rosenstock-Huessy as a fact consequent to the magnificent human capacity to speak, for that capacity allows us also the choice not to speak, or to speak falsely. The emphasis in this lecture on truth and dissemblance in human affairs, and the consequences, is one of its more striking and unexpected features.
2. Everything a person does, or says, or thinks, or creates in addressing reality is part of an ordered process involving, at the most fundamental level, only four forms or modes of expression, and throughout our existence there is a constant permutation among these four fronts, each with its particular role and timing. When the natural balance or equilibrium among these fronts fails, trouble always ensues. This is clearly a startling schematization, which is at the heart of Rosenstock-Huessy's work, and one that requires explication.
3. Central to understanding how mankind progresses in all areas—politics, arts and sciences, religion, social norms—is recognition of the role of the imperative in language, and also the vocative, the importance of which is largely missing in our inherited, ancient Alexandrian grammar table— "I love, you love, she loves, we love, they love," etc. —in which all of the persons and moods are presented as equal.

These three points—the prevalence of dissemblance, the four modes of expression, the centrality of the imperative mood—are not just inductive generalizations; they are embedded characteristics of humankind as a whole, for all cultures and all times. They are universals, but they also have a historical dimension, which is to say they are part of human history, including so-called pre-history, and only gradually came into being, although Rosenstock-Huessy is not hesitant to refer to them as part of a lawful process, in the sense of fixed and irreversible laws of human society, discovered and described, not enacted.

The four fronts, referred to in item number 2, above, are revealed above all in speech or language, and more specifically in descriptive grammar. If that sounds simplistic, the reader should not be deceived. The phenomenon that Rosenstock-Huessy delineates is complex and does dynamically and comprehensively illuminate the human condition. Although these four modes of confronting and describing reality—whether it be to disclose or to dissemble—have a number of names, each of these elements has a discrete core identity that underlies the various names. Once one is alerted to this finding, one sees the process everywhere, in different guises at all levels. Whether it is an entire nation-state, society at large, or an individual, this grammatical quadrilateral still applies.

Along the way, we must be disabused of certain fantasies that cloud the picture, the most important being, perhaps, the notion that thought is independent of language, indeed superior to language, and that the brilliance of the thinker is allegedly limited by the inadequacy of language to reflect his supposed depth of insight. According to this assumption, first we think and then we speak, as though the thought is independent of language. But for Rosenstock-Huessy there is no human faculty superior to speech. Speech, not reason or the mind, Wayne Cristaudo has written in his work on Rosenstock-Huessy, "is the real basis of thinking." "Speech," for Rosenstock-Huessy and Franz Rosenzweig, "was primarily a creative, revelatory, and redemptive power, and not merely or essentially a descriptive one."[2]

It is necessary, too, to let go of the dualisms that have dominated Western philosophy since the time of Plato, or at least since Descartes in the seventeenth century: subject and object, mind and matter, idea and reality, and so forth. We may indeed be sometimes a subject and sometimes an object, but human experience is hardly exhausted by that duality. It is not only incomplete, it is a false limitation that has done untold damage. We can never get rid of the subject/object split, Rosenstock-Huessy concedes, but by enlarging the picture we can put it in balance and perspective.

Each of the terms in the title of this talk—logic, language, literature—Rosenstock-Huessy makes clear, has common synonyms. So he

2. Cristaudo, *Religion, Redemption, and Revolution*, xi, 55: "The idea that language is an obstacle to reality" is for Rosenzwieg and Rosenstock-Huessy "but a vestige of naturalism's blindness to the way in which we make and respond to our world."

also speaks of unifying into a single cosmos "thought, speech, and literature," and he refers as well to "thought, language, literature," and "logic, linguistics, literary criticism." The terms "thought," "logic," and "philosophy" are more or less interchangeable here, as are "language," "speech," and "linguistics," although speech for Rosenstock-Huessy most often refers to that most basic and defining capacity of human beings, not simply to a branch of learning. "Literature" is ambiguous because it is not always evident when by "literature" Rosenstock-Huessy means poesis, i.e., creative writing, whether it be a lengthy novel or a sonnet, or when he means the academic study of literature. There is, in any case, considerable overlap in the finest cases of literary criticism and literature.

"Thought, language, literature" would be the most correct title, Rosenstock-Huessy reflected, but alas, "the alliteration of the three 'L's proved too strong an enticement. Thus," he writes, "my mind fell into the trap of language at the very beginning, and I am giving myself away as a pointed example of language's power over a man's logic." (68–69)

Properly understood, the thousands of languages of mankind, Rosenstock-Huessy remarks, are "one great and marvelous disclosure of the human mind." He credits the work of Wilhelm von Humboldt as an inspiration for this realization. With Humboldt, Rosenstock-Huessy believed that to understand human speech we must study it as a "finished product," not as a process in formation. Hence, to look to the children's nursery for an understanding of speech, to study how the child gradually masters his or her mother tongue, is a form of reductionism and is completely misleading. "It is in the highest reaches of our own intellectual life that we must look for analogies when we try to discover the energies which created speech."(68) This point is brilliantly elaborated in Rosenstock-Huessy's small book *The Origin of Speech*. In the present lecture it is a passing comment.

PHILOSOPHY

Philosophy cannot be successful without philology, Rosenstock-Huessy asserts, and vice versa. That is, there can be no separation between logic and language, or thought and speech. Language, logic, literature are merely "various forms of crystallization" in a single process. Such an argument, he recognizes, is heretical in philosophy (or it was in 1935 when Rosenstock-Huessy wrote this paper), but he cites as predecessors

Thomas Carlyle; John the Disciple "in his character as the author of the Gospel of St. John"; Friedrich Schlegel; J. G. Hamann; and in the twenty years preceding 1935, "Majewski, Ebner, Buber, Cuny, Royen," who have all developed "forms of thinking" that may enable us to describe the underlying unity of thought, speech, and literature.[3]

It has been the foolish pride of philosophy that it was "beyond speech and not at all at the same level." Language, it has been claimed, is merely material; thought is in the realm of the ideal, in the Platonic sense. Philosophy or logic may aspire to be the science of truth, Rosenstock-Huessy acknowledged, yet those truths, nonetheless, must be expressed in language, in books and articles subject to critical examination. Despite that fact, whenever a critic, such as Carlyle, called the supposed elevated thinker "a mere myth-weaver or a sartor resartus like any poet," philosophy paid no attention. "The logician, proud of his scientific character, prefers symbolical logic to the modest confession that he is a writer of books and a speaker of words."(68–69)

It is relevant to note here that the subordination of philosophy to language was a twentieth-century phenomenon, occurring in different guises, such as the analytical school in Britain and the structuralists on the Continent. Much of this work, however, sometimes referred to as "the linguistic turn," dissolved into cynicism, relativism, or even nihilism, lacking in moral content. Rosenstock-Huessy's aims were far different. In 1962, twenty-seven years after his 1935 lecture at Dartmouth, he wrote about Ludwig Wittgenstein:

> "Wittgenstein's approach . . . excludes from consideration the actual truth or falsity of any statement" aside from formal matters. "Further, the things that are likely to be of greatest interest to living human beings in time—those that require decisions and action—are outside the scope of logic and linguistic analysis. . . . [For Wittgenstein] what a living person does or should do about any statement is not the province of philosophy. . . . The idea that words and other symbols have a reality of their own, or that they are, or can be, active and actuating powers

3. Probably a reference to Erazm Majewski, *La science de la civilisation* (Paris, 1910) and to Ferdinand Ebner, *Das Wort und die Geistigen realitäten* (Innsbruck, 1921). Martin Buber is a well known author on speech philosophy and was a major contributor to the journal *Die Kreatur*, along with his friend Rosenstock-Huessy. Probably a reference to Albert Cuny, *Études prégrammaticales sur le domaine des langues indo-européennes et chamito-sémitiques* (Paris, 1924) and possibly to Gerlach Royen, a Dutch scholar, *Die nominalen Klassifikations-systeme in den Sprachen der Erde* (1929).

> that derive from, preserve, foster, and even make human history—that may bring people together or plunge them into war—is not acceptable to Wittgenstein."[4]

The thinker can never invent a wholly new language to serve his purposes. However original a philosophy, it must deploy existing language. On the other hand, the philosopher, like the poet, may give existing words new meanings, although the old meanings cling, and sometimes the intended new meaning is stillborn. The mind of the philosopher can be a "seedbed" of new languages, in the sense that new meaning is created. In fact, Rosenstock-Huessy writes, "to think means to translate from one language into another better language."(71) It must be accepted, too, that "thought" does something to language. It may kill words, for example. If this is true, it should be one of the tasks of philology to inquire what logic does to language.

> Logic can no longer remain indifferent to the fact that it has duties toward language. That is why we wish to speak here of thought, speech, and literature as one united effort of mankind to disclose or to conceal the truth. . . . They are rays of one fire burning in man to communicate to or to hide from his fellow man his share of truth. And we throw out [i.e., put forth] the hypothesis that thought, language, and literature, insofar as they are means of concealing or revealing truth to ourselves, to a partner, or to all men, are ruled by the same laws."(71)

More than two thousand years of philosophic disdain for rhetoric or oratory, since Plato, has led us to believe that thought and literature are separate activities. We exercise our reason by reading or writing articles and books, but the "intermedium stage of *speaking our mind* is rarely inserted." (Italics added). Hence, the illusion is born that we can somehow think outside of the realm of speech. "The modern thinker conceals from himself the fact that no thought can come to the ken of the majority of men except in listening." We partake of the reasoning process by listening and answering. It is the "electric induction of the dialogue" that makes us partners in the search for truth. But once this social situation is over,

4. The comment on Wittgenstein is from an entry that Rosenstock-Huessy wrote for the *American People's Encyclopedia* (Chicago, 1962) that can be found in the microfilm collection, Reel 11, 545, 107, accessible now at www.erhfund.org. It is one of about seventy brief essays he wrote for that work. For more on Rosenstock-Huessy's writing for the *Encyclopedia*, see below, chapter 10, "Rosenstock-Huessy Meets Jelly Roll Morton."

"we are empty again."(73) The reciprocity of listening and speaking was a central theme in Rosenstock-Huessy's thought, best exemplified in his 1944 essay, "The Listener's Tract."[5]

LANGUAGE

The philologists and linguists, those specializing in language, as distinct from the philosophers, have their own problems, which is revealed by the organization of the field of languages in higher education. Typically, one can study a language and never be offered any "linguistic principle."

> Modern linguists do not think that the power of language is intimately connected with the power of truth. They do not assume that, as Aristotle said, truth is the obvious aim in speech, and lying only secondary. The whole idea of levels in speech depending on its nearness to truth is unheard of. The science of truth and the sciences of languages are separated. Language is thought of as being a tool, a gadget at man's ready disposal to serve him whenever he wishes to put up [i.e., put on] this or that air."(69–70)

LITERATURE

With regard to the third group of activities, literary criticism and comparative literature, and also creative writing, Rosenstock-Huessy reinforces the notion that often the most profound remarks relating to language and philosophy are made by those specializing in literature, "which fatally remain unheeded by logicians and linguists." The philosopher has traditionally shown "utter contempt for oratory" because he dismisses it as merely language, and not logic. Yet, consider, Rosenstock-Huessy writes, the philosopher or

> any speaker on the platform tries to speak his mind in a lasting way, and . . . therewith, he is struggling with the living word in a unified effort. He has to think in the monologue we call thought, he has to speak to an audience by which he gets involved into a dialogue, and he is hoping for a lasting effect by which his words

5. "The Listener's Tract," which survives in a typescript from 1944, was published for the first time in Rosenstock-Huessy, *Speech and Reality*. The work is reprinted in entirety below, chapter 8.

> shall become detached from the moment and take on the power of outlasting more than one occasion.(72)

We see in this example the three-fold character of words: "In the monologue the man is thinking aloud; in the dialogue, he is speaking to his hearers[;] and in the pleologue . . . he speaks for future recollection." Pleologue, Rosenstock-Huessy explains, is a kind of speech that can be presented to more than one audience. In time, the monologue branched off into the supposed separate realm of thought; the pleologue gave birth to literature. Monologue, dialogue, and pleologue are separable only superficially, since all three are present at the same moment when a speaker stands at a podium.(72)[6] In other words, the unity of these disciplines is derived from the primordial act of speaking. Philosophy is a form of literature and literature a form of philosophy.

The image of the philosopher thinking inwardly and supposedly always aiming at the truth is fallacious. First of all, "we discover as many new things about ourselves or about the world or about our beliefs through speaking out and writing down as by thinking inwardly," and inward thought is as susceptible to deceit as any other human process. The philosopher or logician is as eager to deceive himself as the orator and the novelist are, and he "uses as many tricks to cheat his own conscience" as the other two do. Detached inward thought is, in itself, "no more proof against the fallacies of passion, prejudice, and interest than speech or writing. Thinking can be myth-weaving exactly as fiction is. And literature struggles for truth just as desperately as thought."(73)

To summarize Rosenstock-Huessy's 1935 indictment of the isolation of the academic disciplines: The self-described thinkers, the philosophers, deceive themselves by the idealistic notion that isolated thought is superior to, perhaps purer than, speech or language; the specialists in language, the linguists and philologists, divorce language from its essential function of conveying truth between men, and treat it as a detached, natural mechanism existing merely for "communication" and subject to analysis on that basis; meanwhile, those specializing in literature, so-called, appear to accept their separation from the philosopher's search for truth, with the result that the study of literature can descend into mere aestheticism or into academic word-play.

6. According to Cargill, "The Communication Theory of Eugen Rosenstock-Huessy," the concept of "pleologue" resembles Chaim Perelman's idea of the "universal audience" (*The Realm of Rhetoric*) and also Michel Foucault's idea of originary texts ('Discourse' 220), which are texts that become the objects of commentary.

TRUTH AND DISSEMBLANCE

In all three forms of the spoken (or written) word—thought, literature, and linguistics or language—man is "essentially concerned with disclosure and velation," as noted earlier, or we might say, concerned with openness and concealment, in relation to himself, to others, and to humans in general. Human beings are distinguished from the animals

> by the one fact that any group, nation, tribe, member, human individual, wherever we find him is occupied in justifying himself to himself, to others, and to the kind. This explains why he is wearing clothes, why he is making speeches, why he is reasoning and why he is writing books. . . . Man is at every moment bound up with his kind in a way no animal is. At any given moment man answers for his attitude by true or false statements. He is perpetually active in disclosure and velation, perpetually passive in enclosure and reception.(74)

In a memorable affirmation of humankind's fundamental sense of accountability, Rosenstock-Huessy writes: "Mankind is present where[ever] a man exists." A person may address himself inwardly, may speak to the ears of another, or may write for the eyes of a million readers, or do all three, but we are conscious that in the end in all three forms of discourse we are answerable to the judgment of mankind as a whole. From one source or another, we crave affirmation. In a sense, we feel we are always being addressed: Who are you? What are you? What is the truth?

Given this understanding, Rosenstock-Huessy argued, "a uniform structure may permeate the mental, linguistic and literary processes by which man answers for his behaviour."(75) At every moment every human being is inescapably answering to God, another person, or mankind as a whole, either by thought, speech, or writing. Rosenstock-Huessy calls this process "answerableness," which is the consequence of the polarity of disclosure and dissemblance, unveiling and veiling. Often "a group acts on behalf of its members, declaring to other groups what it stands for. . . . The calls, expressed in these declarations, may reflect intentions, or memories, complaints or war-cries, doubts, or certainties, desires or fears. It is always an apologia pro vita sua, whether a nation, a great poet, or a burdened conscience explain[ing] to Geneva [i. e., to the League of Nations] or to posterity or to God what they are actually compelled to become." "Compelled to become" Rosenstock-Huessy insisted, repeating the phrase, "because the alleged activity [i. e., agency] of man is greatly exaggerated by all those thinkers who forget man's answerableness." Rosenstock-Huessy placed little stock in our alleged agency when in fact our freedom is "pretty much limited to the choice to conceal or to disclose the truth" of what is happening to us as we are carried along in life. As he would inform his young students in the Dartmouth classroom: "Your aims are not your destiny." The most a man can say of himself is that although he did not really "make himself or his so-called actions . . . he was indeed able to decide about his amount of hypocrisy about his actions."(75) "Our contribution to our biography is essentially our decision how far we can go with the truth. We all cannot go very far."

We are shaped by life and by nature; our only truly free action is contained in "the myth-weaving or truth-disclosing business." As an answerable creature, thought, language, and literature are our greatest actions, and it is these actions also that bring about change and transformations in society. What happens in the world is constantly determined by a man's choice to succumb to fear and thus dissemble, or by his courage to tell himself or others the truth of what he sees.

It takes real physical energy to tell the truth in the face of the prevailing conventions, Rosenstock-Huessy emphasized. Much lying is just weakness because we lack the nerve to come out with the truth. Thus, the balance between honest reportage and the security of self-justification or rationalization is weighted in the direction of the latter. Lying, concealment, or reticence is usually easier than truth telling. Weakness makes us obdurate at a moment when if we only felt strong or healthy enough we would actively listen and be open to change. The saving "spark" which we are capable of sending into "the network of electric current in the community" tragically does not come because we feel too weak and too weary. Thus we sink back into the safety of compromising.(76)

On the other hand, dissemblance is only possible because society is in fact based on truth. The liar depends upon the social solidity established by those who have told the truth in the past. "Like cold as compared to warm, or ill as compared to healthy, lying is nothing in itself, but a possibility furnished by the existing precedents of truth." The hypocrite plays safe and survives by quoting old truths said by others at critical times; the energizing truth of the moment that he might reveal he keeps safely hidden.(76) What a challenge to humankind Rosenstock-Huessy presented! We must all be as fearless and forthright as biblical prophets. Is this cause for hope or despair?

THE FOUR-FOLD REALITY

In a person's encounter with the world or with reality, four modes of behavior are possible, Rosenstock-Huessy argued, two spatially (the inner and the outer) and two temporally (the future and the past). These also fall into grammatical forms, the imperative, the indicative, the subjunctive, and the perfect. A person can:

- hear a command, i.e., listen to an imperative calling for new action in the future. Oriented in time, he is acting, in Rosenstock-Huessy's terminology, *prejectively.*
- intend to make a move, i.e., to take action in the world in accordance with a description outlined in the indicative mood. Oriented in space, he is acting *objectively.*
- announce or express an emotion, i.e., delve into his interior life, in the subjunctive or optative mood. Oriented in space, he is acting *subjectively.*
- remember or recall an experience, i.e., carry forward an aspect of the past in formulas and ritual or in accordance with tradition. Oriented in time, he is acting *trajecti*vely.

These four modes or moods, each with a particular characteristic on the coordinates of space and time, in any healthy person may recur in sequence or be held in relative equilibrium and harmony. Together they reveal a universal structure basic to humanity.

> To point forward and backward in time and to look inward and outward . . . in space are four perpetual situations of man. In any given moment, a living being is exposed to the possibility of repeating the past or cutting him[self] off from his past, and [he] is given the choice to withdraw into [his] inner self or to look and lose himself in his environment."(78)

What fascinated Rosenstock-Huessy, and what he wrote about again and again, is how these four most fundamental fronts in life—future and past as aspects of time, inside and outside as aspects of space—are constantly revealed in speech. By looking deeply into the forms of grammar, he believed, we have a means of arriving at a more complete and accurate understanding of the human situation than is typically offered by the social sciences as presently organized. The study of the forms of speech and language brings us insights into the deepest layers of existence. These four stances—prejective, objective, subjective, and trajective—are also a key to grasping the fundamental unity of philosophy, philology, and literature, as we will see.

With regard to literature, it is significant that the traditional division of poetry into epic, lyric, and dramatic is paralleled as well in the grammatical forms of indicative, optative (or subjunctive), and imperative. Lyrical poetry, for example, is close to the subjunctive, and distant from the indicative, whereas epic poetry with its narrative form is presented more or less in the declarative sentences of the indicative mood. Finally, the "march of dramatic action fits well into the scheme of a grammatical imperative." What drama and the imperative have in common, Rosenstock-Huessy writes, drawing examples from ancient Greek drama, is that both "are pointing forward to an unsettled future."(77)

With reference to any moment of speech, or any sentence, we can ask: "How far it is concerned with the description of an outward process, or wishes to reflect an inner movement, or pushes forward to a solution in the future, or is reproducing the past."(79) These vectors of time and space, which are integral to life, are, of course, normally intermixed, exactly as we switch in speech or writing from the past perfect to the present tense, from indicative to optative. Most important, there is "an identity," Rosenstock-Huessy claimed, between "the grammar of society" and "the grammar of language."(79) In other words, a full understanding of human speech provides us with a general means of interpreting the processes of human affairs, a means of roughly diagnosing social sickness and health. It is an identity that is repeated, Rosenstock says, "on higher and higher levels of life."

In literature we see the division of "inward lyric, outward epics, backward-looking formula and forward-pushing drama."(79) By "formula," or better, the formulaic, Rosenstock-Huessy refers to the elements in poetry that are frequently repeated to evoke the past, such as memories and implicit quotations, the "unavoidable elements in any poetry" that turn the audience to the past.

A surprising comparison may be made, too, between literature and the procedures in a courtroom, where all of the same elements of our relation to time and space can be found, although divided into an ensemble of separate parts. The formulaic in a legal battle, for example, consists of the wearying repetition of "whereas" and "whereas" and "furthermore as regards to," on and on for pages, citing prior law and prior facts that have the same effect on the reader or listener as the famous recurrent formulaic phrases in Homer. A "quieting influence is secured," Rosenstock-Huessy notes, "because the past is fully represented and resumed, the known precedes the unknown, and before our speech turns to the future, we dwell in the past."(78)

Whether it is poetry or prose, the same quadrilateral of elements will always be present: "Indeed, nobody can speak one language only. Man's reality is at least fourfold."(80) Even lying or concealment is so divided into time and space elements:

> The four forms of lying tell the same story. Fiction, lying, hypocrisy, and cant are four styles of concealing our truth. The imperative is the form which abhors lying most. For to use cant means only to repeat participles and formulas, to lie means to conceal external facts, fiction is the arbitrary invention of inner sentiments, but a hypocrite dissembles the imperatives of his actions.(80)

Cant, then, insincerely repeats formulas from the past; lying rearranges exterior space; fiction invents from interior mental space; hypocrisy falsifies the motives that are leading a person to act in the future.

Turning now to the prose of academic disciplines, which is at the other extreme from poetry, there are as many forms of language as there are in poetry. Poetry, Rosenstock-Huessy argues, is divided into narrative, formulaic, lyric, and dramatic elements, with affinities respectively to the indicative, the participles of the past perfect, the optative or subjunctive, and the imperative. These same grammatical forms of imperative, indicative, optative, and participle are found also in the four types of prose, as distinguished from the poetic: namely, human expression in oratory, science, philosophy, and history, each with their alignments in space or time.(80)

Oratory, or political speech, is the "articulation of an imperative" pointing to the future; it puts us in the prejective mode. "Mathematics [i.e., scientific statement] analyzes relations in [exterior] space and accomplishes the creation of a language perfectly objective." "Philosophy reflects on our inner [interior] thought," and is thus typically subjective. History, as a division of prose, is a special case, and its classification can be confusing. History obviously looks backwards in time and tries to conjure up the past and quote the utterances of the past as faithfully as possible, but as a scholarly discipline in the modern era history must be sharply distinguished from the mere carrying forward of the past by ritual, formula, and tradition, as in a chronicle. Since the beginning of the twentieth century, history is characteristically written in the indicative, upholds objectivity as a standard, and tends to see itself as a branch of "science" in the broad sense.(80) Hence, it does not purely represent the trajective mode, a complication that we will come back to.[7]

Be that as it may, it is vital to reiterate here that these two major realms of discourse, scientific prose, on the one side, and poesis or the creative arts, on the other, although encompassing much of modern human culture, do not exhaust the functions of speech in society. Clearly, non-fictional "scientific" prose, as a whole, is the home of external observations, and not an expression of our wishes and desires, or of our inner emotions. For the latter, we look to poetry or poesis, i.e., to creative writing, to be the guardian of our inner processes. Yet, however grand in what they achieve, however vast the territory they cover, poetry and scientific prose are "in charge" of only two of the four modes of our conscious life, namely "the elating optative of our inner self and the analytic indicative of the external world."(80) Both, it will be noted, including even historical writing, are grounded in our inveterate division of space into inner and outer, interior and exterior. But humankind also lives in time; indeed for Rosenstock-Huessy, we live predominantly in time, not space, and he explicitly identified himself as a "time thinker." Prose and poetry, absorbed in the spatial order, are thus but half of the totality of human experience and expression.[8]

RITUAL AS PAST, IMPERATIVE AS FUTURE

Where, then, in the grammar of human society is time represented? Past and future appear in two other types of speech that are *no less important* than scientific description and creative writing, but insufficiently recognized: "the past by ritual, the future by all the imperatives mastering our life, beginning at the bottom with [*a mere traffic direction*] 'keep right,' and ending at the peak with 'do right.'"(81) The bookish tradition of two

7. I discuss Rosenstock-Huessy's views on the essential purposes and role of historical writing in chapter 6, above, "Heritage vs. History."

8. Rosenstock-Huessy wrote extensively on the nature of time in a number of different contexts. See, e.g., *Christian Future*, 167–74; "Teaching Too Late, Learning Too Early: "Man is peculiarly a temporal being, ever but an exile and pilgrim in the world of space," 91–92; and "Time-Bettering Days." For commentary, see Leithart, "The Social Articulation of Time."

thousand years has misled us because we do not regularly encounter ritual and the imperative in the classroom, the lecture hall, the library, or the laboratory. One can read a whole book or listen to a long lecture and hardly notice an imperative, Rosenstock-Huessy observed, although looked at more broadly the observation is dubious, since teaching in all fields is rife with assignments, a form of the imperative. Still, Rosenstock-Huessy asks, Can ritual and the imperative really be equal on the scales of life to art and science, to mathematics, literature, and philosophy? Indeed, for sanity, balance, and health, it is essential that they be, whether we are focused on the individual or on whole nations. But these relatively invisible forms must first be made visible.

The imperative is not found so much in books as it is in everyday spoken language, in the give and take of simple human interchange. Similarly, ritual, "the powerful realization of the past," persists in countless ceremonies, observances, re-enactments, monuments, and traditions, spoken and performed, which are not always recognized as such. The occurrence of the formulaic, the function of which is "to guard against the inroad of an uncertain future," is found not only in obvious liturgical forms but in all forms of legal practice, and this is true in the United States above all, where tradition may appear to be most eroded. The lawyers, Rosenstock-Huessy pointed out about his adopted country, are the "priesthood" of the formulaic. In fact, modern democracies find their most sacred ritual in parliamentary speech and procedure. At all occasions, whether suitable or not, the "[will] anybody second?" "the motion is carried," and so on and so forth, show the tremendous power of the formula for binding society together. It is this binding power which alone deserves to be termed religion.(81)

Citing the linguistics scholar Antoine Meillet, Rosenstock-Huessy notes that religious ceremonies practically always use a language that differs from that which we employ in the ordinary course of life. But "it is a logical mistake to seek the ritual outside the speech and to ascribe a special speech to the ritual. The special speech *is* the ritual."(82, ital. added) You can almost measure a person's religiosity by the number of occasions when he recurs to the solemn language of ritual.

This is not the place to elaborate further on the supreme importance of the imperative in Rosenstock-Huessy's work beyond its brief delineation in this 1935 address to Dartmouth College colleagues. Suffice it to say that he has written dozens of pages on the imperative and the vocative, i.e., the address in the second person, including in his work on human development. Child rearing, for example, begins always with imperatives, that is, the injunctions delivered by all parents to their children from the moment of birth: "Johnny, go to sleep, eat your porridge, love your sister and brother, tell the truth, obey your elders." As adults, too, we are constantly waiting to be summoned by those whom we feel have the knowledge and authority to tell us what it is necessary to do, including among the summoners our own conscience. Otto Kroesen has shown how the function of the imperative in Rosenstock-Huessy's thought is comparable to the theological notion of revelation (a form of divine address) and analogous to the experience of falling in love or of being moved by love. The common thread is that meaningful action always begins with our being spoken to or addressed and commanded in some fashion.[9]

To recapitulate, from the standpoint of human experience all reality is either situated in the past or anticipated in the future and is deemed to be either inside or outside of a framework that we establish or acknowledge. The present for Rosenstock-Huessy is an artificial human construct. "This means four original approaches to reality, and four different aggregate states for the speaker."(82) Such is true of nations, as well, which if they are healthy have their legislation (future imperatives), their sciences (outward, objective studies), their arts (inward turning, subjective literature or painting, sculpture, music, etc.), and their anchors in the past manifest in rituals, holidays, monuments, observances, historical documents, and the like.

The simple quadrilateral of future (imperative), outward (indicative), inward (optative, subjunctive), past (participles and formulas), Rosenstock-Huessy concedes, may appear to lack subtlety. Turning, then, to a different approach, he drew a parallel with four basic human attitudes: "plasticity, conventionality, aggressiveness, and elation. A man is plastic under the impact of an imperative[;] he is aggressive where he dissects the world by figures, forms, and the calculus[;] he is elated where he trusts his inner revelations[;] and he is conventional or repetitive where he reduplicates the past."(82) These are the potentialities of man whether he is revealing or concealing truth. And whether it is language, thought, or literature, as described earlier, the same "forming principles" will apply, creating the unity asserted in this lecture. Man realizes his ends by a plurality of moods, and in the study of man it is essential, among

9. Kroesen, "Toward Planetary Society." The meaning of revelation and love in the work of Franz Rosenzweig (and implicitly for Rosenstock-Huessy) is expertly delineated in Samuel Moyn, *Origins of the Other*.

other things, to listen to his own remarks about himself. "He knows more than the indifferent scientist about the tragedy in and around him."(83) Rosenstock-Huessy spoke of the foregoing as "discoveries," and he believed these findings can have far-reaching results as a method for studying history, psychology, sociology, and more. In his 1946 work, *The Christian Future*, he said of this cross of reality: "This is not symbolistic fantasy or arbitrary schematizing, but something that has grown through two thousand years."[10]

The discovery is illuminating about man and the world, a new way of seeing ourselves, but perhaps of limited application as, let's say, the basis of policy or the ministration of therapy. We have learned, basically, that human beings must continually and always deal with choices of past and future, to be, for example, in specific instances conservative or progressive, or in times of crisis even reactionary or revolutionary; and in space, we must choose to be inside or outside of innumerable social and political configurations, or in different words, to choose between "them" and "us," the difference between who is inside and who is outside. These are conflicts more or less imposed on us as part of the human condition.

Our modes of personal existence, too, framed less in terms of conflict, may be reduced to the spatial and temporal forms described as subjective, objective, trajective, and prejective, all functioning harmoniously. This is a somewhat different quadrilateral. We muse inwardly and attack problems outwardly, engage in rituals and observances carried forward from the past and respond to charges handed to us for bettering the future. In this 1935 lecture, Rosenstock-Huessy does not take up the problem of the variable conditions of the cross of reality, the difference between the uneventful norm, let's say, a driver's shifting gears in a car for a smooth ride, on the one hand, and on the other, being unjustly ticketed in a speed trap and forced to act.

No person escapes these directional stresses and choices, although there are plenty of systems, especially Asian, such as Buddhist practices, that advise men and women to find quiet in the still present, shutting out the worries of where and when. These various methods from several traditions for finding inner peace and equanimity (at least momentarily), a state that G. K. Chesterton referred to as the "ecstasy of indifference," only prove the rule, that to be human is to be sometimes uncomfortably stretched on the vectors of forward and backward, inward and outward, an

10. Rosenstock-Huessy, *Christian Future*, 166n.

excruciation from which some yearn to escape, at the risk of figuratively leaving this world. Equally vain over the long term are therapeutic goals of social or psychological "adjustment," which means somehow removing the tension of conflicting directions. "Realization," Rosenstock-Huessy writes, "is approached not in one way but by a plurality of moods," an assertion that suggests, perhaps, less torment from this situation and more joyful opportunity for choice.(83)

THREE APPLICATIONS

Rosenstock-Huessy was convinced that the discovery of the four-fold nature of our relation to reality will have "far-reaching results for history, for psychology and sociology." He referred to it as "a sure method" for tackling problems, yet he feared that without any examples of practical application the new categories may appear to be too abstract. In response to this awareness, he offered three quick examples that aim to make the method tangible: one from language, one from philosophy, and one from literature.

With regard to the first, the usual scheme for teaching a language divides the tenses, the moods, the pronouns, and the declension: I love, thou loveth, he/she/it loves, we love, you love, they love. For presenting a foreign language, this practice may be permissible, Rosenstock-Huessy allowed, but it is a terrible model for understanding our relation to our mother tongue, for which we ought to know "the deeper coordination of modes and tenses and pronouns."(83) A "thoughtful grammar, a philosophical grammar," would stress that three forms of the verb are related to three states of personality. The synopsis, reflecting a universal sequence, properly should run: "ama, amem, amat": i.e., love! or love me! in the imperative; I would love or do I love? in the subjunctive; he loves, in the indicative, reflecting a new reality. "Here we have genuine and direct forms." Our own language, according to Rosenstock-Huessy, "should be disclosed to be our living self, not a pedantic bed of Procrustes."(84) The implication is that the teaching of English, for example, to native-born American children should shun the mechanical detachment of the ancient Alexandrian grammar table—I love, you love, he loves, etc.—and turn instead to life as it is actually experienced: first, we are told to love, then we may fall in love with all of its turmoil, and if we are lucky we do love. Rosenstock-Huessy deplored "the disguise of truth by our grammar books." Our mother tongue, he writes, "should be presented to us as the introduction into the secrets of personality."(96) "Of all the dogmas of antiquity," he wrote in another paper, dating from 1945, "the grammatical dogma is the last to persist. The schools have shelved Euclidean geometry, Ptolemaic astronomy, Galenian medicine, Roman law and Christian dogma most radically. Ancient grammatical dogma still dominates."[11]

Turning from language to literature, as a second example of what his discoveries might yield, Rosenstock-Huessy asks that we examine a nation's mental health, so to speak, by the quality of the "equilibrium" between the four tendencies of "describing, and thereby dissecting[;] of singing and thereby elating[;] of listening to orders and thereby changing[;] and of thanksgiving and thereby perpetuating reality."(84) Any special literature, Rosenstock-Huessy proposes, can be characterized by "the proportions that are shown between its four central moods."(84) Onesidedness in a nation's literature is no small matter, of concern only to specialized critics; it can result in "fatal suppressions of reality" and cause social, political, and economic disaster. (96) This is one of the themes of Rosenstock-Huessy's major work in English, *Out of Revolution.*

In the nineteenth century, there was a blossoming of novels, of science, and of historical research. At the same time, however, liturgy, prayer, and rituals were practically dying out. This disequilibrium was filled by looking to the writing of history as an evocation of the past, which is not the same, obviously, as a vital or lived continuation of the past into the present. Rosenstock-Huessy did not use the word "tradition" or "heritage" in this 1935 lecture, but their decline is implied. Turning to historical writing as the remedy for the decline of tradition was a goal of the so-called Romantic historians of the nineteenth century—such as Bancroft in the United States, Macaulay in England, and Guizot in France—but ultimately, as historians defined themselves as practitioners of a kind of objective "science," the reliance on historiography had exactly the opposite effect of what was intended. Toward the end of the nineteenth century, the writing of history accompanied the "triumphal march of the natural sciences, those clearest outposts of our outward tendencies." It could not hope to keep the full balance, because it remained enclosed in the general field of prose. Historiography in our time is a "subspecies in the sphere of prose," and prose is "always analytic, dissecting, aggressive." In another paper, written at almost the same time as the "Uni-versity of Logic, Language, Literature," entitled "The Predicament

11. "Grammar as Social Science," 98. Searls, "Who's Number One?" a short piece in the *Paris Review*, is especially good on this subject.

of History," which Rosenstock-Huessy presented at the meeting of the American Historical Association in December 1934, his thoughts on history are more fully developed.[12]

> It is no mere guess when we assume that the health of an individual and the wealth of nations may depend on a balance between prose, poetry, ritual, and imperative. This can be expressed grammatically by saying that any individual or group must remain capable of shifting freely and at the becks of fate from the subjective "I" to the objective "it," and further to the listening "thou" and to the remembering "we."(85)

It is arguable that in the United States today, we are truly at an excruciating moment, in the temporal realm stretched between the pull of a radically new future and a mired obdurate past, and in the spatial realm torn between factions and unsure of where we belong and with whom we want to associate. We are also subject to a great deal of lying.

Finally, an example of the application of the grammatical method to philosophy. Nothing is "so well safeguarded by philosophers as the naïve arrogance of the school that [holds that] reality can and has to be divided into objects and subjects. This division is taken to be the division of the world. Alas, the world would not survive this division if it were to be taken seriously."(85) In truth, the attitude in which we face the outward world as a subject is merely "one perfunctory and transient function or mood among other functions and moods." A person looking forward, for example, cannot know of any such division of the world. "He acts . . . under the compulsion of an imperative. He is initiated into the future because he is still plastic. He hears a command. The great fact of any ethical imperative, whether coming from above or below, from out or inside, is that I am not the subject [i. e., not the speaker] of the imperative . . . which [i. e., that] I hear."(85)[13] Rather, I listen to it.

Descartes's famous axiom *Cogito, ergo sum* has the "innocent form of a scientific and prosaic statement" because the philosopher wished to express all the truth about himself in the style of the indicative. But when Descartes resolved at the age of twenty-four to devote his life to philosophy, he surely was not taking this step in the descriptive attitude

12. "The Predicament of History," a paper that Rosenstock presented at the meeting of the American Historical Association in Washington, D. C., in December 1934, which was published a few months later in the *Journal of Philosophy*. See chapter 6, above.

13. See chapter 4, above, "The Structure of Significant Lives."

of the *cogito, ergo sum*. Descartes, in fact, listened first to an imperative, "the old imperative of the serpent: *Cogita and eritis,* [Think and you will be.]" Clearly this first "*Cogita*" was not spoken by Descartes himself. It was spoken *to* him, not *by* him. "And when he listened to this call he was in that moment neither an 'I' nor an 'it,' neither a subject nor an object." Subjects and objects cannot "*obey* to human speech."(86, italics added). The "I" differs fundamentally from the "thou" that receives the command; the "I" is the source of the command to act, the speaking subject. The hearer of the command is neither subject nor object. "The things which the philosopher is *called forth* to think about are his objects. He himself is something which is neither subject nor object" at that moment of decisive change.(86, italics added). He is a preject.

It is a good thing, Rosenstock-Huessy emphasizes, that man can "never dream of becoming a subject *pur sang* or an object cog in the machine. It is always a degradation when a human person is treated as an object. And it is always an impermissible deification when he thinks of himself as a prima causa, as a real subject. Did he make himself?" Even before we can introduce the division into subject and object we must first be the recipient of a command, that is, we must be listening to a "you" or a "thou" that flies towards us "like a projectile from another, stronger arm's bow. Under the spell of being addressed I find myself in the plastic attitude which allows a man to be transformed into something different from what he was before."(86) When falling in love, we are commanded by cupid's arrow. One of the great values of Rosenstock-Huessy's cross of reality is that by transcending the simplistic subject/object distinction we are obliged "to limit scientific thought to its proper field and time," an urgent necessity in 1935 and a necessity still more today. "Nobody can use his mental powers in one 'style' only."(96)

The universal acceptance of an experiential reality beyond subject and object, Rosenstock-Huessy believed, can only be achieved by offering new terms that have a chance of becoming just as embedded as subject and object. Hence, his coining of "prejects" for persons in the position of "you-s" or "thou-s" responding to an imperative, and "trajects" for those who see themselves as participants with others in a common past and who are unified in the "we-participle."

The concept of prejectivity, Rosenstock-Huessy acknowledged, bears a resemblance to the concept of "*Geworfenheit*" found in Kierkegaard and Heidegger, but he had no desire to align himself with either of those thinkers.[14] His main concern was to insist that we are far more often governed by prejectivity, as, for example, in a positive response to a call for change or to a revelation, and by trajectivity in our conservatism, than we ever are by either scientific objectivity or mystic subjectivism.(87)

BOUNDED OR LIBERATED BY THE CROSS

What must be granted is that there is no standpoint outside of the cross of reality from which we can view it, a transcendental language that somehow has escaped these four fundamentals of reality. There is no Archimedean point beyond or outside of this nexus. Rosenstock-Huessy would be the first to acknowledge that he is himself in the middle of it, and you, the Reader, are similarly entangled, as am I.

Whenever we begin "to listen or to think from one of these four angles of [our] real life," we become a different person, and all four angles are perpetually needed. In my personal case, for example, I have been inspired by Rosenstock-Huessy's lectures and wish to act on their message in some fashion, prejectively; I am moved by them emotionally, weighing their conclusions, and my imagination is stimulated, subjectively; I am also analyzing the lectures as a critic in a detached, scientific fashion, to some degree objectively; I regard his lectures as worthy of preservation and want to ensure their continued study, as I am trying to do by reporting on them here, trajectively.

"Any one phase of speech or style does not suffice to express our full experience of the life within and outside, before and behind us." Indeed, the deepest errors are the result of the belief that we can rely on only one, as the rationalist trusts only objectivity or the mystic only subjectivity. Even marriage, or at least a real marriage, Rosenstock-Huessy writes, depends upon these four styles: "(1) the divine command 'love me'; (2) the elation of the honeymoon; (3) the hard reckoning of household economy; and (4) the security of the evening chatter and the common holidays."(88)

14. "*Geworfenheit*" usually translated "thrownness" was used by Martin Heidegger to describe the accidental nature of the infant's arrival in the world, without choice over timing or circumstances. This is a rare instance of Rosenstock-Huessy, in his English writings, referring to Heidegger. Speaking to his new colleagues at Dartmouth College in 1935, he may have felt that he could not simply by-pass this philosophical luminary. The two men were nearly exact contemporaries. Heidegger notoriously was an active Nazi sympathizer, a position that Rosenstock-Huessy despised. According to Cristaudo, *Religion, Redemption, and Revolution*, 287, Rosenstock-Huessy denounced Heidegger as "Nazi scum."

Turning reflexive now, near the end of his presentation, Rosenstock-Huessy admitted that the process of making known his discovery is not itself immune from the four-sided structure of "Plasticity, Reduplication, Aggressiveness, and Elation." The new terminology of "prejective" and "trajective" must become more than his "subjective" theory. It has to "enter the field of merciless competition and selection in the schools" and survive. Thus, we have to ask, are these terms indispensable for our understanding of the world, or is this an abstract theoretical exercise? His new method, Rosenstock-Huessy claimed, will at least have to run through all the different styles of self-expression until it can "feel its way back into the Great Tradition," which has unfortunately enshrined the duality of subject and object as though they were exclusive.(89)

Rosenstock-Huessy insisted that "thinking takes time." Truth emerges as part of a process. Yet this fact is largely ignored because in school truths all appear to be pre-existent and everlasting. But, he asks, what is the process of how they came to be? How does the truth grow? "Nobody can, shall or may think all the time! And we incorporate truth not without re-thinking the same problems." "Thinking takes time" refers to all of the possible qualities that color time, and in particular to the stages, which for Rosenstock-Huessy have the status of a law of life, from "impression to obsession to expression to definition," which is equivalent to the movement from imperative, to the subjective uncertainty of the subjunctive, to the participles of the epic or narrative recounting, to the detached, objective indicative--a procession through Thou, I, We, It. Thought, Rosenstock writes, is "a sociological and biological process. . . . It can only be realized by circulating through a number of phases or stations. Thought, speech, writing are creatures and behave like all other creatures."(90) A lecture course that Rosenstock-Huessy taught at Dartmouth was exactly on this subject, which he called "The Circulation of Thought." One version of it was recorded on tape in 1954, consisting of about forty hours over twenty-six sessions.

As I alluded to earlier, the proceedings in a courtroom drama exemplify perfectly for Rosenstock-Huessy the elements of the cross of reality formed by the medium of space and time in which we live, although in a trial the four parts are temporarily separated. "The plaintiff argues on the objective break of the law; the defendant urges his subjective right to act as he did; the precedents bring up the past in order to enable the present court to form an opinion how far the case is the reduplication of former events. Finally the decision comes down upon the unsettled new and shapeless prejacent case and presses it into a legal form."(91) Thus, Rosenstock-Huessy concludes, the due process of the law contains all the elements of the mental process he has hitherto described, with the difference only that in the courtroom the phases are filled by different persons, rather than being the expression of a single individual. "It is a complete misinterpretation of the process," he asserts, "to take these people as speaking the same language." Each is singing a different tune.

Drawing on his early scholarship in the history of law, Rosenstock-Huessy painted in this lecture a vivid picture of a generic murder case in a medieval court room, full of drama, which I can only refer to here. The due process of law, in Rosenstock-Huessy's argument, comprehends the different styles of the human disclosure of reality "because it is one of the models of complete human speech." It condenses into the proceedings of one day "facts and feelings, memories and plans which stretch out over indefinitely more space and time," and the definition or decision that results "is the quintessence of this condensed process." It comes at the end, as it ought to. The philosopher similarly, like a courtroom judge, has no authority to speak the last word first. Of course, as a teacher he can dictate to students, but that is not the practice of philosophy, which occurs when one is not sure of his community. Persuasion is the proper process of research in the social sciences. "He who begins with a definition tries to escape from the rules of this process. He can be a mislocated legislator whose will for power seeks an outlet in writing and teaching. But he is no social scientist. For he declines to think loudly and to make thereby acceptable to his collaborators his process of reasoning."(94)

Eighty-five years ago, Rosenstock-Huessy hoped that the new names "preject" and "traject" would be widely adopted. When he died in 1973, however, this terminology was as alien or unrecognized as it was in the 1930s. In 1935 he accepted that these new names were still at the "frontier between [the artist's] studio and [a] museum" in man's art of thinking, en route from the moment of inspiration to the ultimate institutionalization. He said, hopefully, "Once there is a word, everybody will begin to believe in the existence of the essence behind it. . . . A name wrested from our lips in honest struggle for truth is in fact in most cases the standard bearer of a part of reality. By its name, a thing is called forth into life and put under the protectorate of the whole of human society."(87) Regrettably, to date most of his ideas have not succeeded in crossing the border from inspiration to the commonplace, as he described the process.(94–95)

A critique of faculty psychology, too, is brought in to support not only the unity of the humanistic disciplines but of our mental personhood as a whole. Reasoning, Rosenstock-Huessy held, is not distinct from will, emotion, and memory. "The standing belief that a person has the three departments of reason, will, and feeling is completely wrong. Emotion, will, and memory are loaded with reasoning processes precisely as objective contemplation is. We are using our mental power equally in art and science, in education and in religion. The picture of a man shifting between will and contemplation," as proposed by Schopenhauer, "or between irrational mysticism and cold rationalism is a caricature of the nineteenth century. The human cosmos is represented to completeness in every microcosmic act of inspiration." Logic, language, and literature are fundamentally unified because we are exposed to the four directions of time and space "in every actual process of thought or speech." The difference between our emotional, our inspirational and our rational state" is one of arrangement, not of complete separatedness."(95) Indeed, "Man is unable to think or to speak without using all four elements simultaneously. It is not the elements that differ in poetry, science, politics or religion. It is their arrangement." (95) At any given moment, we are engaged on all the four fronts of life, employing or undergoing inspiration (the imperative), imagination (the subjunctive), analysis (the indicative), and faith (ritual and formula).

A PAUSE AT THE "LAW" OF FOUR

Without doubt, some of Rosenstock-Huessy's faculty audience in 1935 would have reacted as did Bruce Boston in his 1973 Princeton dissertation: The cross of reality is "too pat, too contrived, too systematized."[15] The listener's or the reader's instinctive response is that the world is more complicated than the cross of reality reflects and that Rosenstock-Huessy is building a castle in the air. From another perspective, what he has framed seems too loose or too general to be useful as anything other than an academic exercise. The ideas may be correct but they are inapplicable. Such criticisms are particularly painful and paradoxical because if there are two things that Rosenstock-Huessy prided himself on, they were that

15. Boston's critique, from his dissertation "'I Respond Although I Will Be Changed'" is cited by Bryant in "The Grammar of the Spirit: Time, Speech, Society."

his thought was always grounded in flesh and blood reality, and, two, that he was not given to metaphysical system building.

The cross of reality may be elusive, but it is not meant to be rigid. Rosenstock-Huessy hated abstract systems and saw man as essentially defiant in the face of any attempt to characterize him in any one way. Predictions based on statistics and polls, he felt, were usually wrong because as soon as a person learns that he (or she) is expected to continue along some established course, he rebels against the prescribed path. Human beings make a point of showing that we are not predictable. The world will not come to an end precisely because the prediction that it will end tomorrow catalyzes us into preventive action today. That is one of the meanings of the motto he proposed for the third millennium, *respondeo etsi mutabor*, I respond even though I will be changed.

What saves the cross of reality from typical characterizations about the nature of man is that it is not, in fact, a law or a categorization. It should be seen as an avenue of freedom from social, political, psychological, historical, economic, cultural, religious restraints. "Cross" may be the wrong metaphor if it is associated with the horror of impalement, as opposed to, for example, "crossroads." It is true that the connection to the suffering Jesus was not one that Rosenstock-Huessy entirely avoided. In *The Christian Future*, for example, he used strong physical words: "Reality itself—not the abstract reality of physics, but the full-bodied reality of human life—is cruciform. Our existence is a perpetual suffering and wrestling with conflicting forces, paradoxes, contradictions within and without. By them we are stretched and torn in opposite directions, but through them comes renewal. And these opposing directions are summed up by four which define the great space and time axes of all men's life on earth, forming a Cross of Reality."[16] Yet even this statement is not altogether existentially gloomy because it ends with "renewal." Rather than "cross of reality," it would be a fairer description to speak of, let's say, "vectors of choice," "arrows of freedom," "options of opportunity." Humankind is trapped only in that we have no hope of escaping the mortal template of space and time, which is the way Rosenstock-Huessy would have it. There can be no metaphysical relief, no talk of transcendence, no talk of redemption outside of this "lovable" world. But we are not unfree.

16. *Christian Future*, 166.

THE MORAL LIFE

Several applications of the cross of reality, or the vectors of choice, have been given. Rosenstock-Huessy also applies it to the question of what constitutes our moral duties, in which freedom is central. Whenever we lecture or teach or write books, we naively extend to all men the general commandment, "Hark, Hear, Listen." The insight that these imperatives are at the core of any realistic ethics is the "finest fruit of the new method," Rosenstock-Huessy believed. For the only possible content of any human ethics—that is, an ethics that does not completely overlook man's most human capacity, namely, speaking and listening—is revealed by attention to the foremost role of the imperative: the call to action. Any set of Pelagian rules for good behavior will always end in utter failure if it aspires to go anywhere beyond pure convention and utilitarianism because it will necessarily deny "man's freedom and our life's incalculability." "The quiver of true ethics holds no other arrows but the imperatives derived from man's talk with the universe. They run all like the first commandment: Hark, give ear! It is man's duty to hear and to listen to the voices of love and wisdom and the law. For the rest he is free.

The fact is, no specified ethical code can hold up under the pressure of an inbreaking new command. For might not a person at any time "hear a voice louder and more true" than all of the earlier injunctions? "The only ethical command which church and society can impose on man is: Give ear, think it over. The first thing society must guarantee to its members is time for recollection and reconsideration."(96–97) One thinks here, of course, of the famous moral teaching attributed to one of Rosenstock-Huessy's heroes, St. Augustine: "Love God and do what you will."

Returning now, at the end, to the original theme of his lecture, Rosenstock-Huessy called for a new and better collaboration among the "disintegrated body" of the human sciences. Language, literature, and thought should aim at nothing less than the "everlasting man who lives under the three commands *Audi! Lege! Medita!* (Listen! Read! Think!)." These three commands, equivalent to language, literature, and philosophy, are "our human dowry. They are our only moral prescriptions of general character. They make human society the delicate, frail, loveable creature it is. And they are only three forms of one command."(97)

What then unifies languages, literature, and philosophy? They all begin with the imperative, which is fundamentally a call to action. Each must follow the same path to truth every time a word is spoken, from the inspiration that comes to us as a command; to the internal struggle as we find our way, a mixture of elation and doubt; to the shared achievement as we find collaborators and supporters, and speak as "we" in a new narrative; to the final stage of detached scientific, objective description, and definitions.

Here, then, we have a new picture of human progress, far from the Cartesian view that locks us into objective description as the only source of truth, and which necessarily divides observation between the subjective and the objective. But man is unified in his quest when it becomes apparent that there are four sources of truth, each necessary and equally valid, and each an element in the structure of grammar. The novelist and the philosopher, the philologist and the poet, the historian and the artist, the priest and the logician—none is superior to the other, despite the pretensions and claims of each. Society cannot afford to lose any of the four angles on reality, lest it perish. And no individual can be whole if he or she attempts to suppress or eradicate openness to the future, harking to the past, the poetry of internal life, or the scientific precision of our relation to the external world of nature.

8

"The Listener's Tract"

[The "Listener's Tract" by Rosenstock-Huessy survives in two not wholly identical typescripts from 1944, according to Lise van der Molen's *Guide to the Works* of Rosenstock-Huessy, and was published for the first time in *Speech and Reality* (Argo, 1970), edited by Clinton C. Gardner. I have not had the opportunity to compare line by line the various versions, typescript and printed. In fact, I have seen only one of the 1944 typescripts, that which can be accessed on the website of the ERH Fund, and I have, somewhat arbitrarily, treated that version as the most reflective of the author's intentions, that is, as my *ur*-text. The text that I have particularly relied on here, to produce this printed version, is yet another version, one distributed online by the late Eckart Wilkens. Wilkens's version was the only digital copy available, hence I seized on it to avoid the labor of re-typing word for word the 1944 text. With regard to words and punctuation, Wilkens follows reliably the 1970 printed text, but he undertook at the same time to reorganize the text spatially, so to speak, breaking up paragraphs into much shorter segments and introducing his own explanatory headings and numbering, all with the goal of making the essay clearer and more emphatic. I have ignored Wilkens's restructuring, creating my own paragraphing (the *ur*-text is scarce on paragraphs), and I have occasionally standardized the punctuation. Wilkens simply followed the printed version with regard to punctuation. In the *ur*-text commas may be said to be randomly sprinkled on to the page, ignoring any known rules of English grammar or rhetoric and seriously confusing the meaning of sentences. When a punctuation "error" is egregious, I have made the needed adjustment without notice to the reader. I have also very occasionally added italics to the text in particular instances, specifically where Rosenstock-Huessy refers to a word as a word, or a sentence as a sentence. For example, "True imperatives are not asking *what*?" Finally, when the printed version (and Wilkens's version that followed it meticulously) has needlessly departed from strictly following the typescript, altering Rosenstock-Huessy's original text, I have restored the original.]

Mr. J. Vendryes has written a beautiful book, *Le Langage, Introduction linguistique a l'histoire.* This book, although written in French, has an index. In this index, the words that signify the acts of hearing, listening, obeying, understanding are not to be found; even the word "oreille," the ear, is missing. This is no accident. Our philology is built around the process of talking, speaking, writing. The process of hearing is left to separate departments, as military training for obedience, understanding to psychology, listening and learning to acoustics and education. All these are arts that deal with language incidentally only. It is, for instance, well known that a voice of the right kind is the most precious quality of a man in command. This, however, is not treated as a universal problem of human nature, but occurs in the soldier's education only.

Let us try to compare the system of hearing to the process of speaking. It is not improbable that the variety and ways of hearing may surprise us. Perhaps, we shall find that the apparatus by which men hear is not at all limited to the ear. Would not such an observation be valuable for the interpretation of speech? Is it possible to limit the process of speaking to fifty percent of one unified process, to the operations that go on in the speaker only? May we limit any metabolism in our body to one arbitrary phase? Does not the final process only explain the intention of the beginning? In digestion, we take it for granted that chaff and bulk are necessary for the inner tract and that only a little amount of the food is retained in the body. Is it not a justified question to ask ourselves how language must be composed in order to reach the listener so that he is set in motion and begins to acquire a fragment of the information and content of that which the speaker has said?

Perhaps this explains why we have to say a thousand times something that the students all grasp once. Perhaps this accounts for the fact usually overlooked that education for science cannot [itself] be scientific. The process of producing scientists is educational. And education is not applied science. To educate means to be a representative of creation. The long-range processes of listening: this is education. Years and decades must go by till the listener has caught up with the speaker in a thorough going education. Our analysis of listening, then, is the basic inventory of the means at our disposal when we educate.

The listener's tract is one-half of the social relation that is established by the process of speech. And this half is as varied, as complex, as the speaker´s tract. We already know that a speaker represents the different fronts of reality by different language, that he communicates imperatival, optative, indicative and adjectival aspects of reality. How far is the listener moved to the same front of reality? How far do we paralyze the communication by overlooking the complexities of the listener's tract?

It may help us to observe, with [Jacobus] van Ginneken [the Dutch grammarian], that in any act of listening and understanding, as of speaking, the human body is involved in at least four ways. The innervation of the whole system of respiration and oration, the gesture system of rump, head and hands, our sense of audition, and our sense of vision, all are occupied. We cannot think or realize certain spoken words, or conceive of certain things, when any one of these systems is occupied by other activities.

By a study of the different types of aphasia [inability to speak] and agraphia [inability to write], it has been shown that in order to hear and to understand, we not only need our ears or our eyes. We also must feel free to innervate our larynx, tongue, mouth, etc., and we must feel able to re-enact some of the gesticulations of the interlocutor, or, in their place, some of the movements necessary to write the words down.

Whenever one of the four innervations, inner respiratory-oral tract, outer gesticulation (or instead, graphical movement), audition, [or] vision is jeopardized, disturbance results. They all are essential in the linguistic process.

Even the smallest unit, one word, is a combination of speaking and listening activity. Vowels are preferably that what we hear, consonants preferably that what we enact in a word. The speaker hears his vowels and produces his consonants; the listener innervates the consonants spoken, unconsciously, and hears the vowels. The brilliant test for this interplay of two processes is found in the transcription of patois in poetry, like that of Molière or Balzac. Satirizing the peasant or Alsatian, the writer is able to transcribe the vowels. Nowhere does he succeed to transcribe the consonants as actually spoken. He fails to innervate, to re-enact the sounds of the consonants as produced by the idiomatic speaker. Not his audition goes wrong—as proved by the vowels—but his participating innervation, in his process of listening. He mishears because he does not enact; and he ascribes a fantastic phonetics to the peasant.

That the graphic picture and written language play a powerful part in modern man´s understanding we all agree. Many words are pronounced on the basis of their arbitrary orthography; orthography changes phonetics. And the reproduction of the written picture is essential to our understanding, in our memory. However, it would seem that vision has always played a great part in language. From the very beginning, gesticulation rivaled with sounds. Gesticulation, in special cases, may take over the whole burden of speech. And it is possible that writing and reading are enlargements on this original share of gesticulation and vision in speaking. That we should be helped in thinking by innervating the movement outside our body as well as inside our body is not far-fetched. When Jesus drew lines with his finger in the sand, with the adulteress standing by waiting for his answer, his was an eloquence of listening in which hearing and writing were fused in one.

The degree of intensity in speech and listening, then, may differ widely. When we sing the whole thorax is at work; when we whisper, we barely open our lips. Many forms of speech lie between these extremes. In a similar way, I may listen with my ear, with my eye or with my whole system. In my own experience, I would say that sounds pierce from the ear right to the heart; pictures, written words and vision, never do this; they register with me in the brain. Frightful news, fear, penetrates under the diaphragm. And the ancients knew this fact very well. The fact that our eyes report to the brain, our ears not necessarily so, would seem to deserve some better attention by educators. However this single point may be, we here only have to record that any listener performs a long sequence of participating enactments in a perfect process of listening:

1. He hears noise, sounds vowels.
2. He re-innervates the speaker's consonants.
3. He registers, records the complete word, sentence, phrase.

4. He recalls the conceptual meaning, its indicative content rationally (for instance, Beethoven's Ninth Symphony when mentioned in conversation, he will store away and classify).
5. He re-enacts the emotions behind the phrase; he is moved.
6. He re-enacts the representations condensed into the word.
7. He re-enacts the processes represented; he does something about the cosmic processes communicated to him, following them up by acts.
8. He gets the word out of his system, forgets it.

The whole process leaves the listener undamaged only when he can go through all the movements during his life. The news is good news for him when he finally can forget about it because he has done something about it, and lives on. To forget a thing which we learned before we remembered, or felt, or acted would be wrong. Never to forget anything is an obsession. There is a time for memory as well as for forgetting. In education, we take little advantage of the two facts as being equally legitimate because we do not openly assign them a moment in time.

The usual experience with instruction, of course, is that it is merely remembered. Although we feel that this reaction is inadequate, and feel like [we are] choked, we do little about this. The reaction—as we now may see—must involve our whole system. Or the listening process has not established a social metabolism. It now makes us sick. The outlet, perhaps, should be tears, joy, laughter, sentiment. Or when our alarm clock rings, the best thing is to jump out of bed. People who do not jump out of bed after the clock rings usually have an unpleasant feeling, like a tremor. They feel shaky because they do not enact the best reaction: to jump out of bed, which would get the alarm out of their system.

Now let us parallel the speaker's and the listener´s efforts.

The listener follows the suggestions of the speaker. He is inclined to re-enact as much of the act of communication as the speaker intended to actualize. The listener tries to mobilize no more and no less energy than the speaker mobilized. The wretched experience of the devoted amateur with the hard-boiled expert always is that the amateur listens, heart and soul, and the expert coughs, with a suppressed yawn. Or the listener is bored, and the speaker shouts, as at an auction. This discrepancy is the most serious disease in society. When two experts talk, both with the augur's smile, it does not hurt. When two boys are intoxicated, everything is fine. It is the discrepancy that endangers our social system because speech is abused, in these inadequate responses, by one of the two interlocutors. It has been a lasting shock in my youth to find out later that the other person was not in earnest where[as] I was.

The protective coloring of youth against this danger is indifference; and it seems to be altogether not unknown in New England colleges. The boys are right. The danger is too great that they incur situations in which the teacher plays [it] safe and leans back. And this fear is behind much of our failures. The discrepancy between the speaker's and the listener's effort, to me seems the central disturbance in the transmission of the cosmic processes through speech. The singer may think that he sings; the listener only hears a noise; no artistic pleasure is communicated. I make contact to get action; the listener stores my communication away in his memory. This bears out a great and striking difference in the attitude of a speaker and a listener in scientific reading. A scientist who is making a statement as the result of ten years of work reaches his listener's memory only, in our modern form of learning. That means that the student places this statement into his organ for historical facts. To remember something transforms it into a part of our historical imagination. Oh yes, we say, that is so, and go on with new curiosity to the next item of news.

Teacher and student never register with the corresponding organ as long as the scholar is a research man and conveys first-hand knowledge. It will always remain second-hand knowledge for the student. He will locate it in his memory whereas it fills the whole system of the scientist. Any philosophy is deteriorated by the fact that it is memorized by the disciples. They store it in a part of their body which is unable to produce similar effects in their own life as the philosophy produced in the thinker himself. Only when the philosopher can get his hearers to do something about it, to feel it, to remember it, and to register, only then has he found heirs to his bequest to posterity.

The paralyzing effect of memory on the true meaning of a word said by a man who means business, who offers this as his last word, cannot fail to produce disastrous effects. The neglect of the need for memorizing would be not less disastrous. It is not enough to do "anything" about it. The disciples of Ruskin followed his challenge to establish a work camp. But when they got American money [for this task], they changed their purpose to building a college for workers. They turned the words of Ruskin upside down, and this quite literally: Ruskin College is an offense to Ruskin's intention. They did something about it. But they did not remember what Ruskin had taught. Ruskin had deep feelings about manual work and its honor. The students had charitable leanings toward the poor. The impulse "to do something about it" is very often today coupled with a perfect misunderstanding of the meaning. And the complete understanding of the idea is found in people who would like to kill the person who does something about it.

The tragedy of Greek philosophy was and is to be found in modern times again, in this misunderstanding of the process of hearing and learning. All the process of thinking in the schools of philosophy is a tradition of dialectical contradiction between teacher generation and student generation, with an endless chain that at the end produced a catalogue of all possible *-isms*. No *-ism*, however, was more valid than any other. They all held sway over one generation. But all came about by the fact that the students stored the words of the master away in their memory. Then, their own living experience came into play, in the heart and under the skin, and this personal experience asked for articulation. And it could find this articulation not in supplementation to the teacher's doctrine, but only in diametrical opposition. Why? Because memory is a faculty to keep the past, and the new experience was articulated abruptly.

The power of recognition that enables us to identify our own new experience with the record of past experience is a power that transcends logic and definitions. The power of identifying us with people who express their ideas in other terms requires a quality of the mind that is much rarer than logic or memory or sentiment. It requires the superior power cultivated by the church and in the family: the power of translating for the sake of mission and education the eternal truth into the language of the times. The power of translating fuses the different ways of understanding. But the memorizing student of Thomas Aquinas or of Hegel was perfectly unable to do just that.

Another tragedy becomes clear when we discriminate between the organs through which we complete our process of listening. This is the dilemma of modern propaganda. We all tell other people, we all persuade and spread the news and blow the horn. This is not propaganda, in any specific sense. To speak means to propagate the world's actions by communication. We propagate when one organ of speech is active on the speaker's side and the listener's organ of hearing is more powerful. When I sing and my listener is an effete aesthetic critic, he will abuse me for my innocent song, which he takes to be a case for scientific analysis, perhaps as a mere critic. Instead of singing with me, he dissects my singing.

The opposite happens when the propagandist cold-bloodedly instills me with an opinion he has calculated to arouse my feelings, and which not even he himself thinks to be true. His mouth, without his deeper system, speaks; my heart listened and my feelings are roused. This inadequacy is so frightening in propaganda. I have to turn here against the American Institute for the study of propaganda that has abandoned all attempts to define propaganda.[1] Or, propaganda is stigmatized as working up our emotions. However, I do wish to work up my reader´s emotions as much as his actions, his intelligence, and his senses. Or I would not educate. Scientific education is nonsense. As far as it is education, all education must create life, habits, understanding, memories, plus feelings. Or it just is not education. And also, it is legitimate to arouse emotions. The only condition is that the speaker himself is moved, too. That he shares the process of the listener to a certain extent. But, in propaganda Mr. Goebbels acts differently. Climbing down from his hustings in the Lustgarten in Berlin in 1932, he turned to his friend Goering and asked: "Did I put in too much heat? Shall I be colder next time?" This is propaganda. All attempts to define propaganda without a negative qualification of the devil in our nature [are] hopeless. The devil tries to get something for too cheap a price. The cool speaker cannot buy and shall not buy a deep sentiment by his standing aloof. This is diabolical. And the lack of courage to recognize that this has been called diabolical for eighteen hundred years, the fervent endeavor on the side of descriptive science to treat propaganda as something more new than bad, more technical than eternal, is, I think, obstructive to its understanding.

The liar is as old as truth. Men have lied ever since they spoke the truth. And lying has various forms. One is the discrepancy between the investment made by the speaker and the speculative results he thinks he may produce in the listener. There are many other forms of lying, hypocrisy, positive lying which in themselves, also, are diseases of speech that are highly enlightening as to the character of speech. The abuse of the listener´s tract by technical means that conceal the lack of animation in the speaker, must be admitted as a special sort of lying that is rampant today because of the anonymity of the modern means of communication.

1. According to *Wikipedia*, the Institute for Propaganda Analysis (IPA) was a U.S.-based organization operating from 1937 to 1942, composed of social scientists, opinion leaders, historians, educators, and journalists. The IPA's purpose was to spark rational thinking and provide a guide to help the public have well-informed discussions on current issues. (N.F.)

Propaganda is impossible where the people who speak together also live together. In a community that shares their lives for a long time, words bear fruit (which is the literal sense of propaganda), and yet, nobody in such a community would be surprised that words beget what they were created for: memories, intelligence, feeling, and actions. It is only when the speaker and the listener know each other less and less that the discrepancy between the effort and sincerity on the side of the speaker and the reactions of the heart of the listener becomes intolerable.

We may draw a list of corresponding features between speaker and listener:

	Speaker	*Listener*
1.	Chats	smiles
2.	Talks	listens
3.	Tells	remembers
4.	Teaches	learns
5.	Sings	feels
6.	Commands	obeys
7.	Argues	understands
8.	Prophesies	carries out

In all social disintegration the relations between the two sides of the process are confused or interrupted.

The purpose of speech is to animate the listener to the degree to which the speaker himself is animated. When the speaker is not animated, it is diabolical to animate the listener. For the purpose of speech is to communicate cosmic processes. And the only guarantee of their correct transportation and spread is the sponsorship by the speaker, in his own service as carrier of the news. The man who expects his listener to do something must have done something about it himself. The man who asks me to feel something about it, must have felt himself that this is heart rending and moving, etc. However, the listener has a great advantage over the speaker. A man who does something because he is moved to act by another man's challenge, does that what he does in response to a human word. And this fact is an incredible relief to himself, because he follows a predecessor. Most of the honor of men is in their listening so deeply that they feel challenged to act as the speaker expected them to act.

It is one of the fallacies of modern argument that free men do not want to act under another´s command. This is a complete misunderstanding. Love your neighbor as yourself and God with all your power is a command that does not take away from any man´s freedom. The words "Love men as God loves you," again is the most emancipating sentence. And *it must be said,* or man is not emancipated to his own full power and liberty.

Robert Frost has a poem about two roads in the woodland and that he took the less beaten track of the two. Superficially, that seems to hint to the fallacious modern idea: Don´t let anybody tell you. The less beaten track might seem to be the track less spoken of. This is not so, for otherwise Frost would not have tried to propagate the truth that man must follow the less beaten track. By writing, printing, and publishing it, Frost propagates this real experience of man´s place in the cosmos and of the action expected from man in this cosmos. We are told to take the track that is new and difficult. We are told. We listen, and perhaps, we obey. The beaten track is not the track that people talk you into; it is the track people advise you to take because it has been taken before. The beaten track is not bad because it is talked about; it is the wrong track because it has been taken before. The track is wrong because it is a repetition, not because it is recommended. And against the speakers that tell the boy, become what we all know men usually become, Frost says the only path that *deserves to be talked about* is the new one. In other words, he draws attention to the fact that recommendations and advice and commands must point to the future, the real, unknown and unheard of future in order to be meaningful. He restores the meaning of a path into the future. He does not dissuade man from telling the young what to do.

History narrates the beaten tracks. And education must avoid the pitfall of suggesting that the track beaten now was beaten when, on it, men made history. Yet, they made history with conviction because a speaker or many speakers had been victors in their teaching the actors of the historical drama. Alexander the Great was the disciple of Aristotle, and Charles the Fifth the pupil of Erasmus of Rotterdam. And Alexander conquered, and Charles the Fifth resigned his crown, both because they had the good fortune of having listened to inspired speech that was victorious. Conviction is more powerful where one man is the speaker and the other the doer. The American educator today is frustrated by the general idea that the speaker and the doer must be one and the same person. How may we teach if this were so? The merciful parsimony of the mental life allows one man to condense his life into telling and another's life into carrying out. To restore the power of teaching, we today must restore the honor of listening.

May I mention a personal experience? After the German defeat in 1918 and '19, life seemed to have gone out of the corpse of the empire. Nobody obeyed. Ten million soldiers, dismissed overnight, tried to act, every one of them for himself, and they tried to work out their individual salvation. Anarchy, absence of government, signified the years usually known as the years of inflation. In trying to find a star to guide me in this night, I decided to serve, to listen. That was the thing not done, not approved of in the day′s tumult. And so, I forbade myself to teach and became private secretary to a man who did not look for a private secretary, but whom I asked that he should allow me to listen. I have never felt better than when I took this step from a scholar to a servant; and serving it was, very literally. So, at least I know what I am talking about.[2]

The listener may go much further than the person who with great effort, and toward the end of his life, knows what deserves to be said and taught. The listener abbreviates the process of formulating, and instead may do something about it. Alexander the Great is the continuation of Aristotle; he is the good conscience, the superiority incarnate of Greek thought over the barbarians. And the amiable and catholic nature of Erasmus, his strength and his weakness, are reflected in Charles the Fifth, who devoured the new book by Copernicus, saved the unity of Christendom for another thirty years, loved his Titian, and gave up his throne, disgusted with the world. What about all the Aristotelians? What about all the humanists following Erasmus? Well, they, in turn, waited for their Alexanders the Great and their Charles Sixth, Seventh, and Eighth. And some of them may have found them. The best Aristotelian, however, testifies less to the mental powers of Aristotle than [does] Alexander the Great.

We have compared the speaker′s ways and the gradation in listening. However, we have omitted one decisive situation between speaker and listener that forms the first phase in the process of listening. The

2. Rosenstock-Huessy describes his role as a kind of assistant editor of the *Daimler Werkzeitung* far too modestly. He was the de facto editor, and his boss was Paul Riebensahm, a much older man on the Board of Directors of Daimler. Rosenstock-Huessy, thirty years old, was his partner in an attempt through this publication to bring peace to embittered labor vs. management relations. Rosenstock-Huessy supplied most of the ideas. The Daimler company has a description of this noble failed endeavor on its website: https://media.daimler.com/marsMediaSite/en/instance/ko/The-Daimler-Werkzeitung-from-1919-to-1920-avant-garde-project-in-a-difficult-period.xhtml?oid=9914426 (N.F.)

process of language is fifty percent speaking, fifty percent listening. Language is not [just] speech, it is a full circle from word to sound to perception to understanding to feeling to memorizing to acting and back to the word about the act thus achieved.

And before the listener can become a listener, something has to happen to him: He must expect. To the silence that precedes the speech, we may compare the expectation that should precede the fact of listening. Silence is loaded with significance. So is expectation. Our education is handicapped by many gadgets that more or less ignore or cut back expectations. The expectation of the listener does not depend on the speaker; he has not spoken yet. It depends on the authority ascribed to the speaker by the world, [by] the other students, by society.

The problem of authority is nearly unknown today as separate from capacity and from administrative power. And yet, the educational process of the average college student cannot be arranged satisfactorily without the solution of how to awaken his expectations. He must be hungry before we can feed him. He is blasé, he is indifferent, he is skeptical, he is shy, he is outside the world of which we talk and into which we try to talk him, the world of eternal life.

Authority only can make him listen; authority, it is true, is often understood to mean power. Now, parents and college deans may force a boy to take a course. They, however, rarely are his authorities for expecting great things to happen. Authority is so more subtle that it enters his system much more through the grapevine telegraph of humor, of gossip, of some electricity in the atmosphere, of the remarks of an uncle, etc. We all know that a child sometimes has authorities who have no power whatsoever, and has people in power who have no authority.

The material sword of power and the spiritual sword of authority are confused today. And few people would believe me when I say that the teacher, the power of an administration and the authorities of social evaluation, all three are at work to educate a student. Because that is so, to me most discussions of college curricula sound void of authority; ignoring the tripartite influences that must collaborate, they either give too much to the teacher or too much to the administration of the responsibilities implied.

We cannot educate without the authority of those who make the student expectant. And I sincerely feel that our students are lacking in expectation because no public inspiration or authority sends them to us. We have before us the task of making the students hungry before we may teach them important things. It is useless to teach those who do not expect to be transformed. They may get memorial verses, instruction, facts. And they will either forget this instruction, these facts, or they will abuse them, only because the ingredient of expectation was lacking that would have made the meal spicy. Not our jokes, not our tricks, can lighten the burden of the student when he is not eager to learn. And why should he be eager when he does not expect the extraordinary?

In fact, his modern authorities all unanimously conspire to persuade him that college education is normal, ordinary, regular, the beaten path, that he gets something for himself there. And we hasten to prove to him day after day how much he gets. The introductory courses are evidence of our feverish anxiety to show him our best things right away. They say that it is no privilege, no service to mankind, no campaign for truth. And so, it degenerates like all selfishness, in boredom, drudgery, and the country club. All this because we have overlooked the first stage in the listener's tract of hearing: his expectations and his authorities that open him up to the important and extraordinary idea that he should listen for four years till he is transformed into a soldier of truth, service, and peace for society. Teachers are not facilities for students so that these may work out their own salvation. Teachers are obstacles and difficulties so that the students may rise to their opportunities for the future of mankind. However, we always mention his advantages, his happiness, his future. And so the college is his last school instead of his first campaign in the spiritual militia.

Since he has been to schools all his life, the college is just the next school, which is rather degrading for the college by the simple fact that he enters a new school now for the fourth time. Could we not think of giving him a recess during which to get hungry for the college as a really new situation? Perhaps he should work one year before coming to college. Or should we make him work during his sophomore year after having taught him the facts about listening and expecting, so that he would not waste his year of practical work, as happens now? Many things could be done; but some things must be done to restore the listener´s alimentary tract that leads from expectation to hearing, to listening, to feeling, to remembering, to doing, and that corresponds to the speaker´s tract of silence, cry, song, story, argument, and command. It is up to educators to discover the curriculum that includes the revival of expectation.

Language is the complete social relation between speakers and listeners. Education is a model and sample, a yardstick, for the innumerable situations in which the student will have to speak and to listen, to expect and to act, to be silent and to command. When we do not give him one complete experience of the whole process from the beginning to end, when we do not tell him and show him what authority, what the power to command, what the freedom to serve, mean, then we cannot call that which we do education.

On the other hand, I do not feel that it is so difficult to coordinate a college curriculum around this rather simple aim, which takes him through the mental phases that homo sapiens, man, because he speaks, has to pass through. We must take him through these phases, show their existence, their validity, their purpose for our victories over the world, and their diseases and decadence by lack of mental faith, love, and hope. And I suppose that that has always been considered the core of the traditions of a Liberal Arts college, of the Humanities, of Science.

How to speak to our students is more difficult than we thought it was. It does not depend on us alone whether we reach his ear, heart, imagination, or not. We teachers and scientists often cannot reach their brain except when the variety of idioms of speech is around them; [the] effectiveness of our teaching depends on the effectiveness of the poetic and artistic life, the loyalties and customs, the family and the politics of the country. We do not succeed because the other, supplementary overtures are not voiced, because the alimentary tract that we call listening needs massaging in all its phases or parts. And [the] difference of poetry, music, prose, mathematics actually plays on the different senses that take part in the process of listening. Only that which we hear with all the powers given man have we heard at all.

We have seen that education is insistent listening and speaking, otherwise, however, just the fresh language of mankind. For this reason, the language of education must always re-unite all professional language, all idioms, into one re-unified, re-translated language of one society. No theory of education is satisfactory because theory is speaking scientifically. Education is the full process of translating, out of the confusion of tongues, in one living language.

On the other hand, education and speech and listening in general now may be placed on one even more comprehensive plane of time and space. This plane is often overlooked when we think of the active processes in speech only. We already mentioned the problem of silence and the problem of expectation that seemed to correspond to silence on the side of the listener. Education takes time out of the years of a student and puts him, for a certain time, in a classroom. Education, then, is stressing the fact that to speak and to listen is impossible without two human qualities: to take time and to give time. Grown-up people take time before they make up their minds. They are silent before they speak. They have taken years to study or to do research.

Youth has an enthusiasm of giving time, to the point of waste. However, the boy who never has wasted time never will become a man. Some abundance of giving his time in good faith is the condition of being young. The problem is, in education, how to make the student faithful enough to give his inner time to the process, and not just his physical appearance. And how to make him realize that the teacher has taken time. The teacher seems to give; the student seems to take. This is not, as we see now, quite so simple. Content is given by the teacher. But the enthusiasm of giving time is all on the side of the listener. The importance of a speaker will depend on how much time he has taken out of his life to have the right to say just this and to make this statement. The importance of the listening process depends on the recklessness with which the listener forgets all time limits, all end of class schedule, and listens, completely forgetful of any end of time. In taking and giving time, speaker and listener restore the injured time and space axes of society. In this sense, speech not only sustains the time and space axes but actually recreates them, and by laying emphasis on the otherwise forgotten elements of the world, speaker and listener insist on the resurrection of the otherwise forgotten by resuscitating life "in the wise" of the word by which all things are made.[3]

Therefore, we are mistaken when we ascribe to the imperative the content of being "in the second person." As the six persons in search of an author in the play of Pirandello, the imperative is in search of a subject. 'Tis said to "whom it may concern"; "go" does not contain the second person "you" or "thou"; what it does is to create this person.

For this reason, the imperative is pure verb without an ending. He who does just this becomes the second person by answering the first person. The listener who says "I will do it" becomes the person to whom "go" was addressed. Before, the speaker took the risk to speak to me without any guarantee whether I was human or reasonable or responsive or available or capable of doing what he asked me to do. That I will go places me in the position of the man who feels that:

1. he should respond, [it] is his business to respond
2. that the thing asked is reasonable

3. "Wise" here meaning, "way," "manner." (N.F.)

3. that he is free to do it (has time)
4. that he is able to do it (feels like doing it)

The listener, then, makes the following statements:

1. That he is meant, he is *selected* to produce the next act in the course of events. *Res ad triarios venit.*[4] Every imperative creates a hierarchy of people by telling: who next, by throwing out a net to catch the next fish who will swim toward the goal suggested in the command, by putting up a flagbearer or carrier or actor for the act that is said to be required.
2. [That] the process suggested by the act is "reasonable" does not mean merely that it is rationally explicable by natural laws; it means that reason requires its coming into being. It is of great importance to see the shape given to the rationality of something in the light of the imperative. It does not give up its rational character; nomothetics [i.e., law-giving] ethics are not non-rational. However, the reasonable is not concerned with causality but with filling a gap, restoring an order, add[ing] the thing missing to a universe otherwise perturbed. The reasonable appeals to an estimate of the situation which only asks for a comparative: Is it better to do this than to leave it?

In other words, true imperatives are not asking *what?*, they are concerned with alternatives: whether or not. Reason in the listener's mind is not in the void of innumerable possibilities. Any superlative answer to the imperatival or suggestive situation is out of the question; the question centers around: Is this imperative better than a world without this act?

The social division between the speaker and the listener discloses its emancipatory character for the doer. Any actor who is not able to hear within himself the clear-cut alternative: Shall I do this, or not do this? Anyone who thinks of three, four, or five possibilities at a time is an intellectual stutterer and stammerer. He puts many questions at the same time. And so he cannot answer. This is the disease of our time: conflicting suggestions in great number. And it is in the face of the imperative that our prismatic reason falters.

And I purposely stress the fact that the respondent to an imperative uses reason only for following up his answer to a suggestion. He uses

4. *Triarii* is the last reserve in a Roman legion. *Res ad triaros venit* translates: "the last reserve has been called up," hence, now it is getting serious.

reason not to find out an abstract truth about fact. He uses reason to find out how to go about a concrete suggestion.

All planning that starts by abstract reasoning and tries to deduce special solutions from [it], twists the order of reasoning. The imperative precedes the use of analysis. The logical analysis is in answer to a specific mandate. Because it is in answer not about an object but about an act that is in search for its author, the use of reason is concrete and boils down to the problem: Is there enough suggestiveness in the proposition to interest the listener? To be interested means to be a partner, to be in it. An imperative asks: are you willing to be a part of this dilemma? Are you willing to be subjected to this act of filling a gap? Of adding something to the universe by doing the *unum necessarium*, the thing that, as my shout or cry suggests, is most needed? "Listen!" "Be interested" is the most general imperative, or the generality behind the imperative. And it is this command that is behind any word spoken to anyone. The imperatival feature remains, then, in all other statements, [whether] of purely logical or descriptive or narratory or lyrical character, as the sedimentation of the imperatival phase of all speech. And this command "be interested" means: Use your reason with a regard to a concrete decision; what reason does, is not to speculate about what to do. It only helps to decide whether to do the act at hand. And reason is at a loss to do much more. All questions of fact are sub-questions in order to decide over an act to be taken in the future. No "facts" make sense without this primate of the future act.

This is true with respect to the facts ascertained by the layman and the facts ascertained by science. When we take the statement, *the darkened moon*, these three words may be pronounced in the following ways:

1. Poetically as beginning a poem: *The darkened moon, and nature looks disheveled*, etc. The poet is under the impression of a disturbance, a great emotional experience.
2. It may be in a story: *We all waited till, after midnight, the darkened moon became visible.*
3. The statement may be in an astronomical treatise: *The clear moon has a blue or greenish light. The darkened moon is from gray to brownish.* The darkened moon here is the logical antithesis to the usual moon. The darkened moon is one object of observation and analysis; the moon in general looks different.

4. Only now, do we come to the proposition underlying all the three styles mentioned: *look, the darkened moon.*

All statements are intonated in a different way. The darkened moon is called to our attention emphatically. *The darkened moon! When shall we look at her?* It is sung rhythmically when we put her in the song of poetic emotion: short long, short long, short long, etc. It is accentuated in the logical opposition: the darkened as against the moon in general. And it is put in its proper place in the story, as determining the order of events. *Emphasis* is used for the command: look at her; *rhythm*, for the emotion; *accent* for the factual definition; and *propriety* for the story.

Now, the emphasis is, to some extent, kept in the three other statements because in all cases the listener is expected to pay attention to the darkened moon as something interesting. The quality of command *Look at her* subsists when grammatical transformation stresses *rhythm, accent,* or *propriety*. When we come to the scientist's treatment of the darkened moon, we meet with certain changes. The emphasis is nearly gone out of the textbook statement because everything about the moon is gathered here. Where, then, is the emphasis in science? However, it is there. It has retreated to the general basis of all scientific data; it runs: *Let there be science!* Without this primary imperative, not one of the statements in a cut and dry textbook makes sense. The sentence now would read: *Don´t be interested in the darkened moon all by herself but only as part of a system of astronomy, or a system of nature.*

The emphasis, in scientific description, has shifted from the new fact observed, *I see the darkened moon*, to the system in which this event makes sense. Instead of science, or of astronomy, we might say, the statement is harbingered in the greater imperative: *Let us be systematic; let us build up a system.* The event behind the factual statement, *the darkened moon looks brown*, on which we insist emphatically, is the event of our being scientific, and becoming more so all the time. The imperative, *Let us be systematic, let us be scientific*, swallows up our gullibility by the small incident of one darkness of the moon. Nevertheless, it is the imperative, *Let there be science*, that commands our statement.

Why do we discriminate between the brown and blue moonlight, between the usual and the unusual appearance of the moon? Because in order to build our system, we take every object apart till it can be put together again systematically. The scientific analysis of the particular is the condition of the systematic synthesis which is our imperative. In this sense, then, all statements of scientific analysis are merely preliminary to the urge of systematization. In this sense, our accents on one and the other object are preliminary. They are, quite literally, *prolegomena*, prefaces, *exordia*, to the thing that really is upon our shoulders. The emphasis is on the big event of the future, the system.

And the indicative does not use up all our breath. We speak, in science or in mathematics, in a formalized, less emphatic way, nearly without sounds, in signs out of which the full strength of the imperative has disappeared because this power is saved up for the day of reckoning, the day of synthesis, the day of systematic victory over our scientific task, in this case, astronomy.

Scientists have said that science predicts. This is too simple. Science could not predict without promising or predicting a system of time and space in which all facts, new and old, are contained in their proper order and sequence. The system is predicting. And the future fact predicted comes in only as a part of the system. The system is the promise of science. For the system makes the emphasis on any peculiar fact superfluous. In its place and date, the darkened moon of 1945 is not more exciting than the darkened moon of 545 BC. Every scientific monograph is a prolegomenon to the system that emancipates us from rash impressions and haphazard observations and overwhelming appearances, by the system. The imperative of the scientific undertaking is filled with all the emphasis that the layman puts on the peculiar event.

However, the objectivity of the sciences is based on the subjectivity of scientists applying to themselves the imperative, *Let there be science*, in the fourfold application:

- I am meant
- it is reasonable
- it is possible
- I am free to do it.

Under the clause "*subjiciendum est,*" it has to be undergone, the individual scientist is swayed by the same reason that the layman uses. This reason is not rationality, but suggestiveness [followed by] his response to a reasonable command or suggestion. The suggestion *Let us have a system* strikes him as reasonable. The powers by which he gives his assent are not at all rational. For the thing has to be done in the future; the science does not exist now. And so it is irrational that he joins the army of scientists. However, this is reasonable. Because in making his choice he has to choose between the possibility of a scientific solution and the sensational unrest of daily surprises in his world. And so it is quite reasonable for society to delegate some men to try their hand in building systems.

Now these same scientists, acting irrationally and reasonably themselves, preach that we should act rationally. This is inconsistent. It cannot be done. And our world goes crazy today because scientists have forgotten the basis of their own actions: that they have chosen, between two irrational possibilities of the future, system or no system, the reasonable path of the system, without guarantee of success. Their choice is ennobled only by their willingness to take the consequences, to be condemned to be scientists, and to stick it out.

This same choice is asked by any bride, any employer, any farmer, in much the same way. Nowhere have we rational choices. Starting from zero and determining among fifty possibilities, always are we, in the use of our reason, restricted to deciding the dual of two alternatives. Or we lose our reasoning power in the thicket of possibilities. The word *rational* does not include the problem of living into the future. It is applicable to objects only. Rationality is impossible when the outcome is unknown, because it lies in the future. And rationality assumes that we remain unchanged and analyze objects.

The future, however, is that situation by which we undergo a change and are transformed ourselves. The entities or selves of scientific analysis are outside myself. The progressive synthesis toward the future appeals to my power to survive myself and to enter a new phase of my own life by outliving myself.

9

Chopping Down the Cross

The magnificent "Epic of American Civilization" fresco mural in the library of Dartmouth College, in Hanover, New Hampshire, painted by José Clemente Orozco between 1932 and 1934, runs maybe three hundred linear feet on several walls and is some ten feet high. It is a wonder to behold and all the more striking because it is unexpected in the far north of this country at an institution not associated with either political radicalism or Mexico.

One of the huge panels, entitled by Orozco "Modern Migration of the Spirit," depicts Jesus Christ in a loincloth wielding an ax he has just used to chop down his wooden cross. The symbolism is evident: the spirit revolting against the dead institutionalization of his message.

The official Dartmouth commentary on this particular image reads: "A defiant, resurrected Christ, painted in acid colors and shedding his skin to reveal a newly enlivened body, returns in judgment to sweep away ideologies and institutions that thwart contemporary human emancipation and spiritual renewal. Orozco presents a Christ figure who not only rejects his sacrificial destiny by felling his cross but condemns and destroys the sources of his agony, military armaments and religious and cultural symbols here relegated to the junk heap of history behind him." I find dubious in this description only the words: "rejects his sacrificial destiny." Maybe.

Rosenstock-Huessy joined the Dartmouth faculty in 1935, a year or so after the fresco was completed, and to my knowledge he never met Orozco. The two men were truly contemporaries, however—Rosenstock-Huessy was forty-seven in 1935, Orozco fifty-two—meaning that both had witnessed the catastrophe of the Great War and the subsequent Great Depression, and both were radical to the core, in the sense that they saw through the usual cant of church and state and academy and were unafraid to address it. In Orozco's case, the civil war in Mexico between 1910 and 1920 only compounded the horrors of what was happening worldwide. His mural attacked unbridled capitalism and ruthless industrialization, militarism, a detached professoriate, bellicose nationalism, and much else.

A *New York Times* article about Orozco (Nov. 17, 2013) quotes from his autobiography where Orozco wrote that provocation was both his mission and a necessity. "Everything should be done against the grain, against the current." Because of this defiant stance, even in Mexico he is not much of a hero. Not surprisingly, Rosenstock-Huessy, a kindred spirit, loved this mural, in particular the panel that in earlier versions elsewhere Orozco had explicitly entitled "Cristo destruye su cruz" (Christ destroys his cross). According to Prof. David Johns, a Quaker theologian at Earlham College in Indiana, Orozco painted this scene three times, "twice as murals . . . and once on a 4 ft x 3 ft canvas." Professor Johns writes: "I can imagine [Christ] shouting with each impact of the blade: 'Ya basta! Enough!' . . . To the violence that destroys and oppresses, to all the laws and institutions that diminish humanity under their power—enough."

So much was Professor Rosenstock-Huessy enamored of the image that he incorporated it into his 1938 magnum opus in English, *Out of Revolution: Autobiography of Western Man*. Of the various illustrations in the book, it is the one of most recent vintage by far, an image barely four years old at the time, "hot off the press," so to speak. He gave the image a new name, "A Secular Christ," and found for it a very ancient lineage indeed. In the caption to it he wrote: "We have added a sentence from Augustine which, strangely enough, empowers us to express this idea: *Crux ergo haec ipsa crucifigenda est*—The Cross itself has to be crucified. (*Epistulae* 241 in the Viennese edition—38 of the former editions.)"

It is unlikely that Orozco was inspired by Augustine. He was simply an artistic genius, full of passion for social and economic justice, to whom searing, apocalyptic images came naturally. Christ chopping down his cross is by no means the only provocative scene in Orozco's "Epic."

For Rosenstock-Huessy, too, seeing "Christ destroys his cross" was not a revelation; it represented for him visually a paradox that is at the very foundation of his thought, captured in *Out of Revolution* and in other writings of his: Death is the beginning of new life, not the end. Christianity teaches us, he asserted, to reach back from the end of time into the present and reform it.

This sequence, with death as the precondition of new life, cannot be dismissed as merely a "religious" doctrine. In one sense, it is an obvious truth about the processes of the world, eminently visible in nature. For renewal there must be decay and death. Paganism and tribal rites of sacrifice going back to pre-historic times possessed this understanding to a degree, but as in the eternal succession of the seasons, that vision is cyclical or repetitive. Nothing is learned that may be carried forward *beyond* what exists in nature. There is no inspiration leading to change. The awareness of death in paganism is not a prelude, not a stepping-stone, to progress. In the absence of faith in resurrection on earth, the greatest fear must be the finality of death without fruitfulness.

The message of Christianity, Rosenstock-Huessy argued, unanticipated in paganism and transcending natural cycles, is that death rather than being the end is the necessary foundation of a new beginning. In *The Christian Future* he made this point emphatically. "Christianity," he said,

> is the founder and trustee of the future, the very process of finding and securing it, and without the Christian spirit there is no real future for man. . . . In apparent doubt whether there is still any future in Christianity, people have been demanding in recent years that we save Christianity from destruction—along with civilization and some neighboring treasure islands. But "saving" Christianity is unnecessary, undesirable, impossible because it is anti-Christian. . . . At the center of the Christian creed is faith in death and resurrection. Christians believe in an end of the world, not only once but again and again. This and this alone is the power which enables us to die to our old habits and ideals, get out of our old ruts, leave our dead selves behind and take the first step into a genuine future.[1]

I was led to the foregoing reflections by a remark made to me several years ago by Russ Keep (now deceased), a student of Rosenstock-Huessy's at Dartmouth in ca. 1950. "I am having recurrent day-dreams," Russ reported (thinking of the contentious migration in 2013 of Argo Books, the

1. Rosenstock-Huessy, *Christian Future*, 61–62.

publishing arm of the Rosenstock-Huessy Fund, into the inventory of the independent publisher Wipf and Stock), "of Rosenstock burning all of his books." Rosenstock-Huessy certainly put his life into his writing and speaking with the utmost seriousness. He wanted to be heard. Yet Russ's day-dream is appropriate to the man. The spirit has to blow free, touching who and where it will, and at some rare moments it may effect revolutionary change, a rejection of a beloved past that blocks a new future.

Rosenstock-Huessy worried foremost about the degeneration of inspiration, the ossification of the spirit, while knowing it is inevitable in this life. Sometimes only profound sacrifice, including death, can bring about the needed revivification. And he worried about the urgency of the moment dissipating into abstract academic talk, removed from living service, which is to say, sacrifice of the self.

He could as well have titled "Christ destroys his cross" "Christ waging the self-sacrifice and suffering it requires of the soldier." Christianity, he said in *The Christian Future*, "is essentially war in peace: it distributes the bloody sacrifices of the battlefront by an even but perpetual spread of sacrifices through the whole fabric of life."[2] Lasting peace will only be possible, he argued, through the constant and regular self-sacrifice in peace time that we witness and admire in war. The giving up of self at the right moment makes possible a new future. Real future for Rosenstock-Huessy is precarious, not a mechanical tomorrow and tomorrow and tomorrow but that which is newly created by human dedication.

When is it timely for an institution, a movement, a regime, a relationship, a tradition, a deity to die? For Rosenstock-Huessy that was the greatest question. "When" is always the greatest question, he said. In the cross of reality we are perpetually caught between our loyalty to the admirable accomplishments of the past and our aspirations for a better future. What to let go of, and *when*, is always the issue. The symbol of the felled cross tells us not what to do, or when to do it, but teaches us only to hold in suspension the realization that even our most cherished beliefs can turn into idols and therefore must be sacrificed to allow for new birth, which is to say, in Rosenstock-Huessy's thinking, new names, new language. In the course of a lifetime we may fall under the power of any number of gods, which "can enslave all the elements of our being. There may be a time," he wrote in *Out of Revolution*, "when we must worship them. Yet when we analyze our whole life between birth and death, we cannot assign the whole life of any human being to a single one of these many deities and powers."

2. Rosenstock-Huessy, *Christian Future*, 26–27.

> No one of them is supreme. Some enter the scene rather late. Science is too severe a god for children. Venus abdicates her authority over old age. Socialism annoys the man of sixty, and greed is hardly conceivable to a young person. The gods pass. When the individual realizes their passing, their unceasing change, he is converted to God—the living God who invites us to obey the *unum necessarium*, the one thing necessary and timely at every moment. This man discovers his complete liberty, the unbelievable freedom of the children of God, who are independent of all specific codes and traditional creeds, because the God of our future and our beginning is superior to the gods he has put around us in the short periods of our conscious efforts.[3]

Christ destroying his cross is a revolutionary act, but not a repudiation of the spirit of his gift to mankind. What is effectively dead or has been sullied or abused must be left behind. We can still go forward, but under new names. Rosenstock-Huessy spoke of the Christianity of the future as traveling incognito, without any name at all because so much of the traditional language of the church has been mindlessly exploited and hence become exhausted of meaning.

That Rosenstock-Huessy re-titled Orozco's image "A Secular Christ" deliberately translates the event from a parochial "Christian" story into a universal truth. The lesson of the felled cross is essentially the knowledge that at the "right" time, which is never predictable, we may find ourselves compelled to solemnly and decisively reject faiths or opinions we once held dear. The image is, then, one more exemplification of Rosenstock-Huessy's personal motto and the guiding star of society in the third millennium: *Respondeo etsi mutabor*, I respond even though I must change. The motto reminds us that we are "responsible for life's reproduction on earth." "Human society has outgrown the stage of mere existence which prevails in nature. In Society, we must respond, and by our mode of response we bear witness that we know what no other being knows: the secret of death and life. We feel ourselves answerable for life's 'Renaissance'. . . . A vital word alters life's course and life outruns the already present death."[4]

3. Rosenstock-Huessy, *Out of Revolution*, 727.

4. Rosenstock-Huessy, *Out of Revolution*, 751ff. The Orozco image "Modern Migration of the Spirit" is easily found on the Web from a variety of access points, sometimes in horribly untrue colors. Here's the best site for a look at the mural as a whole <http://www.dartmouth.edu/digitalorozco/app/> For a single shot of Christ cutting down his cross, see: https://hoodmuseum.dartmouth.edu/objects/p.934.13.21

10

Waiting for the New Future

The greatest temptation of our time is impatience, in its full
original meaning: refusal to wait, undergo, suffer.
—Eugen Rosenstock-Huessy, *The Christian Future* (1946)

I drive in a rush to the train station, exercising my will, foot on the accelerator, drumming my fingers on the steering wheel as I am irritatingly compelled to pause at a red light. Again, pressing forward, and into the parking lot. A rapid walk up the stairs into the station and once more an enforced pause, waiting for the train to arrive. Finally it's here, five minutes late. I march into the railroad car, stow my bag, sit down, and suddenly, my will is nullified. The train rolls forward, but I have no accelerator pedal, no way of rushing. The engine will keep its pace, indifferent to me. I sit patiently, allowing myself to be carried forward, with no active power in the matter.

It was an abrupt transition from agent to patient, from exercising will to enduring the, dare I say, luxury of passivity. I am not in control. To the train engineer I avow, "your will be done," and hope for the best. I can only wait for arrival. My thoughts are free to wander as they cannot wander when I am relying on my own will. The luxury is in being wheeled, rolling along, like an infant in a carriage.

The snow fell, making travel nearly impossible. Motorists were stranded, flights cancelled, trains delayed. Millions of individual wills were frustrated, the plans of mice and men *gang aft agley*, mostly voided altogether. Of course, life itself went on. There was no more dying than usual in the great cycle of nature, but life was more of the passive than the active variety. Rather than moving ahead, we were stalled, unable to continue on our chosen paths. One might say, using old-fashioned terminology, it was because of this great act of God or act of nature. To whatever we attribute it, we suffered rather than acted.

"Suffer" has two meanings at least, and one of them is almost totally lost in common speech. We are familiar today primarily with "to suffer" meaning to endure pain. Oh! how he suffered from that toothache. But the original meaning does not imply pain necessarily. It implies only passivity, i.e., what happens *to* us as opposed to what happens *because of* us. In the King James Bible "suffer not the presence of fools gladly" suggests not pain exactly but a kind of experience of which we are meant to exact control: Don't let fools impose on your valuable time. Suffering as undergoing.

"Suffer", "passion", "patience" all meant that which was the inverse from the act of willing. Patience, a form of waiting, is the antonym of agency. The patient undergoes; the agent acts. The passion of Jesus was the inverse of the actions of Jesus. If we set a goal, are intent on exercising our will to achieve it, and our effort is blocked, we are reduced to waiting, maybe reconciled, maybe restlessly frustrated. Often nature enforces waiting upon us. We wait for a pregnancy to come to term; nine long inflexible months. It is said that women learn patience from this experience. We sit in a death vigil, waiting for the moment of expiration. Those are the momentous waiting times, when we are most aware of our helplessness in the face of awesome forces that are miraculous and beyond our control. We wait for a bone fracture to heal; we wait for sundown and the night; we wait for a house plant to grow. Waiting for the plane to land after much circling, we are subservient to human design. Waiting for the crops to grow, to God's design. The publicity for Saul Bellow's first novel, *The Dangling Man*, summarizes the plot: the story of a man who puts his life on hold as he waits to get drafted into the army. He is suspended between past and future by the government.

Much that is vitally important to us cannot ever be *willed* into existence. The late Leslie Farber in *The Ways of the Will* has a revealing list of states in which our willing is fruitless:

> I can will knowledge, but not wisdom; going to bed, but not sleeping; eating, but not hunger; meekness, but not humility; scrupulosity, but not virtue; self-assertion or bravado, but not courage; lust, but not love; commiseration, but not sympathy; congratulations, but not admiration; religiosity, but not faith; reading, but not understanding.

We have to wait to love and to be loved. All the popular songs recognize this: "You'll know when it *happens*." At moments of crisis, we can only pray for courage, which in the end we may lack. People may mourn their loss of religious faith; they cannot will it back into existence.

Farber, for many years a practicing psychoanalyst, asked, what happens to a man "who turns for help to his will to achieve those qualities of being that cannot be achieved, or even approached, by means of will?" If not allowed their own time, those powers that can never be willed gradually atrophy. We have all seen caricatures of men (usually men), the CEO in his private jet let's say, who never succumb to passivity, except perhaps in the barber's chair, and turn into monsters.

The fictional couturier Reynolds Woodcock, portrayed by Daniel Day-Lewis in the superb film *The Phantom Thread,* is a special example. He is a domineering creative genius who has nearly lost his humanity because of his obsessive nature, rescued by a woman who brings to the surface his underlying neediness for nurturing and passivity. Farber argued that an over-reliance on willing was a major source of neurosis in our time. In fact it has consequences beyond just psychological damage.

I am guessing that in the course work towards an MBA degree, there is not much emphasis on learning to wait, as a true state of being not merely a clever strategy. Psychologists speak of an action bias, the tendency toward action over inaction, the urge in a crisis "to do something." You plant a seed; then what are you supposed to do? Not much more than keeping it watered and weeded.

William James referred to a now forgotten book by one Annie Payson Call, *Power Through Repose*, which espoused, he said with approval, the gospel of relaxation. This is not the same as will-lessness, as in some Buddhist practices that cultivate equanimity to an extreme. The "ecstasy of indifference," G. K. Chesterton called it. The world needs our will, when timely, to engage with, improve, and transform unacceptable conditions. We are called to minister to this broken planet in loyalty to those who came before who had the same constructive goals and to those in the future who we hope will look back to us with respect. But along with the act of willing is knowing when not *action* but waiting is the only sane stance. We have done what we can for now. Waiting is not the same as resignation, which implies giving up entirely. They who only stand and wait, as Milton said, also serve. Thy will be done on earth as it is in heaven is a prayer for cooperation.

Modern society lacks a name, Eugen Rosenstock-Huessy wrote, for the "not yet" attitude. "Teachers, priests, and parents sow seeds into those entrusted to their care. How does such a sower live after his seed is in the earth? Is he as unconcerned as the viewing public which just watches?"

> It is almost unbelievable that we should use pale, nondescript expressions for the sower's time of expectation. I can hardly make myself understood to my readers when I maintain that the whole future of our planet depends on making this "not yet" (Latin: *non iam*) time [a necessity] to bear fruit. We need to learn to live in that strange time after our will and skill have already done all they could, in which we await the result."[1]

Waiting is not a mere strategy for achieving an end, as though the future can be ambushed. That would make waiting instrumental, a disguised form of willing. Waiting is not a means to an end. It is a moment, an hour, a year or many years when we are open to receiving that which cannot be willed, that which can be given to us only as an "unbought grace" (in Burke's phrase), a moment of recognition, unsolicited yet often more valuable to the soul than that which we think we urgently need.

New technologies, Rosenstock-Huessy wrote sixty years ago, make possible instant gratification. As a rule, he said, technological innovation has three consequences: it widens the space, shortens the time, and destroys a familiar living group. The goal of these innovations is precisely the elimination of waiting time. But the universally peaceful, communitarian planet we crave in this third millennium of our era is not attainable, he argued, in an environment devoted to the god of speed. It is necessary "to replace the groups destroyed by technology, and to do that we must voluntarily slow down." The future planetary peace will arise from a "voluntary patience, an unexpected and technically unnecessary slowing down." In the strife of politics and nature it is only the living generation that asserts its will. "Every peace, however, will connect several generations in such a way that the will of any one generation will become unimportant. . . . One generation after the other has to be won

1. Rosenstock-Huessy, *Planetary Service*, 89.

over explicitly and induced to conclude peace. . . . Peace can be concluded only step by step." Fundamental, permanent changes require the concurrence of three generations, which takes time to effect.[2]

Peace is not an armistice, a mere cessation of combat. "Three generations have to be pulled and led into a peace before it has come about."

> Peacetime always feeds and fills our consciousness with several lifetimes. . . . That is why peacetime can be produced neither by you alone nor by all of your contemporaries. . . . Every peace which is more than an armistice connects and unifies people who have belonged to different ages.

The dominance of media, of the immediate, has left people famished for this kind of peace, which we experience primarily at holidays and celebrations. Marx complained that the proletariat refused to be radicalized because of their adherence to the "opiate" of inherited religion. The opiate of the moment is media, which may fuel protests but dumbs down a deeper awareness beyond the latest sensation. Technology "uses up our common time," and then, in trouble, what are we to do: run to the online media as consumers and order up a new future? How do we create a new future? Most fundamentally by speaking and listening in a context without time constraints and without prescriptions and planning.

In times of war and contention we single-mindedly strive to win as fast as possible. In times of peace the model is not the soldier, who must act fast, but the craftsman who takes his time. He or she must wait for inspiration. There is a difference, then, between technological time and fruitful time. To fulfill the planetary task of the third millennium, we will need available *both* experiences of time: having no time and having "an eternity at one's disposal." We need both the expediency of the engineer and the random, unplanned timeless openness of the artist who waits for what may be given.

In this "age of acceleration" we have forgotten how to wait. But the god of speed gives way when, against all expectations, we take our time. "After a new step in technology we should always go slower, or the sheer excess speed will leave no time for the next living group to gather itself together." We cannot be forced to love each other. It has to grow. "To beget and to create, . . . we must renounce the whole armory of war," its

2. Rosenstock-Huessy, *Planetary Service*, 101–4.

single-minded determination of the moment. "Love disarms; suffering overpowers. God's passion is the high tide of his creative power."[3] (108).

3. Rosenstock-Huessy, *Planetary Service*, 106–8.

11

Eugen Rosenstock-Huessy Meets Jelly Roll Morton

Prof. Eugen Rosenstock-Huessy meets Jelly Roll Morton? Not exactly, but if we interpose Francis P. Squibb Jr. (1927–2003) between them, the meeting comes close. Squibb attended Dartmouth College, majoring in philosophy, and while at Dartmouth became an admirer of Professor Rosenstock-Huessy. Graduating in 1949, he went on to earn a master's degree in Philosophy at the University of Illinois. That is the start of one narrative of Squibb's life, which we will come back to.

The other narrative is that he was a jazz musician and promoter of that musical form. Following a stint in the U. S. Army from 1950 to 1952, Squibb edited and prepared jazz records for William Russell in Chicago and became known in the area for his musicianship. Then in 1954 a twenty-five-year hiatus began that was more literary than musical. From 1980 to 1985, however, late in life, Squibb returned to his first love: he was appointed Curator of Printed Music at the William Ransom Hogan Archives of New Orleans Jazz at Tulane University. The obituaries for Squibb in 2003 remember him mostly for his work on the history of jazz, mentioning among other things that he wrote liner notes for important jazz recordings, such as Jimmy Witherspoon's *Evenin' Blues*.

In the same vein, the eighteen boxes of Squibb's papers held by the University of Chicago Library are valued because of his work in jazz history. According to the library cataloguing record, the Squibb collection consists of discographies, printed and handwritten music, correspondence, interviews, songbooks, liner notes, photographs of black musicians, and so forth. In addition to letters to Squibb from other musicians, the collection includes valuable photocopies of correspondence and music by jazz greats. Prominent in the collection are items relating to Scott Joplin and Ferdinand "Jelly Roll" Morton, d. 1941.

Now what about Squibb's day job? From 1954 to 1964, with his Master's degree in philosophy, he was managing editor of the *American Peoples Encyclopedia* (APE), a reference work published by the Spencer Press in Chicago and first copyrighted in 1948. Various revised editions followed for which it is hard to find precise documentation, but by 1957 the *American Peoples Encyclopedia* was published in twenty volumes. At some point before the 1962 edition appeared, the Grolier Company, publisher of U. S. family favorites like *Encyclopedia Americana* and the *Book of Knowledge*, acquired the *American Peoples Encyclopedia* and a comprehensive revision of the set was undertaken.

It was then as editor that Squibb hearkened back to his old learned professor, commissioning Rosenstock-Huessy to write more than seventy entries for the 1962 edition of the encyclopedia. The titles of these entries are listed by Lise van der Molen in his indispensable *Guide to the Works of Eugen Rosenstock-Huessy*, and the texts of the entries are duly reproduced in the website www.erhfund.org, copied from the earlier microfilm. Van der Molen had to do a considerable amount of digging to determine which entries were by Rosenstock-Huessy, since not all of them are signed, and the surviving correspondence between Squibb and his revered professor is slim. Hence, the list published in the *Guide to the Works* cannot be considered complete. Dr. Van der Molen has in hand the facts needed for a definitive list, which may one day be available. A few of the entries reproduced initially in the microfilm collection of works by Rosenstock-Huessy and now incorporated in the ERH Fund website, such as the essay on the "University," are not listed at all by Van der Molen, although from the content there can be no doubt of the authorship.

It would be tedious to list here all of the topics Squibb and Rosenstock-Huessy settled on, but the choices are highly revealing of Rosenstock-Huessy's deepest concerns, whether he viewed the subject positively or negatively: "Pierre Abelard," "René Descartes," "Dialogue," "Ralph Waldo Emerson," "Michael Faraday," "Name," "John Henry Cardinal Newman," "Friedrich Nietzsche," "Paracelsus," "Revolution," "Claude

Henri de Saint-Simon," "Giovanni Battista Vico," "Walt Whitman," to cite a few. Some of the entries are about relatively obscure figures, leading one to surmise that no one above Squibb was paying much attention to what properly belonged in an "American Peoples" encyclopedia: "Karl Sudhoff," "Johannes Vahlen," "Hans Vaihinger," "Valentinus," "Michael George Francis Ventris," "Karl Adolph Vernet." These entries were all necessary in Rosenstock-Huessy's view, however, because they reinforced arguments he made in other entries. The story of Paracelsus cannot be told without mentioning Sudhoff, for example. In other words, many of the entries by Rosenstock-Huessy are interconnected and support one another by cross referencing.

There are also a few surprise entries by Rosenstock-Huessy: "Vampire," "Zen," and "Ludwig Wittgenstein," for example. The Rosenstock-Huessy Archive at Dartmouth even has a few manuscripts of entries intended for the encyclopedia that for one reason or another never made it into print. But, perhaps understandably, for all their variety there is no evidence that Squibb asked Rosenstock-Huessy to write on jazz or blues.

In these large format encyclopedia volumes most of the entries, whatever their length, occupy just one or two pages. Van der Molen sometimes listed Squibb as the "co-author" of an entry, which he confesses was an arbitrary and perhaps unfounded assumption. It is true that good editors are sometimes virtual co-authors, but these essays, although highly compressed and written in unadorned, straightforward prose, have Rosenstock-Huessy stamped all over them, and Squibb's contribution, if any, must have been minor and confined to mechanics. The requirement of merciless concision in composition of this sort forced Rosenstock-Huessy to single out quickly what he judged was the enduring significance of a life or what he deemed the essence of a topic, and predictably his judgments were often unconventional.

It is a bit surprising that Rosenstock-Huessy, the historian, was not asked by Squibb to summarize and comment on at least a few major events in European history. The entries for which he was commissioned are almost all biographical or philosophical. It is likely that some other editor of the encyclopedia, not Squibb, was responsible for entries on history.

Professor Rosenstock-Huessy accepted this work not because he was struck by its enduring importance but because, like many retired academicians in those days, his income was insufficient, and Squibb was offering, at a few hundred dollars an essay, a respectable way to increase it, if only temporarily. Whatever the motivation, we have to be grateful to Squibb for eliciting this revealing writing by the great man. Indeed, if all of Rosenstock-Huessy's *American Peoples Encyclopedia* entries were to be collected into a little book, it would be a valuable, highly readable, trenchant sampling, in not more than 250 pages, of the author's stance on a range of subjects. Such a work is all the more needed because, according to Raymond Huessy, who owns two sets of the APE, in editions after 1962 some of the more controversial of the entries by Rosenstock-Huessy were replaced with "standard information," in Ray's words.

There is one more chapter regarding Francis Squibb and Eugen Rosenstock-Huessy. In 1965 Squibb left the encyclopedia and moved from Chicago to Tuscaloosa, to be the editor-in-chief of the University of Alabama Press, where he remained for the next fifteen years. It can be deduced from that fact that the publication by Alabama in 1969 of *Judaism Despite Christianity: The "Letters on Christianity and Judaism" between Eugen Rosenstock-Huessy and Franz Rosenzweig*, edited by Rosenstock-Huessy, was no fluke. In fact, it seems there was even talk in the 1960s of Alabama publishing the complete works, but the author, eighty years old in 1968, no longer had the stamina to oversee thousands of pages of translations and the like. The chance of a lifetime had thus come too late. Rosenstock-Huessy often mused about the significance of timing in life, quoting Shakespeare's "ripeness is all." "When," he said, is always the greatest of questions. How many worthy endeavors fail because they are simply too early, and how many opportunities are fatefully lost because the moment has passed. He called for a science of timing, that is, a more developed recognition of the "too early" and the "too late" as a recurrent element in the biographical study of success or failure.

During their many years of collaboration, Rosenstock-Huessy and Squibb may have talked about jazz. Did Rosenstock-Huessy appreciate Jelly Roll Morton? Alas, we know nothing about that. He was certainly devoted to music and referred to it in many different contexts. I once heard him say that his ideal retirement would be to live in Milan and regularly attend the opera at La Scala. Some of his favorite metaphors were drawn from music. He told his students that each should aspire to be a note in the great symphony that is the history of humankind—an elevating but far from easy demand.

The power of music exemplifies the nature of authentic listening for Rosenstock-Huessy. Between the listener and the music there are no barriers. In a lecture to Barnard College girls in 1962, he said: "In music, the individual person is of no importance. And that's a condition of her listening to the music. It's the exclusion of the personal which makes music possible. . . . God created one universe permeated by sound and swallowing up your little resistance." Music has nothing to do with the brain. "It has to fight the preconceptions of your brain." In general, "to listen means to break down the barriers of the visible world. And you cannot listen to God, or to religion, or to poetry, or to wisdom, or to a command given by a commander in the field, if you cannot for one moment deny that there is a wall between the speaker and the listener. For this one moment, the man who makes the sound, . . . and the man who intercepts it must be united." Thus, "in any speech recurs the musical experience that the listener and the speaker form one body politic . . . ." "God has given us this faculty of melting down—in humility, in obedience, in enthusiasm, in conviction—the walls of our being." The thought is as applicable to Jelly Roll Morton as to Janacek.[1]

In *Out of Revolution* Rosenstock-Huessy addressed the mystery of how it was that Bach, Mozart, and Beethoven all arose in German-speaking culture. Why this particular supreme concentration of genius? One answer is that the Lutheran Reformation, including Luther's own writing of scores of hymns, was among other things a reaction against the visual focus of Roman Catholicism. Sermons and hymns were the Lutheran way, or let's just say, listening in church as opposed to looking. That insight holds even though Mozart was a Roman Catholic because of the overwhelming influence of Bach. Rosenstock-Huessy warned regularly against the perils in modernity of a culture so heavily centered on the visual, on what fascinates the eye as opposed to the more profound response we have from that we learn through the ear. Walter J. Ong's wonderful Terry lectures at Yale, published in 1967 as *The Presence of the Word*, took as its epigraph a quotation from Rosenstock-Huessy's *Soziologie*: "Experiences of the first order, of the first rank, are not realized through the eye." Similarly, as an epigraph to his poem "I Am Not a Camera," W. H. Auden quoted from Rosenstock-Huessy: "Photographable life is always either trivial or already sterilised."

Old encyclopedias, like old textbooks, are an extremely perishable genre of printed matter. Regularly revised to keep up with the latest information, the earlier versions are simply trashed as being superseded. Almost no libraries collect such works and because their monetary value is nil they do not circulate in the used book market. There are a

1. For the Barnard lecture, see chapter 1, above.

few exceptions, like the ninth edition of the *Encyclopedia Britannica*, published in the late nineteenth century, which will always be valued because of the brilliant scholarship of some of the longer contributions. The *American Peoples Encyclopedia* can expect no comparable fate. It is doomed to oblivion.

Francis Squibb's devotion to Rosenstock-Huessy is notable but not uncommon among the professor's students. On the occasion of Rosenstock-Huessy's 70th birthday in 1958, Squibb sent to his mentor a letter so personal and private one hesitates to bring it to light, but I think it is relevant to an understanding of Rosenstock-Huessy as well as Squibb. The letter, undated, was probably written just after Sunday, September 21, 1958. A group of Rosenstock-Huessy's former students organized a three-day birthday celebration for their professor that weekend at the farm in Tunbridge, Vermont, of Bob and Anne O'Brien. Squibb seems to be alluding to that event in the letter. Rosenstock-Huessy lectured on each of the three days.

Brackets indicate my insertions. The letter is handwritten on both sides of a single sheet.

> Dear Eugen, on your 70th
>
> There is so much that I want to say, and fortunately so little space: a few words may be better. I do not feel you are retired, since in the many years since I was privileged to hear you, you have continued to live in my memory—that part of my memory that has led me into the best of which I have been capable. If I am ever able to say or do—in any way, to help some other person as you, perhaps without realizing it, have helped me: only then will I feel that I will have at least in part discharged my debt —my obligation. You are the most honest person I've ever met, heard, or read. I am profoundly grateful that I have known you, a little; it saddens me that I cannot be more, the better to do you honor—but I try to be better, & I try to understand, [—] too many words & not the right ones: I will never forget you, & you will be part of whatever I may become. I hope this may be something worthy. (over) As my wife Mary could tell you, I have instantly "invoked" you at moments of importance—I am proud that in her brief glimpses of you this weekend she has [*illeg.*, come?] to share my admiration and devotion. As I have said to you before, you are (for me) DARTMOUTH—I cannot imagine the place without you. I cannot imagine myself without having known your words, & struggled (I still struggle) to understand

& to apply them. Although I was not privileged to share as much with you as many students, I regard you as my best friend— & I feel that this will always be so. Perhaps all the above can be disregarded: it boils down to the fact that you made me aware of life & its potential as no one else, & for this I owe you my life itself! Your devoted student & friend,

Francis Squibb

[What follows is a single entry by Rosenstock-Huessy from the 1962 *American Peoples Encyclopedia*. This piece was not signed, for a reason that becomes evident in the text. I have introduced a couple of paragraph indentations not in the original.]

EXISTENTIALISM, a poorly defined doctrine in philosophy. It is popularly understood to be a school of philosophy that began with the Danish philosopher Sören Kierkegaard's revolt against systematic philosophy as exemplified for him in the philosophy of Hegel; thought of in this way, existentialism is supposed to have reached its greatest development in Germany and France after World War I, with Karl Jaspers, Martin Heidegger, and Jean-Paul Sartre among the major figures. Actually, however, existentialism is less a school than it is a tendency, or a manner of approaching philosophical problems, that has existed at least from the time of Socrates, and probably from an even earlier time.

Thinkers, poets, and others not immediately identified with the intellectualized existentialism that gained popularity after World War II under the aegis of Jean-Paul Sartre are usually [i. e., often?] described as existential. Sartre himself has objected to being called an existentialist, since this word has been loosely applied to a wide variety of thinkers, many of whom completely disagree with each other on most issues.

At least four different approaches may be discerned in twentieth-century existentialism, with a considerable degree of interlocking among them. The most commonly noted division exists between the Christian existentialists and the atheistic existentialists. But both "Christian" and "atheistic" are misleading in this context: a leading Christian existentialist like Gabriel Marcel, for example, probably would feel a closer affinity to the atheistic existentialist Jean-Paul Sartre than to what he might call "conventionalized Christianity"; Sartre probably would feel a closer identification with Marcel than, for example, with the logical positivists who share his tendency to aggressive atheistic protest. Marcel, a Christian, probably would feel closer to Martin Buber, an existential Jewish theologian than to Jacques Maritain, a leading representative of Neo-Thomism.

Neo-Thomism is the third existentialist group and involves an explication of what the Neo-Thomists consider the existential aspects of the thought of St. Thomas Aquinas; the other important Neo-Thomist is Etienne Gilson, the noted medievalist. Both Buber and Marcel are important exponents of the "philosophy of dialogue" (sometimes called the higher grammar and philosophy of meeting), a fourth major tendency in twentieth-century existential thought. The other major figures in this school are the Jewish philosopher and theologian Franz Rosenzweig and the Christian philosopher of history Eugen Rosenstock-Huessy, who of the four was the most germinal since he was the first to explore this line of thought (in the essay "Grammar of the Soul," 1916, in *Angewandte Seelenkunde*, 1924) and was the most penetrating and versatile in applying it to his life and work (see Dialogue). With the exception of the Neo-Thomists, the philosophers of dialogue most successfully avoided the taint of cultism that characterized much of the existentialist movement after World War I, particularly in France after 1945.

Life as the Existentialists See It

Despite the immense areas of disagreement among existentialists, it is possible to discern certain themes which, however variously expressed, seem common to them all. All agree on the contingency of human life. Man shares life, but "life is that process which produces corpses" (as defined by the German physiologist Rudolph Ehrenberg) and "we think because we are going to die" (Rosenstock-Huessy). Death looms large: it is one of the "existential moments" (in Kierkegaard's phrase) that cannot be avoided or shared. Sartre is at some pains to stress the fact that no one can die for anyone else. Because of this, say the existentialists, it is folly for the philosopher or the artist to imagine that his system of thought or feeling is in any real sense objective. Objectivity is possible only for God; since the atheistic existentialists deny the existence of God, or even the possibility of His existing, there is for them no such thing as objective truth; for the Christian existentialists it is deemed presumptuous for any man to claim possession of objective truth. For Kierkegaard, Hegel was wrong in thinking that he was not himself a character in his massive system. René Descartes, the great "scientific rationalist," began his system with the single assumption, "*cogito ergo sum*" (I think, therefore I am). The "I"—Descartes himself or any other thinker—is presumed to be a constant: Descartes was ashamed of his pre-rational life as a child and he imagined that having reached rational maturity he could speak of himself as "I" with perfect objectivity. (See Descartes, René).

Not so, say the existentialists. Both Hegel and Descartes delude themselves into thinking that essence (the abstract it-ness of a thing, person, or idea) precedes existence (the concrete thou-ness of a thing, person, or idea). For the existentialist, existence precedes essence, which means that a person lives (is involved in contingent change, and can himself change so as to be different than before) before he dies (is no longer able to change or to be changed, and is therefore knowable for what he is, or was). Until a person dies, he can always change his essence; hence his essence (his Being) cannot be known until after his death. Kierkegaard's title, *Stages on Life's Way* (1845), expresses the existentialist's awareness that the "I" of the thinker is not the same throughout his life: that the "I" changes as the thinker moves through the stages toward his own death, the awareness of which becomes the beginning of his thought. The interpretation of the Crucifixion is, in this light, important to the Christian existentialists. Throughout His life, Jesus never would admit He was the Christ; only on the cross would He admit that He was God; also, the "death" of Christ on the cross becomes the true beginning for any Christian—these are but two phases of the significance existentialists have seen in this important event in human and divine history.

Realizing that he will die and that at that moment he will cease to be a mystery and will become knowable (although perhaps with difficulty), the existentialist feels that everything he does, thinks, or says is of the utmost importance because by his actions, thoughts, and words he is creating in life what he will have become in death. The existentialists also believe that however they may strive, they will, in death, fail to "measure up"—either to God's wish, or to their own self-conception. Only God's grace could help, and this is denied by the atheists. Sartre's reaction to all this is nausea (the title of his first novel). Dread and anguish are felt by others. The existentialist maintains that the vices, the "seven deadly sins," the willful avoidance of life through alcohol and narcotics, and the like, are literally ways to avoid facing one's own death and its implications—for the existentialists believe that their doctrine consists of conceptions so fundamental as to be known intuitively by everyone.

What can man do in such dreary circumstances? It would be suicide to give up simply because the cause is hopeless. He must act. He must decide. He must commit himself. For the grammarians he must "speak himself into existence"—must enter into a dialogue, a meeting, with others of faith and so break "the chains of nothingness" (loneliness and estrangement). The slogan "*Cogito ergo sum*," which ignores time and contingency, is replaced (by Rosenstock-Huessy and others) with the contingent, time-conscious "*Respondeo ne moriar*" (I respond lest I die).

Influence of Existentialism

For the existentialists themselves existential thinking is considered the redemption of philosophy. Apart from the lunatic aspects of the Sartrist cult in France after World War II the movement had considerable influence, although less in the United States and Great Britain than in Europe. If the influence of such existential non-existentialists as Friedrich Nietzsche, Franz Kafka, Rainer Rilke, Albert Camus, Miguel de Unamuno, André Malraux, Reinhold Niehbuhr, and many others were considered, the ultimate impact of the tendency might be considerably greater than the detractors of existentialism were at mid-twentieth century willing to admit. Existentialism also influenced formal philosophy, particularly metaphysics and ethics. Metaphysicians found refreshing the existentialist stress on "nothingness" as distinct from "being," and in existentialism's philosophy and theology of crisis and decision ethical relativism was formidably challenged.

[At the end of this entry, as in all of the encyclopedia entries, there is a bibliography or list of references. About twenty titles are cited, which I am not reprinting here but which should be considered an integral part of the entry, even though we will never know to what extent the list represents actual preferences of Rosenstock-Huessy's or are merely standard sources.]

12

Man, the World, and God

ROSENSTOCK-HUESSY AND HIS FRIEND Franz Rosenzweig, the great Jewish thinker, together asserted the most fundamental axiom of all: God, man, and the world are all real and existent, whether we like it or not or know it or not. Each is to some degree autonomous, and most of the trouble in the world begins when philosophers, or theologians, or scientists, try to reduce any of these three separate powers into only one or two.

All that we know and experience, or can claim to experience, is exhaustively divisible into just three elements: man; the world around us (including both human creations and nature); and God. No one of them is totally reducible into the other. The atheist attempts to reduce God to nature; the humanist reduces God to man. But God is He or She who speaks to us in a time of crisis and is an irreducible reference beyond man. Man, too, is not reducible to nature. Man is not like any other animal. Exclusively, with reference to the world and nature around him, he lives in time, conscious of his ancestry, the time before us, and conscious of his mortality, his limited future physical existence. He consciously speaks to the future, whether in prophetic books or lessons told to a grandchild, and responds to words spoken 2,000 years before he was born. We are part of nature but also eternally separable from it.

MAN

The first is the easiest to grasp. Each living person feels his (or her) individuality, his separateness or apartness from the things around him. We are aware of our personal consciousness, and from infancy are aware that we are personified by an individual name bestowed upon us by those who came before. Through the process of, first, listening and then speaking, we also acknowledge the consciousness of the other human beings that we encounter. The experience of meeting another person is clearly not the same as greeting any other element in the world, even creatures as intelligent as dogs, let alone a flower or a rock or a telephone pole. Beyond meeting, loving another person to the degree that we put their welfare ahead of our own is quintessentially human.

Human beings are "distinguished by a proper name," Rosenstock-Huessy writes, "unlike the classifiable things of the outside world: trees, tables, stones, or houses." Because a man or woman can be addressed or spoken to, they can answer yes or no, assent or dissent, and hence reveal the power to resist, which is the source of our confidence in being free. In any ordinary sense, leaving aside the poetic, nature does not speak and does not listen. For Rosenstock-Huessy *speech* is far different from mere communication. An animal may communicate but it cannot make a promise, a commitment to an action in the distant future. Speechlessness is the very definition of nature. As distinguished from ourselves, we interpret nature, indeed the world as a whole, as being determined at some level, bound by material causality. The world is thus objectified and part of a causal chain; we, on the other hand, are subjects, and we experience ourselves as responsible agents. That part of man which science reduces to predictability—a high body temperature can kill; failure to nurture an infant with skin-to-skin contact can destroy its humanity; all statistical data; all psychological research, especially behavioral studies—capture only a fragment of the whole man or woman.

Despite the explanations of evolutionary theory— explanations that for investigatory purposes *have no choice* but to begin by defining man as simply part of nature—we know as persons that we remain an irreducible mystery. Evolutionary theory provides an intriguing path of inquiry, which keeps thousands of dedicated scientists busy "explaining"— in accordance with the rules of scientific procedure—our strange presence, but these findings do not begin to satisfy a reflective mind regarding the origins and destiny and human consciousness. Because it is intellectually ungraspable, to describe humans as formed over tens of millions of years, or to say each of us is made up of billions of atoms, these so-called objective "facts" are equivalent to irrelevant fantasy; they are beyond imagination. They are not in the least defining of a living person, and certainly not capable of being the basis of any practical action in the world.

On the one hand, it is true that no one can doubt man is part of nature. We eat and breathe and reproduce like other mammals; we are born and die after a relatively short period of life. Ashes to ashes, dust to dust. Indeed, it is fine, even wholesome, to picture ourselves as one with the material cosmos upon which we are dependent and to feel a semblance of kinship with all the other creatures of the earth, from elephants to ants. On the other hand, only a dunderhead would not acknowledge in himself aspirations, relations, dreams, including our capacity to love, that transcend mundane time and space, and that make our apartness unique in the universe.

It can be stated dogmatically that man is not entirely reducible to nature or to the world, and never will be, although within the extremely narrow program of science and its glorious faith in its mission it is essential that man be seen in that simplistic way as the basis for investigation. A scientist following his established method has no choice but to dismiss as extraneous that which is neither material nor subject to quantification, that which is outside of the standard investigatory program. The *sciences* of man, whether biology or psychology, to be legitimate must as a matter of principle and strict practice assume or posit that the scientific method is adequate to fully comprehend man, that is, to make him altogether simply part of nature. Science is, however, only one way of viewing and examining the world, out of several other possible ways, albeit a wonderfully productive (and often beneficial) way.

Here are a few words from a lecture series by Rosenstock-Huessy dating from a short book written in 1935, *The Multiformity of Man*:

> Man has succeeded in mechanizing his world. He has organized nature. For its very effectiveness, his deed raises the issue of man's own position in nature with new acuteness. Man himself becomes a greater mystery than ever before. The question arises quite afresh how far man belongs to the natural world and how far, therefore, he can become organized in a social world.

THE WORLD (INCLUDING NATURE)

If man knows himself as different from flora and fauna and atoms and cells, he also does not doubt the reality of and influence of the external world, by which we must include not only nature but also the history and society that envelop us. I, as an individual, experience not only rain and shine, hurricanes, earthquakes, ocean waves, and snake bites, that subject me to their consequences, I also experience political upheavals, wars, the poles of city and farm, music and the arts, and all the happenings that the morning news floods us with every day from every place on the globe. As with nature, so with history and society. We are part of it, but we do not individually cause it. This situation may be encapsulated in the statement that in relation to the world, we are both subjects and objects, we act and are acted upon, we see and are seen. It is an old theological doctrine that man was put on earth to be conscious of the Creation, such that God could see in the awareness of the human mind His handiwork reflected back to Him. The natural world would be beautiful without man, but the concept is vain and empty. Without man, there would be no beauty and no history, only the unperceived unending cycles of nature, with no imagined goal.

Man, it may be said is super-natural. Understanding him requires not just science but the humanities, Shakespeare and Cervantes, Beethoven and Bach, Matisse and Michelangelo, to mention just a few heroes out of thousands to whom we have to turn for wisdom and understanding that is beyond quantification or measurement.

GOD

The above describes preliminarily the first two elements, man and the world, as the fundamental components of existence. Surely this is complete without gods and without the autocrat in heaven with a white beard who commands the waves and determines our fate. For Rosenstock-Huessy, however, God is a compelling reality who cannot be looked for in space, that is, in a place, but only in time. Nor is He in time a continuous presence, at least not for most people. We are aware of Him (or Her, if one wishes) only at rare critical junctures, and we call out to God especially at moments of weakness and suffering. We hear God sometimes as a hidden or masked internal voice that inspires us to speak out and to listen, across millennia, sometimes upholding a standard of righteousness we call conscience. We also hear God in the words of others spoken at the right time that move us to action. Rosenstock-Huessy defined God as "the power that makes us speak," referring to a level of utterance beyond mere functional communication and mere chatter, that is, makes us speak out. Speech at the level Rosenstock-Huessy had in mind is a form of action, when we are called upon to sacrifice, to take a stand, to serve, to express love, to condemn. At the highest level, think of a judge in a courtroom pronouncing a person "guilty," or the bride in the marriage ceremony uttering, "I do." Those are spoken words with great practical consequence, and such speech in different contexts defines our existence.[1]

The pathway to God is through the gods, the deities and powers that we unthinkingly worship daily, the powers that govern our lives and to which we are willingly obedient—be it the quest for money and love, or our marching off to war again and again, or our subservience to technology, or our succumbing to lust, the worship of celebrity, devotion to family, friendship, beauty, speed, fortune. Academics worship learning and scholarship. The Greeks and Romans personified most of these powers and others as gods. Only by first recognizing our own inveterate polytheism, which exposes our persistent capacity for worship and our sense of dependency, can we take the next step of freeing ourselves, when it counts, from bondage to lesser divinities. We supplicate the supreme power that at crucial moments can help us to transcend the lesser deities and liberate us from limited attachments. Acceptance of our polytheism is the necessary pathway to monotheism for Rosenstock-Huessy.

> None of the multiple deities who demand our thanks, thought, and service can enslave all the elements of our being. There may be a time when we must worship them. Yet when we analyze our whole life between birth and death, we cannot assign the whole life of any human being to a single one of these many deities and powers. No one of them is supreme. Some enter the scene rather late. Science is too severe a god for children. Venus abdicates

1. Bade, "Living Theory": "With his discussion of how language establishes relationships, using as a primary example those two little words 'I do,' Rosenstock-Huessy was not simply making a comment on speech act theory, an example of a performative verb, he was saying that language brings you and another person into a relationship that in the case of 'I do' alters not just one's own life but that of another; it establishes not just one relationship but multiple relationships backwards through the past as well as forward into the future with kinship ties, and that by establishing such relationships it reveals its political basis. 'I do' has the power to bring together people of different (and perhaps antagonistic) genders, families, classes, castes, nations, races, and religions."

her authority over old age. Socialism annoys the man of sixty, and greed is hardly conceivable to a young person. The gods pass. When the individual realizes their passing, their unceasing change, he is converted to God—the living God who invites us to obey the *unum necessarium*, the one thing necessary and timely at every moment. This man discovers his complete liberty, the unbelievable freedom of the children of God, who are independent of all specific codes and traditional creeds, because the God of our future and our beginning is superior to the gods he put around us in the short periods of our conscious efforts."[2]

In *Revolution, Redemption, and Revolution*, a book largely focused on Rosenstock-Huessy, Wayne Cristaudo writes: "Our orientation through life is bound up with the powers we are ruled by or —what is essentially the same thing—the powers we serve. . . . All people seek orientation throughout their lives and are thus responsive to powers greater than themselves. Those powers we serve are our divinities. . . . To know someone's faith, we need merely to observe what and whom they serve. . . . [Faith is] an existential condition and . . . not something with which philosophy can dispense."[3]

Rosenstock-Huessy had contempt for any objectification of God, as in jejeune questions of whether or not He exists, as though God were a unicorn. He would say to his students who were caught up in such debates, "God doesn't care whether you think He exists or not." God is part of the real world of broad adult *experience* across the globe, not an abstraction in metaphysical speculation. Theology in Rosenstock-Huessy's view was a superseded science, although it has a glorious and instructive past. Surrounded in uncomfortable mystery because He cannot be fitted into the narrow path of the Enlightenment program of science, which does not tolerate mystery, we have to accept that God just *is*. He doesn't have to be talked *about*. His relation to us is often much too private. He is revealed in time, often as the basis of hope for the future, and in accountable speech. When we are seduced by the devil, He is an invaluable resource.

Outside of the objectifying program of science we are left with the traditional language of prayer, petition, praise, which is a fundamental and ineradicable part of the speech repertoire of all humankind that takes God for granted and is at the center of "religions." These forms of speech, which at times of terrible crisis even the most committed atheist will fall

2. Rosenstock-Huessy, *Out of Revolution*, 723–27.

3. Cristaudo, *Religion, Redemption, and Revolution*, xi-xii.

back upon, are simply part of our humanity and as embedded in human experience as the five senses. Some people may feel that we inexplicably "see" God in the beauty and wonder of nature, whereas others see only chemistry, physics, and biology. The latter is in no sense more "true." Equally commonly, people will hear the divine in transcendent and transporting music, the magic of which cannot be analyzed away. Freud dismissed such phenomena by characterizing them as "oceanic" experiences, which is nothing but an apt metaphor, sparing us from the embarrassment of appearing to be superstitious in a secular, scientific age.

In Rosenstock-Huessy's view it is silly to try to strip away religion from the actuality of the world. It is a given in all human societies and will not someday somehow be vaporized by "reason." To be "opposed" to religion, as we see advocated in some recent books, is like being opposed to the seasons of the year. One may wish, politically, to limit religion's power to affect public policy, let's say, or to determine social norms, but religion is not going to go away as a result of human "progress." It might even be said that it is so pervasive throughout the planet and always has been that no one can truly stand outside of it and try to banish it by fiat. Atheism is also a form of religious belief. Religion is part of human existence. That does not mean that theocracy cannot rightly be left far behind. For Rosenstock-Huessy religion is a historical reality, just as God is a historical reality, leaving aside supposed theological proofs of God's existence, which Rosenstock-Huessy believed were beside the point. Cristaudo is excellent on these questions. "Atheism's claim that we are godless . . . arises from the fact that atheism is a philosophical doctrine. The gods, though, are not philosophical constructions; they are no more born out of the philosophical mind than babies are."[4]

In our sporadic, unpredictable relations with God, He is not an object and we are not an object. God is always a person with whom we are in dialogue, that is, a subject who addresses us with imperatives. "Norman, where art thou?" "I am here, Lord." "Go forth and save the world." We serve God both by bringing about a new and better future and by conserving what is precious from the past. In these modes, as actors in time, we are neither subjects nor objects, but *trajects*, speaking for the past, and *prejects*, speaking for the future, to adopt Rosenstock-Huessy's coinages.

I personally do not consider myself a "believer" in any conventional sense. However, I have often thought that if there is no God, even

4. Cristaudo, *Religion, Redemption, and Revolution*, 131.

a symbolic god, suicide is the only honorable choice. The history of humankind over thousands of years and right up to yesterday is marked by unspeakable horrors, the terrible pain and suffering of millions over the centuries, which cries out to heaven. If this is what has to be, if unrelieved injustice and unbearable pain is the norm, how can one go on? Implicitly, to go on living we need a glimmer of hope, which is based on the progress we can see, and above all, on faith, which is the progress we cannot see and which depends upon trust in the unknown God, who can be addressed and addresses us. "When men fall silent the stones will cry out, for God must be present," Rosenstock-Huessy said.

In this context I think of an untitled poem by Adam Kirsch from 2005 where, as a last resort for justice, we have at least the "mute Accuser." If God is the power that makes us speak, we thereby have transferred to us the responsibility of overcoming His muteness and speaking out.

> Once the first infant's taken by the heel
> And swung by laughing soldiers so his brain
> Bursts like a fruit against the ghetto wall,
> The name of the Father is not named again;
> Then we demand the Judge, who may not save
> But metes out the reward and punishment.
> We stop petitioning when we observe
> The peaceful old age of the commandant,
> Teaching us that we must be satisfied
> With a Recorder who lets nothing slip—
> Till human bones that human teeth have chewed
> Or throat-slit mummies in a frozen Alp
> Resurface to remind us of the million
> Victims that decompose for each preserved,
> And that the mute Accuser is the one
> God we might still believe in or deserve.[5]

In his interpretation of the most famous section of Michelangelo's Sistine Chapel ceiling Rosenstock-Huessy explicitly argued that God is waiting for humanity to continue His work:

> Michelangelo shows God creating Adam, and keeping in the folds of his immense robe a score of angels or spirits. Thus at the beginning of the world all the divine powers were on God's side; man was stark naked. We might conceive of a pendant to this picture; the end of creation, in which all the spirits that had

5. Kirsch's poem was published in *The New Criterion*, Nov. 2005.

> accompanied the Creator should have left him and descended to man, helping, strengthening, enlarging his being into the divine. In this picture God would be alone, while Adam would have all the Elohim around him as his companions.[6]

The novelist Julian Barnes in *Levels of Life*, observed: "When we killed—or exiled—God, we also killed ourselves. . . . We were right to kill Him, of course, this longstanding imaginary friend of ours. . . . But we sawed off the branch we were sitting on. And the view from there, from that height—even it was only an illusion of a view— wasn't so bad." Without God we have no ultimate point of reference. We used to be able to say, we are all God's children; we are all equal in His sight; we are all part of His creation. Now what do we say: "We are all evolved equally?"

The errors of dozens of philosophies and world views may be found in the simple fact that one or the other element of this triad—man, the world, and God—has been ignored or conflated. Most commonly these days, both autonomous man and God have dropped from view, and we are left only with nature, in the form of physics, biology, and evolutionary science. A man or God independent of nature would be super-natural and that is a prohibited status. A scientist *in his work* has no need of the God hypothesis and no need of an entity somehow separate from nature in the form of man. Consider, however, this scientist is not beholden twenty-four hours a day for fifty or sixty years only to the rules of the scientific method. Those are work rules. He was once a child in a family knitted together by love; he may be now a father and husband, conscientiously devoted to the welfare of his wife and children beyond even his own personal well-being. Like no mere animal, he loves and sacrifices and prays, calls his octogenarian mother every week, and sometimes draws reassurance from the thought that his father, long deceased, would be proud of him. It was not science that *motivated* him to become a scientist and that sustains him daily; it was a sentiment, like love. When he is in his lab or his office, he feels the deepest loyalty to the mission of his discipline, his science, the community that constitutes his profession, to its integrity and to his fellow toilers in the same field around the globe. In other words, he swims in a medium that is not reducible to quantified, measurable nature and in which, as a person, God is a presence,

6. Rosenstock-Huessy, *Out of Revolution*, 727.

whether or not acknowledged, who upholds him. Reducing the triad of man, nature, God to nature alone distorts and falsifies the reality of life in its wholeness. There is a profound difference, Rosenstock-Huessy often pointed out, between the science and the scientist. Refer to his words on "Soul, Body, Spirit," chapter 5, above.

If God and man cannot be folded into nature alone, neither can nature and God be folded into man, or man and nature folded into God. The Western theological and religious tradition includes a number of examples of the argument that God is not only the creator and sustainer of the universe, but also its essential being. At the least, God's omnipotence and omniscience asserted in theological language crowds out the independence of man and the world. Autonomous reason, in this theorizing, is subject to God's sovereign will, and there would be no man and no world without God's instant to instant sustenance. Obviously, this is idealist speculation of one brand or another and precisely the kind of airy, abstract thinking that Rosenstock-Huessy mostly ignores because it is not rooted in real life and mundane experience. Just as the teacher of creative writing advises his students, "write about what you know," so Rosenstock-Huessy implicitly and sometimes expressly advised his listeners and readers: Value your direct knowledge, trust your experience, grade and rank your knowledge. The product of the laboratory deserves no privilege over the validity of what you know from direct, personal experience. The filter of education also can destroy our ability to receive our experience as primary evidence.

Finally, we cannot shrink God and nature into man alone by telling ourselves that God is merely a projection of infantile wishes and a fantasy, a myth, and that the world and nature have no inherent meaning outside of ourselves. Is it all sound and fury signifying nothing? The outcome of such thinking is inevitably relativism and reductionism leading to nihilism and despair. Is nature subject to unlimited manipulation? Must we despair? Only if we are guided solely by intellect and not by revelation, or grace, when powers outside of ourselves move us to faith, hope, and love, despite cynicism. We must never forget that it is incumbent upon us, as free men and women, to make a better world. We are responsible. God underlies this aspiration willy-nilly. Rosenstock-Huessy liked the quotation commonly attributed to Sallust although he found it elsewhere: Myths are truths that never were but always are.

Miscellanea

Political Classification; Barack Obama as a Man of Destiny; Revolution and the Advancement of Mankind in the Second and Third Millennia; Some Comments Regarding Rosenstock-Huessy for Jeffrey Hart; Voluntary Service as an Antidote to War; On the Universal History of Humankind

POLITICAL CLASSIFICATION

People ask about Eugen Rosenstock-Huessy, "Was he a liberal or a conservative?" It is a desecration of his thinking to fit him into either of those categories, to attach to him either of those stagnant labels. If his schema of the cross of reality means anything, it is that a person who is whole and not stunted, who is capable of responding freely to what life presents, who can shake off the ideology of yesterday, the person, that is, who is living within *time* as well as space, will find himself (or herself) called upon at one crucial moment in his life to identify as conservative and at the next crucial moment to be what the world calls a liberal, a progressive, or even a radical. It is who we show ourselves to be at any given moment that ultimately counts, not the tag.

Anyone who allows himself to be wholly defined by abstractions, by party names, is soul dead, convenient and harmless though these terms may be in the ordinary give and take of politics. "Principle," Rosenstock-Huessy once said, "is what I thought yesterday." He was not thereby declaring himself to be unprincipled, but recognizing simply that tomorrow he might be faced with a decision, a discovery, a crisis, that would lead him to trash all of his carefully worked out ratiocinations. Suddenly circumstances change, and we realize that we are now asked to be different, to abandon our old beliefs, perhaps in a small way to affect the course of history; at this one time, to rise to the occasion; to save the world.

Rosenstock-Huessy's motto, "I respond although I must change" (*respondeo etsi mutabor*), is all about being open to new moments, to being larger than the label that is applied to us. The moment you call me forever a liberal or a conservative, I will show you that I am more than both of these terrible limitations on my freedom, whether to respond to the demand of a new future or to protect a vital inheritance. Thus, human beings defy objectification. This is the weakness of most social science prognostication, as Rosenstock-Huessy pointed out. How do you know what I will be tomorrow?

Recognizing the importance of stages in life, he quoted with approval the wisdom often attributed to Churchill (but apparently originating with François Guizot), that a man in his youth who is not a radical has no heart, and the man in old age who is not a conservative has no head. This is a generality but it brings home the truth that the generations need each other for balance.

I heard Rosenstock-Huessy once respond directly to the question of whether he was a liberal or conservative, utterly silly though these terms are from the perspective of the level at which he spoke. Wonderfully, he said he was a "counter-reactionary." I interpreted this to mean that he was opposed to those who sin against the holy spirit, those who try to smother the baby in the cradle, those who trample upon the new shoots in the ground, those who fail to recognize the new vitality, those who mock the new life that resurrects from the dead that has the power to shape the future for the better.

> Every form of civilization is a wise equilibrium between firm substructure and soaring liberty. Childlike people praise the liberty and ignore the substructure. They do not ask the price of one's privileges. Pacifists, liberals, Protestants, Socialists, in their genuine passion for improvement, forget the equilibrium that underlies a civilization. Mankind always stands on the edge of barbarism and universal warfare.

~

BARACK OBAMA AS A MAN OF DESTINY

No one saw more deeply into the "intelligible sequences" of the history of the West than Rosenstock-Huessy. In particular, he understood that profound change in human affairs can never be effected without sacrifice, almost always bloody. It is a weakness of the liberal outlook to believe that the way forward can be through peaceful evolution alone. That ideal is worthy and must be sustained, certainly, but the human heart can be obdurate, and a reformed future, in the end, inevitably requires mortal struggle to be realized, whether we like it or not. The title of Rosenstock-Huessy's masterwork in English, *Out of Revolution: Autobiography of Western Man*, drives home the point.

Unfashionable though such a view is these days, Rosenstock-Huessy saw design in history—not dropped down from on high but as a consequence of human passions. "Our passions give life to the world," he wrote. "Our collective passions constitute the history of mankind." The history of the past two millennia, he believed, which may appear to be "a crude encyclopedia of all possible methods of government and public morals, is at closer inspection one ineluctable order of alternating passions of the human heart."

The ineluctable order becomes apparent only in retrospect, in the linking of seemingly disparate events, sometimes over very long time spans. The revelation of the connectedness between the progressive actions of succeeding generations is what gives us hope that good will prevail, although never immediately. Nothing of importance in history is achieved in anything less than three generations of effort, Rosenstock-Huessy argued.

Anyone who does not hear in Barack Obama's speeches the echo of Martin Luther King Jr., is surely tone deaf. But more to the point, the real suffering endured by activists in the Civil Rights movement, culminating in the assassination of King when he was only thirty-nine, was the absolute precondition of Senator Obama's successful run for the presidency of the United States forty years later. Martyrdom, from Abraham Lincoln to King, confers on events irreversible seriousness amidst the multitude of ephemeral strivings in history. A platform is erected that can never be wholly abandoned. "He who suffers wins in politics," Rosenstock wrote. "The martyr does not obtain the victory personally, but his group, his successors, win in the long run."

The holiday calendar of any nation may be compared to a sacred creed, another topic about which Rosenstock-Huessy wrote extensively. The federal holiday "Martin Luther King Jr. Day" was signed into law by President Reagan in 1983 and despite some rocky beginnings it is now observed in every state. The universal acceptance of that holiday may well be considered a defining addition to the liturgy of our national religion. The ground of future growth now so well watered by the blood of martyrs, the nation awaited only the person to embody the dream.

REVOLUTION AND THE ADVANCEMENT OF MANKIND IN THE SECOND AND THIRD MILLENNIA

The conservative bias of the patriotic organization Daughters of the American Revolution (DAR) has been satirized with the jingle: "We are the daughters of the American Revolution, and we will never be the mothers of another." Any sensible person knows that revolutions are perilous because of their uncertain outcomes. To blithely preach revolution, as the Communists did, verges on nihilism. Think of the peasant wars associated with the Protestant Revolution, the turmoil in England at the time of Cromwell resulting in the first beheading of a king, the Terror during the French Revolution, and the horrific party purges and the extirpation of the kulak in the Soviet Union under Stalin. Even the *comparatively* benign American Revolution, before the era of total war, had huge unremembered costs in mortality and suffering.

Writing in 1938 when Communism was rife in the United States and Europe, Eugen Rosenstock-Huessy warned in his classic work, *Out of Revolution:* "It is always astonishing to find bankers, scholars, parsons enthusiastically awaiting a new revolution without divining the satanic character of all revolutions, whether it comes from the left or from the right. God certainly does not grant to a revolution what he gives to thirty or forty years of loyal collaboration in peace and law."[1]

The DAR has a point because a true *world* or *total* revolution—as opposed let's say to a bread riot, a coup d'etat, the deposition of a dictator, or some other violent transfer of power lacking in universal ideals— is always, in Rosenstock-Huessy's definition, "once and for all." There will, in fact, never be another American Revolution. The Christian Church,

1. *Rosenstock-Huessy, Out of Revolution, 16.*

England, France, Russia were permanently and irreversibly changed by singular revolutions never to be repeated.

Because of the largely beneficial results in the long term, revolutions may be too easily glorified as worth the cost, since it is indisputable that such radical change cannot be achieved by peaceful protest or negotiation. It is necessary to walk through the valley of death to reach the desired end. Yet any reader of Edmund Burke knows how much of value is irretrievably lost by revolutionary transformations. Nonetheless, these entirely unpredictable volcanic eruptions are sources of creative power that must be judged affirmatively in the scales of history, ultimately bringing improved wellbeing to all of mankind, indeed liberating human powers that were hitherto unrealized, and in each case giving birth to a new type of man.

Events mimicking a true revolution can be manufactured. Quasi-revolutions are commonplace, and indeed the word "revolution" is now attached to the most trivial happenings and commercial products. Even in the case of indisputably major events, evidencing courage and nobility—for example, the unseating of a dictator in Egypt early in 2011— it is a question whether the action is properly called a "revolution" when there is no evidence of a cultural or political bequest that is a necessary step forward for *all humankind.*

Political upheavals with the goal of catching up to the West —or let us say, the best of the West, leaving out what is undesirable—i .e., of gaining the rights and liberties and practices of liberal democracies, such as the free choice of vocations, the rule of law and parliamentary procedure, religious freedom, the entrepreneurial spirit, equality for women, and the organization of labor, not to speak of all that is enshrined in the United Nations Universal Declaration of Rights of 1948— such upheavals are not themselves "revolutions" if the word is to retain the precise meaning that Rosenstock-Huessy gave to it. But the terminology is not important if the substance is understood. "Revolution" is a convenient word. What must be understood is that the rights and liberties we refer to now as bedrock are all the result of a connected series of bloody, world revolutions in Europe in the past one thousand years.

When considering the five great European world revolutions beginning in the eleventh century, exclusive of the American Revolution—the Papal or Gregorian, the Protestant, the English, the French, and the Russian— it helps to consider that it is nonsense to declare oneself "for" or "against" revolution. One might just as well be for or against ocean waves. We have no choice in the matter. The great European revolutions were not predictable or controllable events. Utter surprise was one of their characteristics; each emerged with the force of a tidal wave, and the timing of each is fundamentally inexplicable. Historians will forever be debating the "cause" or the "causes" of the French Revolution, which is symptomatic of the profound mystery of its emergence, and so for all of the others. The great revolutions deserve continuing study, and the professoriate has illuminated much about the motivations behind them and the underlying issues, but we will never be able to divine the point at which men become willing to spill blood for a cause or an idea. And make no mistake, as Rosenstock-Huessy points out, there can be no revolution without those willing to die for the cause.

In the absence of "scientific" explanation, we fall back, retrogressively it might seem, on teleology. Science, of course, has expunged teleology, which is as it should be in dealing with the material world, the world after the fact. But men are purposeful. They have missions and goals that take centuries, even millennia, to be fulfilled. The dreams and ambitions of the human spirit leap over space and time, and men and women can be inspired (inspirited) by commands issued far away and long ago. Speech is the embodiment of the human spirit, in Rosenstock-Huessy's conception, and great inspiring utterances echo through the ages, transformed and translated as necessary to serve an immediate purpose. At what point there will be a coalescence of the spirit such as to produce martyrs for the sake of a new and better future can never be systematically known or anticipated.

The only meaningful context for such moments is the story of humankind as a whole —not so-called world history, which is to a large degree the child of political or multi-cultural correctness— but a coherent narrative of where mankind has been and where we are going, within which a pattern of human ideals unfolds. This is sometimes called Universal History, and the great European revolutions fit into this narrative with a design that is evident in retrospect, with each revolution in dialogue with the preceding one, and each listening to the implicit command: "there is work still to be done to fulfill human destiny." Such is the picture that Rosenstock-Huessy draws in *Out of Revolution*. The book is important not because of the individual interpretations of six revolutions, brilliant though those interpretations are, but because of the pattern as a whole in relation to what has been called our journey through time.

Rosenstock-Huessy was never tempted by Marxism, and he despised the Nazis from the start. He is not classifiable politically and seems to transcend the usual polarities. It is ironic that because he wrote a book about the singular creativity of the European revolutions in the second millennium, he was superficially assumed to be pro-revolution! In fact, much of his thinking was moored in Christianity, and he saw in the events of the second millennium another stage in the working out of the Christian revelation, a fulfillment not unlike the Joachimite or Johannine prophecies of three great ages. The third millennium of our era, in which we are now living, figured in Rosenstock-Huessy's thinking as much as the first two. His universal history begins with the tribes of ten thousand years ago. The advent of Christianity is the neck of the hourglass that links the modern world to the ancient, including the tribes, the Egyptian and other star-gazing empires, ancient Israel, and the Greeks.

From this perspective, the European world revolutions were a vital, if calamitous, stage in the universal history of mankind, and are not recurrent. The third millennium in its progress to a planetary society will certainly have its share of wars and travail, but it is hard to imagine the eruption of revolutions comparable to those of the second millennium in Europe, or to the American Revolution, which were associated with the development of nation-states and made huge social, political, and economic leaps with influence far beyond the borders of the West. The spirit will speak to us in the third millennium in different forms and unexpected ways, as usual, and transformations there will be, but not in accordance with the old patterns.

The closest Rosenstock-Huessy came to prophesying a true revolution in the third millennium of what he called "our era" (formerly referred to as AD, and now more usually CE), is in his various discussions of the first stage of man's emergence into the life of the spirit, namely the era of the tribes. Each of the great European revolutions drew inspiration and authority from reaching back to a specific earlier time, as for example the Protestants adopted the first century of Christianity as their standard. For Rosenstock-Huessy, such reclamation from the past is not arbitrary or accidental but essential to progress. In the third millennium, the *era of tribalism* will provide that guidance. The tribes, he said, invented speech, using that word in the refined meaning Rosenstock-Huessy gave to it; and they invented marriage and the family. These both require resuscitation in the coming centuries. The tribes also lived necessarily in deference to nature, over which they had little control.

> Following the paths of the wild animals was the first political power that enabled these groups to become a little larger than the small group of husband, wife, and children. The relation of the tribesman to the animals is one of spiritual gratitude for their directing powers, for the work done for them, because the elephant, the lion, and the fox, etc. were superior to men.

The most imaginable world revolution in the third millennium will produce a new order of mankind in relation to the natural world. It is obvious that with nine billion people living on Earth, which is the anticipated number by 2050, and all of us struggling to improve the conditions of life, we will need to be much more mindful of our impact on the natural environment if we are not to exhaust or destroy the bounty around us on which we remain dependent.

Our inspiration in the third millennium will be our repossession of the achievements of indigenous peoples in the era of pre-history. To gain the authority to save planetary society from ourselves, we will need to think back to the beginning. Perhaps, then, it is a harbinger of this inspiration that Bolivia, according to John Vidal writing for the *Guardian* in the U. K., "is set to pass the world's first laws *granting all nature equal rights to humans*. The Law of Mother Earth, now agreed to by politicians and grassroots social groups, redefines the country's rich mineral deposits as 'blessings' and is expected to lead to radical new conservation and social measures to reduce pollution and control industry." Constitutional rights will include the right to continue vital cycles and processes free from human alteration; the right to pure water and clean air; the right to balance; the right not to be polluted; and the right to not have cellular structure modified or genetically altered. (April 10, 2011). If Bolivia manages to implement even a fraction of its radical program, which springs from the spiritual as well as the practical concerns of the country's present-day Native American population, one can imagine the titanic struggle with capitalism that is bound to follow in every country, and it will be violent. It is notable that Chile, too, more recently has embedded environmental protections in its new constitution.

The problem with capitalism, Rosenstock-Huessy argued in *Out of Revolution*, is not, as the Marxists claimed, that it exploited wage-earners; the benefits it has ultimately brought to the standard of living of workers are obvious. Capitalism's persistent failure is that it neglects to reproduce or replace what it exploits and exhausts, whether it is the soil, the fish stocks, or stable families and communities that are the nursery of reliable and capable workers. The capitalist was "freed from all responsibility for the political, moral and educational order of his country. . . . Lumber, electricity, a man's talents, can be commercialized; or they can acquire a past and a future, enter the real life of the soul, as soon as we feel responsible for their reproduction."

> Suppose all the kinds of raw material we use in our business begin to grow scarce: rubber, wood-pulp, children, poets; forest fires begin to destroy our timber, and drought our fields. . . . At that moment the employer becomes deeply interested in the process of "Reproduction"; a new world opens before his eyes: a world of change. The circular process of raising rubber, replanting forests, educating foresters, resettling the country, begins to present itself to the minds of the businessmen who up to that time had thought of nothing but the logs they bought from the farmer who needed cash.[2]

"The World Revolutions," Rosenstock-Huessy wrote,

> all start without reference to [*geographical*] space, with an absolute programme for the whole of mankind, and a vision of a new earth. They all believe themselves to be the vessel of eternal, revealed, definite truth. Only reluctantly do they come back to the old earth. Every revolution makes the painful discovery that it is geographically conditioned. . . . All great revolutions presuppose a colossal effort of human liberty and free will. They all arrive at their limits because they underestimate the freedom of their neighbours. The Great Revolutions never take into account the fact that mankind cannot act all at once. They overestimate the capacity of humanity for simultaneous change.[3]

One can only hope that whatever the practical limits of Bolivia's aspirations, the result will be a legacy for all mankind.

2. Rosenstock-Huessy, *Out of Revolution*, 73–90.
3. Rosenstock-Huessy, *Out of Revolution*, 457–58.

SOME COMMENTS REGARDING ROSENSTOCK-HUESSY'S CHRISTIAN BELIEFS FOR JEFFREY HART

[Jeffrey Hart (1930–2019) was a professor of English at Dartmouth College for twenty years. He also was an undergraduate at Dartmouth for a couple of years (before transferring to Columbia), during which time he took a class or two from Professor Rosenstock-Huessy and thereafter was an admirer for life. He sent me some writing of his own regarding Rosenstock-Huessy and some questions. Below are my responses. I do not still have what he sent to me that prompted these remarks, but his queries may be inferred.]

Rosenstock-Huessy did not see himself as an "emigre," and even less as a "refugee." He resigned his professorship at the University of Breslau immediately upon news of the triumph of National Socialism at the beginning of 1933 and decided to *immigrate*, as he said, to the U. S. It was obviously important to him that it be understood that he didn't flee, that he did not wait to be driven out, that he resigned in protest.

You raise the question of questions, "Was he really a Christian?" Someone should write an entire essay on that. Peter Leithart in one of his articles on Rosenstock-Huessy notes rightly that there are contradictory statements from the man. Here are just a few "bullets," to use corporate-speak, that remain with me.

1. Rosenstock-Huessy's *Fruit of Our Lips* (recently published by Wipf and Stock in a new edition, edited by Raymond Huessy) will one day be recognized as one of the ten or twelve most vital and enduring books ever written about, or I should say, for Christianity, in a class with the *Confessions* of St. Augustine or the *Imitation of Christ*.
2. He was keenly aware that he lived in what he called a "post-theological" age and that most of the traditional language of the church had become empty of meaning. Hence, he took it upon himself to give new definitions to the old vocabulary that with its overtones of the supernatural and mystical no longer seemed "true" to moderns. It was an effort at translation, and no one has ever done it better. You can see this especially in "Soul, Body, Spirit" (reprinted in chapter 5, above). That word "soul," which philosophers and psychologists rightly mock when it is treated as a material thing for which empirical evidence must be mustered, is there transformed into a

self-evident truth. Or as Rosenstock-Huessy said in another place: When Thomas Paine wrote, "These are the times that try men's souls," he wasn't talking about men's minds or men's bodies.

3. He disliked the classification of Christianity as a "religion," because that characterization immediately raises images of church buildings and pews, priests engaged in hocus-pocus, so-called miracles, and so forth. He wrote extensively about architecture, about ritual, about liturgy, and had a profound appreciation of such matters, but none of that should be confused with the Christian revolution or revelation (the same) of two thousand years ago. He, like one of his favorite authors, G. K. Chesterton, saw no need for "miracles" that break the natural order. The natural order itself is a gigantic, continuing miracle—that the sun rises and sets every day, that the acorn gives rise to the oak, the birth of a child. He admired William Blake, who saw a universe in a grain of sand. And as we know, human speech is the greatest of all miracles, which literally moves mountains. Once in class he alluded to divine grace in a way that removed all of the sanctimony around it. "Grace," he said (I am not quoting verbatim), is when you are feeling depressed and alone, and then out of the blue a friend calls you and invites you out to a meal. Conversion, he said, is simply re-orientation, and so forth.

4. He argued that the Christian revelation is universally applicable. It should not be segregated into just one of the several so-called world religions—Hinduism, Islam, Buddhism, etc.—as though they are all roughly equivalent, which is just modern relativism. Christianity brought to light elements of life that apply to all men (and women) at all times and everywhere, a "driving power," never to be permanently reversed. He saw the moment when Jesus lived as the neck of the hourglass of human history. Tribal, Egyptian, Jewish, Greek, Roman achievements and understanding, painfully acquired, all now gathered into a liberation theology that has defined the third millennium as it did the first two AD. In his remarkable recorded "Make Bold to Be Ashamed" lecture, he asserts that the importance of Jesus has little to do with the Sermon on the Mount, but everything to do with the art of timing.

5. So, Resurrection in the flesh is the "body" of the Christian church alive today, quite ambulatory, after two thousand years. What need of Paul's five hundred eye-witnesses. Resurrection in the flesh is a

regular occurrence. Love's triumph over death is a regular occurrence. These are not philosophical abstractions, concocted in someone's head. Jesus did it first and taught us all that it can happen, and hence we can have faith that despite doubt and despair, love and truth and goodness will triumph in human history and affairs. Hence, we have direction, a command.

6. "Whenever two or three are gathered in my name, I am with you" (Matthew 18:20). You must know the inspiring union song, "Joe Hill," written by the novelist Alfred Hayes as a poem and later set to music:

    I dreamed I saw Joe Hill last night
    Alive as you or me
    Says I, But Joe, you're ten years dead
    I never died, says he
    I never died, says he . . . .
    The copper bosses killed you, Joe
    They shot you, Joe, says I
    Takes more than guns to kill a man
    Says Joe, I didn't die
    Says Joe, I didn't die
    And standing there as big as life
    And smiling with his eyes
    Joe says, What they forgot to kill
    Went on to organize
    Went on to organize . . . .
    From San Diego up to Maine
    In every mine and mill
    Where workers strike and organize
    Says he, You'll find Joe Hill
    Says he, You'll find Joe Hill . . . .

This is a "Christian" song, consciously or unconsciously, about death and resurrection, although Jesus is not mentioned. He doesn't need to be. Christian truths are so deeply integral to our culture that the overt preaching of doctrinal Christianity and institutional church attendance are no longer defining of a "Christian" culture. Christendom ended in the trenches of WWI, not to speak of the Shoah, but "Christianity incognito," as Rosenstock called it, or "religionless Christianity" in Dietrich Bonhoeffer's words, persists in International Courts of Justice, in Doctors without Borders, in the Nobel Peace Prize, in scientific endeavor (very Christian, if you understand it), and in a billion small efforts to remake the world for the better with every soul on the planet prized.

Even deeper, Judaeo-Christian understanding truly superseded the great Classical inheritance, although much of academe still thinks of the Renaissance as the wonderful intellectual opening that finally did away with supposed medieval darkness. Rosenstock-Huessy had little patience for the Renaissance worshippers, who were blinded by their adulation of the glories of Greece and Rome. In a typical mortal thrust, he said (I am not quoting verbatim) "and with the Renaissance came the revival of the glories of the ancient world, including human slavery." As a gift to mankind, the Renaissance wilts in comparison to the Reformation, a far greater revolution as he demonstrated in *Out of Revolution*.

VOLUNTARY SERVICE AS AN ANTIDOTE TO WAR

Public Law 111–13, the "Edward M. Kennedy Serve America Act," signed by President Obama in April 2009, got little attention from the media and compared to other legislation is a minor concern. The very existence of the Corporation for National and Community Service (CNCS), the agency that administers the wide array of Federal voluntary service programs, is annually threatened by some Republicans. The new national service act has many merits. It addresses real and serious problems, with an eye both to those who will receive help of one kind or another and to those who will be providing the services. "Disadvantaged youth," for example, may receive services that will give them a better break in life, and some of them will be recruited to perform services, such as disaster relief. When unemployment for those in their twenties is rampant, the opportunity for any kind of work experience has obvious benefits.

Those over fifty-five are similarly incorporated into the mission of the Serve America Act, both as doers (Silver Scholars, Encore Service, etc.) and receivers. The problem of the unemployed is at least mentioned, although the Act does not strongly address that recurrent suffering in our midst. There is always the fear, in fact, that national service programs will end up displacing permanent paid workers, an outcome that the Act expressly prohibits.

The Civilian Conservation Corps of the 1930s often gets mentioned in this context, which at its height in 1935 had 500,000 boys in uniform, but from our perspective today the CCC had serious flaws. Among them was its categorization as a relief program, restricted to those in dire need.

It thus segregated "disadvantaged" and "court involved" youth from the nation's youth as a whole. However glorified the program is in retrospect for its accomplishments, people at the time were wary of CCC boys, just as they are today when there is talk of placing half-way houses in middle-class neighborhoods.

Rosenstock-Huessy, who had had experience in Germany in the 1920s organizing voluntary work service programs (before he came to the U. S. at age forty-five), saw into these issues profoundly. In 1939 he gathered around him a group of Harvard and Dartmouth students (and even a few Radcliffe women), with the intention of launching a permanent national program of voluntary work service that would integrate the social and economic classes, rather than divide them. One of these students, Frank Davidson, fresh out of Harvard and with connections, convinced President Roosevelt that the "means test," which excluded the well-off from the CCC, should, as an experiment, be abandoned.

With the quiet blessing of the administration and the enthusiastic support of Eleanor Roosevelt and the ardent anti-Nazi journalist Dorothy Thompson, Camp William James, a mixture of CCC boys and Ivy Leaguers, was launched in Sharon, Vermont, in 1940, with the avowed purpose of being a pilot program for a transformed national service corps. Rosenstock-Huessy was its intellectual leader. Camp William James lasted less than two years, for various complicated reasons, the main one being the entrance of the United States into the war against Germany and Japan, which gave young men something else to do of far greater urgency.[4]

Rosenstock-Huessy named the camp after the great American philosopher because he admired James's eye-opening essay, "The Moral Equivalent of War," which was first published in 1910, more than a century ago. Most talk of national service eventually gets back to James, but few service programs take the risk of heeding him literally. James was unquestionably on the side of the peace-mongers, as was Rosenstock-Huessy, but neither man blinked at the profound and virtually ineradicable roots of the bellicose spirit in humankind, or shrunk at mention of the virtues that war promotes—yes, virtues—which cannot be dispelled by anti-war bumper-sticker sentiments. War is the greatest metaphor we have for high seriousness, courage, determination, comradeship, and sacrifice, hence such rallying cries as the "war on poverty," the "war on cancer," or the "war on terror," the last of which is rejected by some

4. The story of the camp is well told in Preiss, *Camp William James*.

because they thought the metaphor was too grand and sweeping (and dangerous) for the purpose. But war, James wrote, "has been the only force that can discipline a whole community, and until an equivalent discipline is organized, I believe that war must have its way."

We are rightly fearful of martial rhetoric, and a relevant fact about the new Serve America Act is that among its many emendations of prior related legislation, what were formerly called "camps" in CCC days are now designated "campuses," and the former "camp superintendent" is now the "campus director." What after all is more pacific than a campus (or so we used to think until shootings have become commonplace on them).

Such changes in terminology may be harmless enough, but both James and Rosenstock-Huessy were after something much deeper than simply giving vent, through the mechanism of service, to charitable and patriotic impulses and to the urge to do good. Social and material needs in the United States are certainly vast, and Public Law 111–13 does a good job of pointing out how much opportunity there is for helping others, but nowhere does it suggest that somehow national service can be an alternative to war.

After a review of many sides of the question, James argued that peace cannot be, or even ought to be, "permanent on this globe" until the nation states that are "pacifically organized" succeed in preserving some of the old elements of army discipline. "A permanently successful peace-economy cannot be a simple pleasure-economy." "Martial virtues must be the enduring cement; intrepidity, contempt of softness, surrender of private interest, obedience to command, must still remain the rock upon which states are built."

James had in mind mandatory universal service and famously proposed that instead of military conscription there be implemented "a conscription of the whole youthful population to form for a certain number of years a part of the army enlisted against *Nature*," from which, he believed, numerous goods to the commonwealth would follow, among them a corrective to social and economic inequality. James's position is sometimes ridiculously misconstrued, suggesting that he wanted to abuse nature, rather than conserve it!

Rosenstock-Huessy addressed questions of war and peace and voluntary work service throughout a lifetime of writing. His formulations, often complex, are varied and cannot easily be summarized here, but some principles are constant. The most basic, perhaps, was his belief that war is the natural condition of mankind—it simply erupts as we stand by helplessly—while peace must be painstakingly created, usually with enormous human effort and always requiring sacrifice, often mortal sacrifice equivalent to the sacrifice in war.

The pacifists, Rosenstock noted in 1946, "are the indispensable antithesis to the ghastly warhoops of the temporal mind. . . . They are right when they abhor war as the order of the world; it certainly is its disorder. The world was created for peace. But they are wrong when they do not add that the act of creating the world is a perpetual act. What we call the creation of the world is not an event of yesterday, but the event of all times, and goes on right under our noses."[5]

Voluntary work service, then, when it seeks to cross borders—such as national borders, social and economic class barriers and boundaries, and racial, ethnic, and religious differences—and assumes all of the associated risks and challenges of such actions, can be the nuclei for a created future. True progress is never automatic. The world needs, paradoxically, a kind of soldiering for peace, Rosenstock-Huessy argued, the traits of the warrior mentality, or the rashness of youth, yet balanced by the more conservative reason of the older generation. "The corollary to the abolition of war is the integration of the soldier's way of life into the mental life of the community." "A moral equivalent of war will not suffice," Rosenstock wrote. "It may have to be a mental equivalent of war as well . . . ." And this mental equivalent is not campus detachment or bureaucratic caution, it is voluntary and risky engagement at the front.[6]

ON THE UNIVERSAL HISTORY OF HUMANKIND

Among the most fundamental and recurrent themes in the thought of Rosenstock-Huessy is his picture of the evolution of human society, or what he called the universal history of mankind, that history that has bearing on the entire globe without regard to the particular interests of nation states and cultures. The decisions of the mayor of Peoria in 1876 is not part of such a history, nor is a battle during the Sung dynasty that had

5. Rosenstock-Huessy, *Christian Future*, 224.

6. Rosenstock-Huessy, *Christian Future*, 231–32. For more on this subject, see my online essay: "The Case for National Service." https://medium.com@etzioni_25175/the-case—for-universal-national-service-guest-column-8fd42810f43c. In 2021 there was new supportive legislation relating to national service.

no implications beyond the local. All that counts are profound changes that are permanent or irreversible and that ultimately impinge on all peoples everywhere.

For Rosenstock-Huessy, the destiny of mankind will be the result only of individual and collective human effort, or more often, struggle and sacrifice, often mortal sacrifice. The tendency of mere "nature" is to run downward, as a garden turns to weeds. Man (including woman) he described as the "uphill animal," defying gravity, defying nature, to achieve peace and order. Destiny is teleological, but it is not irreversible. There is implicitly in human history a direction, because men dream, but there is no certainty the promise will be fulfilled. The future of mankind hangs on human "resolve," a weak reed. Every living soul has a duty to contribute to this great end.

Because he believed unwaveringly that humankind has a destiny, namely unity and peace, there has to be a visible process striving toward that glorious end, often blindly. Universal history is a single integrated narrative, a passing of the torch, not a congeries of incidents of coups and battles, tribes and nation-states, plagues and migrations, innovations and inventions, empires and democracies. Our destiny can be reached only by means of active, ongoing endeavor and sacrifice by individuals and groups determined to create a better future. Christianity was prophetic in its universal message of peace, i.e., the end, the destiny, the promise of Man was proclaimed in the Gospels, and the task of mankind is to fulfill this destiny. In other words, where we should be going is well known. We have to close the space between what we hope will be and the present. Rosenstock-Huessy loved Chesterton's poem *Ballad of the White Horse*, with the refrain,

> For the end of the world was long ago,/And all we dwell to-day/ As children of some second birth,/ Like a strange people left on earth/ After a judgment day.

The advent of Christianity was the narrow neck of the hour-glass of "man's pathway through time," with ten thousand years of prior human experience pouring into it, but lacking in direction or meaning. Israel, as adapted and enhanced by Christianity, provided the basis of both unity and direction, and also gave meaning and purpose to the human story.

The first millennium CE or AD was devoted to establishing the Christian church in Europe and supplanting paganism, mired in its cyclical view of history, its polytheism, and its decadence. Rosenstock-Huessy wrote a great deal about the Church Fathers and the Middle Ages and knew that history intimately. Note that it was in about 350 AD that the Church invented a wholly new calendar with the birth of Jesus as Year One, and it is an extraordinary fact that every corner of the globe now accepts as a practical matter that the present year is 2022, an example of the quiet universalization of the Christian message, although not consciously accepted in those terms. In fact, much of what are considered civilized standards in 2022 are unnamed inheritances from the Christian era, which proceeds now anonymously.

The Christian mission was to preach the gospel to *all* peoples, a previously unheard of ambition. The forms that Christianity has taken and will take in the third millennium will be, to some degree, new creations, what Rosenstock-Huessy called in *The Christian Future* "Christianity incognito," i. e., people working toward the realization of the Christian prophecy without even identifying with Christianity or being aware of the tortuous history behind their endeavors for peace and betterment. Rosenstock-Huessy detested the blithe invocations of abstract so-called "values," such as "peace" or "justice," as though such concepts were just available for the picking without there having been any previous embodiment or incarnation on which this "value" rested—an unfortunate inheritance from Greek idealism.

In Rosenstock-Huessy's imaginative schema (not his alone), the first millennium was the era of the Father, the proclamation of one God, which certainly does not mean that all of the lesser gods just disappeared. Far from it. They are still with us and the most important always will be, Mars being one of them, and Venus, too. It is just that we know they must be and can be transcended, their worship checked.

The second millennium, the era of the Son, of salvation, was not only the period when nation-states were formed and came into power, France and England very early, but also the era of the European revolutions, which Rosenstock-Huessy described so powerfully in the eight hundred pages of *Out of Revolution*. The promise of Christianity in elevating men (and women) as the partners of God, of man as created in God's image, is realized in the succession of revolutions which one by one liberated us from constraints on our freedom—established inequality, slavery, racism, tyranny, economic oppression, theocracy, misogyny, and on and on, each revolution incomplete with regard to all of the elements of true human dignity, but the next one expanding the list. Rosenstock-Huessy did not cite it, but the 1948 United Nations Declaration of Human Rights is a good list of what was achieved, once and for all, in the second millennium, at enormous cost of life. Obviously, these rights are ignored daily, but a standard has been enunciated and a consensus achieved to which we can refer with meaning. And it is permanently impossible now to undo these standards without outcry.

Today it is asked, are not universal rights no more than an imperial ambition of the West, not the true product of global consensus? There is certainly no consensus. Authoritarian or tyrannical regimes have reasons to dispute the validity of universal rights born in the West, charging that they are merely masks for power. I do not know how Rosenstock-Huessy would respond to such a debate, implicitly that between liberty and order. Whatever the issues, he stood for the blossoming of the human spirit and was the enemy of repression.

The essential point is that human rights are an achievement, not some kind of automatic progress of which we are merely spectators. And they are a standard that was won only by the efforts of countless brave souls slaughtered in the process. Rosenstock-Huessy would say that there can be no true, lasting progress without martyrdom—such is the reality of the reactionary resistance, the forces that are always arrayed against necessary change.

The task of the third millennium, the era of the Holy Spirit (which Rosenstock-Huessy said we now euphemistically call the human spirit), is to create the "Great Society" when mankind is able to live in peace but also maintain cultural, ethnic, religious differentiation. Rosenstock-Huessy rejected the concept of One World, which represented to him the tyranny of a world government and homogenization. Man must flourish in all of his beautiful differentiation—in fact, it is one of our fundamental drives to differentiate ourselves from others—yet we can be moved by the spirit towards brotherhood. There will be borders and boundaries—it is a natural human instinct to distinguish inside and outside, us and them, we and they— but they will be porous. Look at the European Union, the amazing permanent outcome to a gigantic catastrophe and hardly even conceivable a century ago.

Rosenstock-Huessy was fully aware, of course, that a schema of three stages of Christian development echoed the prophecies of the Franciscan monk Joachim of Flora in the twelfth century. He saw St. Francis as an epoch-making figure, a Christian who was the antithesis of the Crusades and the inspiration for a spiritual pivot leading up to the Reformation. Prophecy for Rosenstock-Huessy was not prediction. There is no lockstep in history. Prophets who emerge sense the future and give warning. Their inspiration may lie fallow for centuries. "The gift of prophecy," Rosenstock-Huessy said, "is the power to embrace a total experience at the beginning." He saw himself as a prophet, I think, a voice crying in the wilderness, "vox clamantis in deserto," the motto of Dartmouth College, as it happens.

War, Rosenstock-Huessy held, is always a problem in space, i.e., a problem of borders, of "us" vs. "them," of "we" on the inside of a boundary against "they" on the other side of the boundary. The voluntary sacrifice required to maintain the peace—when members of a nation deliberately cross these borders, not as invading armies, but in fellowship—has the potential to ward off violent conflict because it is no longer possible to determine easily who "we" are and who "they" are. The globalization of the economy can have the same effect, although it remains a question whether international trade in fact prevents war. The generations, mothers and fathers and sons and daughters, cooperate in creating bridges that may transform foes into friends. It is no accident that we see in recent years not only "Doctors Without Borders," but other groups or professions adopting the same criterion of disparaging borders, such as "Reporters sans Frontières" and "Diplomats Without Borders."

In *Out of Revolution*, published more than eighty years ago, Rosenstock-Huessy anticipated totally the full globalization of the economy. It is one of the central themes of the book: "Economy will be universal, mythology regional. Every step in the direction of organizing the world's economy will have to bought off by a great number of tribal reactions," he said in 1938. I think of Islam today in this regard, in that globalization leads people to want to protect their cultural roots from being washed away in the flood of commercialization and modernity, and they may react violently to the incursion.

To bring this all together, we have to go back some 10,000 years BC, from the achievements of the first human societies, tribal culture, then pass through the early astral civilizations, such as Egyptian, Chinese, or Inca—astral because everywhere such societies look to the heavens for guidance and revelation— then to ancient Israel, which rejected both tribalism and the astrological temple cultures. The Greeks, too, have a special place in this pre-Christian, pagan world. Although Rosenstock-Huessy had classical training in a German *gymnasium* and could have taught Classics at the university level, all of his life he battled against the reverence of the ancient Greeks in European culture. Scholars and others simply failed to see the sharp limitations and defects of the Greek achievement, especially insofar as it has been influenced by Parmenides.[7]

Each of these early phases in mankind's evolution, which Rosenstock-Huessy has written about extensively, were periods of enormous creativity, with legacies that we still depend on. He spoke of the "reconquest of our era," or one might say the perpetual reconquest, because again and again we have to go back and re-invigorate or resuscitate the best of what we inherited that is "now" threatened. This is a perpetual cycle of forgetting and recovery. Tribal culture, for example, invented accountable speech and marriage (including the incest taboo).

Here is Rosenstock-Huessy in *Out of Revolution*: "With a conscious economic organization of the whole earth, subconscious tribal organizations are needed to protect man's mind from commercialization and disintegration. The more our shrinking globe demands technical and economic co-operation, the more necessary it will prove to restore the balance by admitting the primitive archetypes of man's nature also."[8]

What holds human history together, what unifies it, is the power of speech. A large percentage of Rosenstock-Huessy's work was on the nature of the miracle of speech, which he sharply distinguished from mere *talk*. We are seriously spoken to and we answer; we are thus called into the spirit of an enterprise that is temporally much larger than ourselves, and in the end we may devote our lives to answering that call. Speech links the generations. It is also, of course, the foundation of peace. At war, the enemies stop speaking to each other. To make peace, they must engage in civil discourse.

The most immediate issue in our time is the future of the nation-state, a great European invention that conquered the world but whose time has passed. "Today [1938!]," Rosenstock-Huessy wrote, "the nations face a dilemma: either destruction through loyalty to their national deity or conversion to a living faith." By conversion to a living faith, he did not mean going to church, but certainly faith in the ultimate unity and harmony of mankind, which the Nazis diabolically opposed and rejected. "Man can never be confined to the worship of any single god. He cries out for the one God of all mankind." "Man will no longer be satisfied to remain shut up within the limits of one nation's institutions and ways of life. . . . The relativity of each nation's particular type and standard

7. See Rosenstock-Huessy, "Heraclitus to Parmenides," which may be interpreted as a rebuke to Heidegger.

8. Rosenstock-Huessy, *Out of Revolution*, 715.

means the end of the modern era and its secular revolutions. The World War [of 1914–1918], with its sequel, the Russian Revolution, was the last total revolution tending to cast all men in one mould. Henceforth, more than one type has to be made accessible to the souls of men. The absolute power of each separate god is gone."[9]

For Rosenstock-Huessy, the two World Wars, 1914–1918, 1939–1945, were a continuous conflagration; the Soviet threat that brought about the Cold War, too. They were the final gasps of the dead era. "The future task is to lead man's life through a sequence of different phases and well-timed allegiances. No single allegiance can claim domination any longer over our whole life. The place of the old Christian conversion will be taken by a solemn and deliberate change of allegiance in mid-life. Man is called to fulfill himself. How can he, if parts of human life remain inaccessible to him?" "A unified [global] society with a multiplicity of tribal characters and national types will be the 'leit-motif' of the centuries before us." Rosenstock-Huessy spoke of this new stage as the Great Society.

~

EXCERPT FROM A LETTER TO CYNTHIA, FEBRUARY 22, 1943

[Rosenstock-Huessy lectured often on Universal History. About ninety hours of recordings, from 1949, 1954, 1955, 1956, 1957, and 1967, have survived. Both the audio and transcriptions may be found on the website of the ERH Fund. And, of course, many of his books, in both German and English, address the subject, most notably *Out of Revolution.*

In addition we have the unpublished manuscript of his "Letters to Cynthia," composed in 1943. Cynthia Harris was a twenty-year-old Radcliffe student who for a few years was, I think it is fair to say, Rosenstock-Huessy's muse. "Disciple" might also do as a description of her standing with the professor, since Cynthia inspired him to send her over two hundred pages of text, elicited, it seems in part, by hearing from her what her professors at Radcliffe and Harvard were propagating, most of which Rosenstock-Huessy disputed. Below is a short excerpt from these letters, on the topic of universal history.Bracketed insertions are mine.]

9. Rosenstock-Huessy, *Out of Revolution*, 729–33.

The speech-creating unit is the first epoch of history, and the Gentiles, the tribes of old, the subject matter of Mr. [Ernest A.] Hooton's [anthropology] course [at Harvard], are important for this reason.

The writing-creating period is the second epoch of history. Great civilizations transformed oral speech into holy writ of their temples, and thereby the temple cities, the second unit of history. Your course on humanism gives you an in[k]ling of such an epoch.

The period which tries to establish the goal to which all peaces thus created by tribes and cities should be directed, is the third great epoch of history. The story of Israel is the story of how the innumerable languages and temples were foiled by one more group which opposed the innumerable cities. Israel insisted that the innumerable was murderous to peace among men, that the wild growth of peaces made it impossible ever to realize the goal implied by the first peace ever concluded. Israel tried to push the nations onto their own logical conclusion. If the very essence of speech was pacification, the final pacification should not be obstructed by the confusion of tongues and temples. Israel, within this confusion, promises singleness of tongue and temple, within a world of polyglot and polytheism.

You easily see how tribal histories and Mexican, Chinese, Greek history are all polytheistic and do not allow to be considered as unified into one universal history without qualification.

This affects the alleged Jewish history, too. The profounder the faith of a Jew, the less will he believe in a Jewish "history." It is all there, in Abraham and at the Sinai, and it has to be lived in every generation, the one truth of the city of Peace, among the polyglot of the heathen, the many idols of Egypt and Niniveh. The perpetual persecutions and pogroms are not a progressive history. They are Israel's risk for her message among the gentiles. Tribe, Temple City, Israel have many histories, in endless repetition. But there is no "singular" binding together the history of Mexico, of Egypt, except by stepping outside their history and viewing them subspecie of a singular unknown to them!

Our own era, the Christian era, is the history of this singular. First the Church transplants the city of peace everywhere among the Gentiles right into the heart of their cities by throwing out their temples and replacing them by the living temple of living souls. The Old Jerusalem's replacement by the New Jerusalem is called Church history.

The era proceeds to replace the many civilizations of the heathen by a Christian World. The pluralism of Mexican, Chinese, Babylonian histories is replaced by the new singular of the World history. This history of the world climaxes in two world wars, which are "global" indeed.

And one more plural has to [be] mopped up and brought into line: the polyglot of races, tribes, classes, still prevails. The social history which begins with the rise of industry, is the beginning of a unification for Mankind's history.

Plural histories	*Singular history*
Tribes	Church history
Temple States	World history
Israel's	Mankind's history

In the light of the singular "history," the plural "histories" can be reread belatedly as containing already hints for a final single evolution. For instance the incessant persecutions of the Jews through all the periods of history lose their static repetitive character somewhat when they are related to the origin, growth, decay, resurgence of the Church.

The great features of Japan, Assur, the Inkas become as we say today significantly "contributions" in the history of one world, whereas, by themselves, they were not contributions at all but dissociations and divisions and "distributive" more than "contributive."

And the primeval man and the retrogressive primitive races of our day may now, in the light of our one History of mankind, be made to converge, whereas, by themselves, these tribes scattered and diverged and split.

The Peace of Man in this world in the power of one speech, is the topic of history. All history can be written under the two aspects of diversity and convergence. All history is pluralistic and monistic, both. Lincoln belongs [to] American history, and [to] the history of the human race. The Daughters of the American Revolution think that George Washington was an American, but he was an English gentleman living in Virginia, too.

I propose to put before you those burdens of history by which all the strophes of it are made known to be parts of one song. I propose to tell you of tribes, temple-cities, Israel, the Church, the World, and Mankind, just enough so that the innumerable histories about some event, some man, some century in some country, do not remain mere diversities. They are all held together by some vital burden. If you can hear these burdens clearly, history becomes as transparent as the song of John Brown's Body. Indeed the burden of John Brown is a wonderful example of the power which history has over us. It makes the dead live again and they have not lived in vain: Their soul is marching on.

The deepest craving of mankind is for this lastingness of peace, this victory over annihilation. Man rears up against nihilism. And in rearing up he towers over death, victoriously. The towers made by his hands are the symbols of his victories over death. All '*ex*'altation, all '*ex*'cellency, all elevated acts or feelings have received their qualification of being "outstanding" from this desire of towering high over death. The so-called higher level, the plane of which Churchill spoke when he said that he would feel "below the plane" of Russia's fight, is the level on which death is overcome, on which man, by an act of peace, creates an evolutionary process, emerging above the plane of futility.[10]

Now the burdens of history differ since those towers over death can be built in three manners or out of three materials.

I. The many tribes of polyglot [history] made peace around their ancestral spirits. They enjoined on their children to keep alive the ancestor forever and forever and forever. The everlastingness of the founding spirit is the one elementary principle of any group. It is based—in prehistory—on the belief that the ancestor, by the faith of the tribe, may be kept alive. Death is denied and life is over-asserted. This negation is literally enacted by putting on masks which show the living play[ing] the part of the progenitor. Masks are hung around the skull of death. And these tribes were successful. Their tombs still exist in which the Old Man was fed. The grave cult is our greatest historical source [material] for tribal history. And so they have been successful; in a time of no writing or books they have deposed their dead in such a manner as to reach us, the living, after many thousand years, in the only possible way.

   Through their investing in the dead a tremendous capital, believing in their perpetuity, they tell us their story today and allow us to rewrite history as a convergence of all their tribal vicissitudes. Rarely has a faith paid higher dividends than the faith of primitive tribes in their masks around death. These masks have survived or have made the tribe survive. The first of the burdens of history might be labeled: *The Masks around Death* or *The Speech of the Tribes.*

II. The temples of the Gods were built on excavated and elevated ground, in stone of the most enduring quality, syenite, granite, etc.

10. *Ed. note.* I am unable to place the quotation from Churchill.

They were [built] to last and they did last. The temples outlasted their gods. We have these temples before us. The men were successful again. These temples and their inscriptions are deciphered by us today. They have fortified life, against the wear and tear of time, and so the fundamentals of these huge temple-cities will be treated in a part on: *The Fortresses of Life* or *The Temples of the Countries.*

III. The goal of all these polyglot and polytheistic worlds was erected by Israel, in its Messianic hope for one God over all countries and through all times. The freedom of man over all times and all spaces ever experienced by him is the freedom of Israel, bestowed on her by her Messianic hope in the God of the Future, the God to come, the God always coming, the God who had created future when he spoke his first word: Let there be light. And Israel was by no means alone in this faith. Although the Messianic God is the star of David and his people, he was hoped for in nearly every other group of people in one way or another. So now we have three eternal burdens:

- The Speeches of the Tribes
- The Temples of the Countries
- The Messianic Gods

Mark well all these burdens made for peace, for lastingness, for continuity. As against a blind struggle without identity, a wild change without result.

IV. The three millennia of our own era inherited these burdens from the ancient world. The Church inherited hers from Israel, the modern world took her clue [cue?] from the civilizations of ancient countries. The future society is dependent on the vitality which it must resuscitate from the well-integrated Peace [of] the clan and family and tribe of old.

The only peculiarity of the God of the Church was that he actually replaced the many Gods in the hearts not of Israel alone, but of all men. And so the part on the burden of the Church must be entitled God of Gods.

V. The World History which Ranke or H. G. Wells proposed to write was a history of the country or countries, of the "world of worlds" as we may perhaps say somewhat poignantly.

VI. And the burden of mankind will have to be its unity over all tribal fissures, as the tribe of tribes, as the Great Society.

God of Gods, World of Worlds, Tribe of Tribes, are the burdens of our era respectively.

Now, the relation of our era to its pre-history appears to be of a somewhat inverted order, as follows:

I tribes	IV Gods (Church)
II countries	V World of Worlds (Globe)
III God	VI Tribe (Society)

And it stands revealed that human history is not going on in the straight line, as most contemporaries are inclined to assume. The movement is more subtle. I and VI, III and IV, and II and V, correspond.[11]

The things which end antiquity are carried to completion first, in the transfer from Israel to the Church. Then and only then, after the Church with her New Testament had become the heiress of the Old Testament, did the Western World inherit the civilizations of Greece, Egypt, China, and Rome, in their global expansion. Oneness is supplemented by a new enterprise, of building the many races of man into one human family. That which was first, the tribe, is the last to be integrated into unity. That which was last to be lived, the messianic hope, was the first to be universalized.

Antiquity and our own era relate like strophe and antistrophe, the last burden of antiquity and the first burden of our era correspond. As long as this antistrophical character of the burdens of our era goes unnoticed, our own era is deprived of its unity, of its claim to be an era at all. The meaning of the Christian era depends on our entering upon its singular character as the antistrophe to all polyglot, polytheistic histories. American history just as much as Chinese history or Spanish history might be weighed down by local issues definitely [perhaps "indefinitely" is meant here]. Then they are extrapolated from the march of time, and relegated to the caleidoscope of ancient histories. This is going on in many history books before our eyes. The destruction of the unity of history was carried to a summit by [Oswald] Spengler. He divided history into six millennia

11. *Ed. note*: Rosenstock-Huessy illustrates by manuscript pencil lines here that I and VI correspond, II and V correspond in the middle, and that III and IV correspond. That is, in pre-history the tribes are first; in the Christian era, the tribes come last, in the third millennium. Similarly, in pre-history the revelation of one God comes at the end, with Israel; in our era it comes first; it constitutes the first millennium.

which all, he thought, achieved the same things, in different areas of the world. History became, with him, the description of different geographical units. And it is an accident that these geographical units should have flourished in different millennia. Another author, Helmold, composed a world in this order: Europe, Asia, America, Australia, Africa.[12] This is the Spenglerian belief, without any unifying chronology or unifying goal. Spengler by leaving us with the semblance of a continuous chronology and by allotting to each civilization the cycle of seasons through one of the assumed six millennia, makes it more difficult to look through his veil of despair. But he despairs of history as a singular completely. And for this reason, the two thousand years of our era became, under Spengler's pen, appendages to the histories of antiquity.

This then is our choice. Either the years 1—1943 repeat the stories of other eras preceding them, or the years AD integrate all eras previous to them. This is the choice which amounts to a mental war. Historians are at war with each other today because by far the majority is tempted by the Spengler-Helmold temptation. Under their rule, history becomes pluralistic, cyclical, the history of endless declines and falls.

To me, this would make the study of history a contradiction in terms. I reject this attempt of plunging the history of our era down to the level of Babylonian or Thailand history. It is suicide and it leads to mythology necessarily. There is no reason to find the truth or to tell the truth if history does not make us free from repeating the old eternal cycles. To me, antiquity becomes incandescent in the light of our era. History makes sense. The materials all wait for us to be integrated into one symphony of all the burdens. You will be in this battle between the modern temptation of destroying history and your faith in history, as long as you look at one history book. Be a good soldier. And give me the opportunity of teaching you the bars of the real melodies which make up history.

Your antispenglerian, Eugen

12. *Ed. note:*This cannot be a reference to the 12th- century historian, author of the *Chronica Slavorum*, who lived before America and Australia were known; so who?

Bibliography

Axelrod, Charles David. *Studies in Intellectual Breakthrough: Freud, Simmel, Buber*. Amherst, MA: University of Massachusetts Press, 1979.

Bade, David. "*Respondeo etsi Mutabor*: Eugen Rosenstock-Huessy's Semiological *Zweistromland*." *Culture, Theory and Critique* 56 (2015) 87–100.

———. "Living Theory and Theory that Kills: Language, Communication and Control." A conversation with David Bade at the Decolonial and Southern Epistemologies Forum, Jan. 28, 2022.

Bailyn, Bernard. *On the Teaching and Writing of History*. Hanover, NH: University Press of New England, 1994.

———. *Sometimes an Art: Nine Essays on History*. New York: Knopf, 2015.

Barnes, Julian. *Levels of Life*. New York: Vintage, 2013.

Becker, Carl. "Everyman His Own Historian." *American Historical Review* 37 (1932) 221–36.

Bergson, Henri. *Time and Free Will: An Essay on the Immediate Data of Consciousness*. Translated by F. L. Podgson. London: Allen and Unwin, 1950; orig. publ. 1889.

Berlin, Isaiah. "History and Theory: The Concept of Scientific History." *History and Theory* 1 (1960) 1–31.

Boston, Bruce, "'I Respond Although I Will Be Changed': The Life and Historical Thought of Eugen Rosenstock-Huessy." Ph.D. diss., Princeton University, 1973.

Browning, Robert. "Paracelsus." In *The Poems of Browning*. Vol. 1: *1826–1840*, edited by John Woolford and Daniel Karlin, 127–35. London: Longmans, 1973.

Bryant, M. Darrol."The Grammar of the Spirit: Time, Speech and Society." In Bryant and Huessy, *Eugen Rosenstock-Huessy. Studies*, 233–60.

Bryant, M. Darrol, and Hans R. Huessy, eds. *Eugen Rosenstock-Huessy. Studies in His Life and Thought*. Lewiston, NY: Edwin Mellen, 1986.

Bushman, Richard. "9 Pro Tips from Richard Bushman." Wheat and Tares, July 21, 2015. https://wheatandtares.org/2015/07/21/richard-bushman-on-mormonism.

Cargill, Meredith, "The Communication Theory of Eugen Rosenstock-Huessy: Speech Pragmatics," (Draft version 9, June 6, 2006), unpublished. It can be found online at http://erhpaperdownloads.blogspot.com/

Cayton, Andrew, "Not the Fragments but the Whole." *William and Mary Quarterly*, 69, no. 3 (2012), 513–26.

Chartier, Roger. "History, Time, and Space." *Republics of Letters: A Journal for the Study of Knowledge, Politics, and the Arts* 2, no. 2 (2011) 1–13.

Chesterton, G. K. *The Ballad of the White Horse*. London: Methuen, 1948.

———. *The Everlasting Man*. New York: Dodd Mead, 1925.

Cristaudo, Wayne. *Religion, Redemption, and Revolution: The New Speech Thinking of Franz Rosenzweig and Eugen Rosenstock-Huessy*. Toronto: University of Toronto Press, 2012.

Cristaudo, Wayne, and Frances Huessy, eds. *The Cross and the Star: The Post-Nietzschean Christian and Jewish Thought of Eugen Rosenstock-Huessy and Franz Rosenzweig*. New Castle on Tyne: Cambridge Scholars Press, 2009.

Cristaudo, Wayne, et al. eds. "Eugen Rosenstock-Huessy (1888–1973): Sociologist, Historian, Social Philosopher." Special Issue. *Culture, Theory and Critique* 56, no. 1 (2015).

Ermarth, Michael. "From Here to Eternity: The Philosophy of History of Eugen Rosenstock-Huessy as Eschatology on the Trans-Modern Installment Plan." In *The Cross and the Star: The Post-Nietzschean Christian and Jewish Thought of Eugen Rosenstock-Huessy and Franz Rosenzweig*, edited by Wayne Cristaudo and Frances Huessy, 307–32. Newcastle upon Tyne: Cambridge Scholars Press, 2009.

Epstein, Catherine. *A Past Renewed: A Catalogue of German-Speaking Refugee Historians in the United States after 1933*. Washington, D. C. and Cambridge, U. K.: German Historical Institute and Cambridge University Press, 1993.

Eugen Rosenstock-Huessy Society of North America. "Recent Publications Relating to the Work of Rosenstock-Huessy, 1973–2013." http://www.erhsociety.org/wp-content/uploads/1.RECENTpubls.relatingtoERH-10.15.13_combined.pdf.

Farber, Leslie. *The Ways of the Will: Essays Toward a Psychology and Psychopathology of the Will*. New York: Harper and Row, 1966.

Fiering, Norman. "Benjamin Franklin and the Way to Virtue." *American Quarterly* 30, no. 2 (1978) 199–223.

———. "The Case for Universal National Service." June 4, 2020. Amitai Etzioni <https:/medium.com/@etzioni_25175/the-case-for-universal-national-service-guest-column-8fd42810f43c>

———. "Heritage vs. History: Eugen Rosenstock-Huessy as a 'Physician of Memory.'" *European Legacy* 24, no. 5 (2019) 511–36. https://doi.org/10.1080/10848770.2018.1562022.

———. *Jonathan Edwards's Moral Thought and Its British Context*. Chapel Hill, NC: University of North Carolina Press, 1981.

———. "The Structure of Significant Lives." *European Legacy* 22 (2017) 406–26. http://dx.doi.org/10.1080/10848770.2017.1291885.

Gay, Peter. *Freud: A Life for Our Time*. New York: Norton, 1989.

Harris, Roy. *The Linguistics of History*. Edinburgh: Edinburgh University Press, 2004.

Headley, John M. "Multiculturalism Reconsidered." In *The Problem with Multiculturalism: The Uniqueness and Universality of Western Civilization*, edited by John M. Headley, 71–79. New Brunswick, NJ: Transaction, 2012.

Hobsbawm, Eric, and Terence Ranger, eds. *The Invention of Tradition*. Cambridge: Cambridge University Press, 1983.

James, William. "The Moral Equivalent of War." In *Memories and Studies*. 267–96. London: Longmans, 1911.

Jones, Ernest. *Life and Work of Sigmund Freud*. New York: Basic Books, 1953.

Kidder, Tracy. *Mountains Beyond Mountains. The Quest of Dr. Paul Farmer, A Man Who Would Cure the World*. New York: Random House, 2003.

Klein, Milton. "Everyman His Own Historian. Carl Becker as Historiographer." *The History Teacher* 19, no. 1 (1985) 101–9.

Koselleck, Reinhart. *Futures Past: On the Semantics of Historical Time*. Translated by Keith Tribe. Cambridge: MIT Press, 1985.

Kroesen, Otto. *Planetary Responsibilities: An Ethics of Timing*. Eugene, OR: Wipf & Stock, 2014.

———. "Toward Planetary Society: Revelation and Redemption in the Work of Rosenstock-Huessy, Rosenzweig, and Levinas," unpublished paper.

Kuhn, Thomas S. *The Structure of Scientific Revolutions*. Chicago: University of Chicago Press, 1970.

Leithart, Peter J. "The Social Articulation of Time in Eugen Rosenstock-Huessy." *Modern Theology* 26, no.2 (2010) 197–219. http://onlinelibrary.wiley.com/doi/10.1111/j.1468- 0025.2009.01594.x/abstract.

Lowenthal, David. *The Past Is a Foreign Country*. Cambridge: Cambridge University Press, 1985.

———. *Possessed by the Past: The Heritage Crusade and the Spoils of History*. New York: Free Press, 1996.

Lowith, Karl. Review of Rosenstock-Huessy *The Christian Future*. *Church History* 15, no. 3 (1946) 248–49.

McKnight, Stephen A. "Voegelin's New Science of History." In *Eric Voegelin's Significance for the Modern Mind*, edited by Ellis Sandoz, 46–70. Baton Rouge, LA: Louisiana State University Press, 1991.

McNeill, William H. *Mythistory and Other Essays*. Chicago: University of Chicago Press, 1986.

Marty, Martin E. *By Way of Response*. Nashville: Abingdon, 1981.

———. "A Life of Learning." Charles Homer Haskins lecture. 2006. ACLS Occasional Paper, no. 62.

Maslow, Abraham. *Religions, Values, and Peak-Experiences*. New York: Viking, 1970.

Morgan, George Allen. *Speech and Society: The Christian Linguistic Social Philosophy of Eugen Rosenstock-Huessy*. Gainesville: University of Florida Press, 1987.

Morison, Samuel Eliot. "The Faith of a Historian." *American Historical Review* 56, no. 2 (1951) 261–75.

Moyn, Samuel. *Origins of the Other: Emmanuel Levinas between Revelation and Ethics*. Ithaca, NY: Cornell University Press, 2005.

Muller, Jerry Z. *The Tyranny of Metrics*. Princeton, NJ: Princeton University Press, 2018.

Nora, Pierre, "Between Memory and History: *Les Lieux de Mémoire*."*Representations* 26 (Spring 1989) 9–15.

Novick, Peter. *That Noble Dream: The Objectivity Question and the American Historical Profession*. Cambridge: Harvard University Press, 1988.

Ong, Walter J. *The Presence of the Word*. New Haven: Yale University Press, 1967.

———. "The Spiritual Meaning of Technology and Culture." In *Technology and Culture in Perspective*, edited by Myron B. Bloy Jr. and Illene Montan,. 29–34. Cambridge: Cambridge University Press, 1967.

Perry, Ralph Barton. *The Thought and Character of William James*. 2 vols. Boston: Little Brown, 1935.

Plumb, J. H. *The Death of the Past*. Boston: Houghton Mifflin, 1970.

Preiss, Jack. *Camp William James*. Norwich, VT: Argo Books, 1978.

Rome, Sydney and Beatrice, eds., *Philosophical Interrogations. Interrogations of Martin Buber, John Wild, Jean Wahl, Brand Blanshard, Paul Weiss, Charles Hartshorne, Paul Tillich*. New York: Holt, Rinehart and Winston, 1970.

Ricoeur, Paul. *Memory, History, Forgetting*. Translated by Kathleen Blame Pellauer. Chicago: University of Chicago Press, 2004.

Rosenstock-Huessy, Eugen. *The Christian Future, or The Modern Mind Outrun*. New York: Charles Scribner's Sons, 1946.

———. "A Classic and a Founder." *Rosenstock-Huessy Papers*, vol. 1, 1–73. Norwich, VT: Argo, 1981. Originally published 1937.

———."The Founder of the Science of Life: The Tripartition of the Life of Theophrastus Paracelsus von Hohenheim, 1493–1541." In "A Classic and a Founder. "17–73.

———. *Fruit of Lips*. Pittsburgh, PA: Pickwick Press, 1978; written originally in 1954.

———. *Fruit of Our Lips: The Transformation of God's Word into the Speech of Mankind*. Edited by Raymond Huessy. Eugene, OR: Wipf & Stock, 2021.

———. "Grammar as Social Science." In *Speech and Reality*, 98–114. Norwich, VT: Argo, 1970.

———. "Heraclitus to Parmenides." In *I Am an Impure* Thinker, 77–90. Norwich, VT: Argo, 1970.

———. "Hölderlin and Nietzsche." In *The Cross and the Star: The Post-Nietzschean Christian and Jewish Thought of Eugen Rosenstock-Huessy and Franz Rosenweig*, edited Wayne Cristaudo and Frances Huessy, 17–20. Newcastle upon Tyne: Cambridge Scholars Press 2009.

———. *I Am an Impure Thinker*. Norwich, VT: Argo, 1970.

———. "Ichthys," in *Fruit of Our Lips*, 31–52. Eugene, OR: Wipf and Stock, 2021.

———. "In Defense of the Grammatical Method." In *Speech and Reality*, 9–44. Norwich, VT: Argo, 1970.

———, ed. *Judaism Despite Christianity: The Letters on Christianity and Judaism between Eugen Rosenstock-Huessy and Franz Rosenzweig*. Tuscaloosa, AL: University of Alabama Press, 1969. Reissued in 2011 by the University of Chicago Press, with new introductory material.

———. "Letters to Cynthia," 1943. Unpublished.

———. "The Listener's Tract." In *Speech and Reality*, 134–54. Norwich, VT: Argo, 1970.

———. "Metanoia: To Think Anew." In *I Am an Impure Thinker*, 182–90. Norwich, VT: Argo, 1970.

———. "Modern Man's Disintegration and the Egyptian Ka." In *I Am an Impure Thinker*, 35–52. Norwich, VT: Argo, 1970.

———. *The Multiformity of Man*. Essex, VT: Argo, 2000. Earlier editions appeared in 1936, 1948, 1973.

———. *The Origin of Speech*. Norwich, VT: Argo, 1981.

———. *Out of Revolution: Autobiography of Western Man*. New York: William Morrow, 1938. There are several later paperback reprints.

———. *Planetary Service: A Way Into the Third Millennium.* Translated by Mark Huessy and Freya von Moltke. Jericho, VT: Argo, 1978. Originally published 1965.

———. *Practical Knowledge of the Soul.* Translated by Mark Huessy and Freya von Moltke. Eugene, OR: Wipf & Stock, 2015. This is a revised edition of the work published by Argo Books in 1988. Originally published as *Angewandte Seelenkunde: Eine programmatische Ubersetzung*, 1924.

———. "The Predicament of History." *Journal of Philosophy* 32, no.4 (1935) 93–100.

———. Recordings of lectures: www.ERHFund.org/online-lecture-library.

———. Review of Crane Brinton, *Anatomy of Revolution* in *American Historical Review*, 44, 4 (1939) 882–84.

———. *Soul of William James, The.* Privately printed mimeograph, Dartmouth College, Hanover, NH, 1942. Reprinted in Rosenstock-Huessy, *I Am an Impure Thinker*, 20–34. Norwich, VT: Argo 1970, with some variations from the original and omitting some footnotes.

———. *Soziologie.* Zwei Bänden. W. Kohlhammer: Stuttgart, 1956–58. A new edition in three volumes, edited by Michael Gormann-Thelen and Ruth Mautner, was published by Thalheimer, 2008–9. *In the Cross of Reality, Volume 1: The Hegemony of Spaces.* Translated by Jürgen Lawrenz. Edited by Wayne Cristaudo and Frances Huessy. London and New York: Routledge, 2017 is a translation of the first volume of Rosenstock-Huessy's *Soziologie*, 1956.

———. *Speech and Reality.* Norwich, VT: Argo, 1970.

———. *Die Sprache des Menschengeschlechts.* 2 vols. Heidelberg: Lambert Schneider, 1963–64.

———. "Teaching Too Late, Learning Too Early." In *I Am an Impure Thinker.* Norwich, VT: Argo, 1970, 91–114.

———. "Time-Bettering Days." In *Rosenstock-Huessy Papers*, vol. 1. Norwich, VT: Argo, 1954.

———. *Die Umwandlung des Wortes Gottes.* In *Die Sprache des Menschengeschlechts.* Vol. 1: 119–42. Heidelberg: Lambert Schneider, 1963.

———. "The Uni-versity [*sic*] of Logic, Language: A Program for Collaboration." In *Speech and Reality*, 67–97. Norwich, VT: Argo, 1970.

Roy, Christian. "Interpretations of History Out of Revolution and Exile: The Correspondence between Eugen Rosenstock-Huessy and Paul Tillich (1935–1944)." In *Paul Tillich im Exil*, edited by Christian Danz and Werner Schussler, 103–24. Berlin: DeGruyter, 2017.

Searls, Damion, "Who's Number One?" *Paris Review.* March 17, 2015.

Smith, Page. *The Historian and History.* New York:Knopf, 1964.

———. "On Writing History." In *Dissenting Opinion*, 52–60. San Francisco: North Point Press, 1984.

Stünkel, Knut. "Nations as Times. The National Construction of Political Space in the Planetary History of Eugen Rosenstock-Huessy." In *Transnational Political Spaces: Agents-Structures-Encounters*, edited by Mathias Albert et al., 297–317. Historische Politikforschung, Bd. 18. Frankfurt: Campus Verlag, 2009.

Van der Molen, Lise. *A Guide to the Works of Eugen Rosenstock-Huessy: Chronological Bibliography.* Essex, VT: Argo, 1997.

Von Ranke, Leopold. *The Secret of World History. Selected Writings on the Art and Science of History.* Edited and translated by Roger Wines. New York: Fordham University Press, 1981.

Weil, Eric, "Science in Modern Culture, or the Meaning of Meaninglessness." In *Valuing the Humanities: Essays by Eric Weil*, edited by William Kluback. Chico, CA: Historians Press, 1989.

White, Hayden. *The Fiction of Narrative: Essays . . . 1957–2007*. Edited by Robert Doran. Baltimore: Johns Hopkins University Press, 2010.

———. "Guilty of History? The Longue Durée of Paul Ricoeur." In *The Fiction of Narrative: Essays . . . 1957–2007*, ed. Robert Doran, 318–39. Baltimore: Johns Hopkins University Press, 2010.

Wolfe, Tom. *The Kingdom of Speech*. New York: Little Brown, 2016.

Wood, Gordon. *The Purpose of the Past: Reflections on the Uses of History*. New York: Penguin, 2008.

Yerushalmi, Yosef Hayim. *Zakhor: Jewish History and Jewish Memory*. Seattle: University of Washington Press, 1982.